1R20
4

TURNING TO THE WORLD

Turning to the World

Social Justice and the Common Good since Vatican II

Edited by
CARL N. STILL AND GERTRUDE ROMPRÉ

McGill-Queen's University Press
Montreal & Kingston • London • Chicago

© McGill-Queen's University Press 2018

ISBN 978-0-7735-5526-6 (cloth)
ISBN 978-0-7735-5527-3 (paper)
ISBN 978-0-7735-5622-5 (ePDF)
ISBN 978-0-7735-5623-2 (ePUB)

Legal deposit fourth quarter 2018
Bibliothèque nationale du Québec

Printed in Canada on acid-free paper that is 100% ancient forest free
(100% post-consumer recycled), processed chlorine free

This book has been published with the help of a grant from the Canadian Federation
for the Humanities and Social Sciences, through the Awards to Scholarly Publications
Program, using funds provided by the Social Sciences and Humanities Research
Council of Canada. Funding was also received from St Thomas More College,
University of Saskatchewan.

We acknowledge the support of the Canada Council for the Arts, which last year
invested $153 million to bring the arts to Canadians throughout the country.

Nous remercions le Conseil des arts du Canada de son soutien. L'an dernier,
le Conseil a investi 153 millions de dollars pour mettre de l'art dans la vie des
Canadiennes et des Canadiens de tout le pays.

Library and Archives Canada Cataloguing in Publication

Turning to the world : social justice and the common good since Vatican II/ edited by
Carl N. Still and Gertrude Rompré.

Includes bibliographical references and index.
Issued in print and electronic formats.
ISBN 978-0-7735-5526-6 (cloth). – ISBN 978-0-7735-5527-3 (paper). –
ISBN 978-0-7735-5622-5 (ePDF). – ISBN 978-0-7735-5623-2 (ePUB)

1. Vatican Council (2nd : 1962–1965 : Basilica di San Pietro in Vaticano).
2. Social justice–Religious aspects–Catholic Church. 3. Common good–
Religious aspects–Catholic Church. 4. Christian sociology–Catholic Church.
5. Church and social problems–Catholic Church. I. Still, Carl N., editor II.
Rompré, Gertrude, 1968–, editor

BX830.1962T87 2018   262'.52   C2018-904233-8
                                             C2018-904234-6

This book was typeset in 10.5/13 Sabon.

*For the Basilian Fathers
who brought the spirit of the Second Vatican Council to
St Thomas More College*

Contents

Editors' Note

Quotations from Second Vatican Council documents throughout the volume are taken from *Vatican Council II: Constitutions, Decrees, Declarations*, edited by Austin Flannery (Liturgical Press, 2014), which provides a revised, inclusive-language translation of the council's basic sixteen documents. Quotations from other church documents not contained in Flannery's collection are taken from translations available online or in print, as indicated, and do not always use inclusive language.

Abbreviations

JM *Justitia in Mundo (Justice in the World)*, 1971
LS *Laudato Si' (On Care for Our Common Home)*, 2015
MM *Mater et Magistra (On Christianity and Social Progress)*, 1961
OA *Octogesima Adveniens (A Call to Action)*, 1971
PP *Populorum Progressio (On the Development of Peoples)*,
      1967
PT *Pacem in Terris (Peace on Earth)*, 1963
QA *Quadragesimo Anno (On Reconstruction of the Social
      Order)*, 1931
RN *Rerum Novarum (On the Condition of Labour)*, 1891
SRS *Sollicitudo Rei Socialis (On Social Concern)*, 1987

The Spirit Lives On:
Reflections of a Council Father

Remi J. De Roo

Half a century has passed since the Second Vatican Council. In retrospect, I can appreciate the period of the council as the most challenging learning curve I have ever known. Let me explain briefly what happened to our church during the period from Pope John's startling announcement on 25 January 1959 to the formal ratification and closing on 8 December 1965.

Nine days after the official opening of the council, the council fathers issued a message to the nations. It is of value to review the intent in that message: "Under the guidance of the Holy Spirit, we wish to inquire how we ought to renew ourselves, so that we may be found increasingly faithful to the gospel of Christ ... We look forward to a spiritual renewal from which will also flow a happy impulse on behalf of human values such as scientific discoveries, technological advances, and a wider diffusion of knowledge."[1]

Assembled from around the world, we council fathers shared our pastoral experience and reflected on the signs of the times. We realized that our previous theological methods had become obsolete. To reach out to the world, we had to reformulate our theology. We had to set aside neo-scholastic, abstract theology in favour of a more invitational style of discourse that would facilitate dialogue with contemporary society.

Nowhere was this more obvious than in the domain that concerns us in this volume: the issues of social justice and the common good. Thanks to Vatican II, growing numbers of disciples have reclaimed the Bible as their own and identified prophetically how the entire church is to be prophetic, missionary, and directly involved in transforming the world and society. The council laid the foundation from which a theology of liberation was gradually elaborated. People suffering from marginalization and oppression rediscovered the sacred scriptures as embracing the cause of those living in poverty.

My previous experience in what we then called "specialized Catholic Action" helped me recognize the profound movement afoot, particularly among the marginalized members of society. Expressions like "the historic cause of the peasants" and "the preferential option for the poor" convey, if only partially, a sense of what I am convinced may well be the most energetic spiritual upheaval emanating from and in the aftermath of the council. Liberation theology, finally recognized as generally orthodox in teaching and juridically legitimate in its application to social structures, is increasingly finding global expression.

The creation and inspiration within the sixteen council documents are worthy in themselves as a compass for both the present and the future. At the risk of overly simplifying this vast and complex body of doctrine and pastoral guidance, I will recall some of the principal teachings of the council, under three headings, with some partial overlapping. I choose these headings not only as historical backdrop but especially as underlying themes that continue to call us to appropriate renewal every day.

Ressourcement. First, I recall the French term *ressourcement.* This entails a refreshing visit and reclamation of our earlier foundations – our origins or sources in tradition and scripture, within the church itself. *Ressourcement* reminds me of what Jesus said to the Samaritan woman at Jacob's well: genuine disciples who worship in spirit and in truth will discover a spring of living water surging up from their hearts.

In pre-Vatican Council times, scripture – the living Word of God – had become somewhat atrophied, even neglected in favour of morality and law. With the assistance of scripture scholars and the influence of the bishops of the Eastern rite, we developed a renewed understanding of revelation. This is no longer identified primarily with the written text of the Bible and the teaching authority of the Magisterium. However vital these are, they are instruments, not ends in themselves. The fullness of revelation is found in the Person of Jesus, the Christ, the Anointed One. He is not merely the Messenger of Revelation but also its very Life. Our previous obsession with narrow academic orthodoxy for too long obscured the fact that the early disciples were known as followers of "The Way," more concerned with living a new lifestyle than with details of catechetics or apologetics.

Dei Verbum (*Dogmatic Constitution on Divine Revelation*) was a direct outcome of our return to the source. It became the basis for renewal in theology, liturgy, ecumenical and interfaith dialogue, and indeed for the promotion of social justice. It will continue to provide us with guideposts for years to come.

The return to the Word of God provided a deepening of the history of salvation, a recognition of the basic need for a more elaborate theology of the Holy Trinity, further reflection on the person and mission of Jesus, and a focus on the indwelling presence of the Holy Spirit in the midst of the people of God. With this refocusing on the Word of God, a renewed vision of the church emerged with a mission both *ad intra* and *ad extra*. A shift beyond the former juridical and hierarchical model toward an unfolding sacramental, grace-filled, pastoral model occurred, with a redirection toward ministries of humble service to all humankind.

This return to our roots also helped me personally to appreciate more fully how the mystery of the church can be perceived as the salvation history of the pilgrim people of God en route to the Kingdom. The Reign of God has begun, but awaits completion at the end of time. We are frail humans in need of constant conversion and communal spiritual discernment. The church is in history, but history is also in the church.

Aggiornamento. The second term is a now-familiar Italian expression, *aggiornamento*, which conveys, among other meanings, a sense of appropriate renewal, adaptation, updating, friendly dialogue with modern culture, and necessary change.

Nowhere more than in *Sacrosanctum Concilium* (*Constitution on the Sacred Liturgy*) is there such a clear, dynamic, and strong rationale for adaptation and renewal: "The sacred council has set out to impart an ever-increasing vigor to the Christian lives of the faithful; to adapt more closely to the needs of our age those institutions which are subject to change; to encourage whatever can promote the union of all who believe in Christ; to strengthen whatever serves to call all of humanity into the church's fold. Accordingly it sees particularly cogent reasons for undertaking the reform and promotion of the liturgy" (SC 1).

Updating the relationship between faith and culture makes manifest how they are intimately linked, as they mutually permeate one another. Biblical revelation and theology require evolution in language and interpretation so as to remain faithful to the original meaning and intelligible to succeeding generations. The discussions that renewed these links created a more open attitude in which cultures honour all traditions and customs, all the way from implementing the vernacular to promoting liturgical dance. The concept of the "People of God" broadened our outlook, from west to east, from north to south.

By returning to the sources – the Word of God, tradition, and the mystery of the church itself – the council fathers were challenged by an obvious need for self-examination and self-understanding. We asked ourselves, "Who are we? What is our mission?" Responding to these queries was imperative if significant renovation was to occur. Our reflections on these questions are manifest in *Lumen Gentium* (*Dogmatic Constitution on the Church*). The updated images of the church in prayer, in relationship with other believers, of the people of God inserted into the world, resulted in the promulgation of three other constitutions: *Sacrosanctum Concilium* (*On the Sacred Liturgy*), *Dei Verbum* (*On Divine Revelation*), and *Gaudium et Spes* (*Pastoral Constitution on the Church in the Modern World*).

The *Pastoral Constitution on the Church in the Modern World* had not even been conceived prior to the council. Its development illustrates how the council participants were led by the Spirit to find a different style and language. It is discursive rather than inductive, inspirational rather than judgmental, seeking to remain in tune with "the joys and hopes, the grief and anguish" (GS 1) of a perplexed and anguished civilization. Underlying this longest of all council documents is a renewed anthropology. Its biblical foundation rests on the concept of the human as created in the image and likeness of God and destined beyond eternal horizons to enjoy communion with and loving embrace of its Maker.

Development. With a renewed understanding of the ecclesial mission in the world, concepts like dialogue, self-examination, and prophetic-priestly leadership by all Christians emerged under a third and final term, *development.* This very idea was formerly rejected as tendentious, if not dangerous. Today it is common currency. Despite entrenched and determined resistance from some influential council members, it gradually came to be seen as the normal form of growth for a living body of teachings. The *Dogmatic Constitution on the Church* proclaims how the Holy Spirit guides the entire body of members through a variety of gifts and ministries, through reflection, contemplation, prayer, and apostolic initiatives, toward ever deeper and greater spiritual growth.

The development described above did not stop with the council. For example, nowhere was the issue of social justice enunciated more forcefully and clearly than at the 1971 Bishops' Synod in Rome. Article 6 remains etched in my mind: "Action on behalf of justice and participation in the transformation of society appear to us as a constitutive dimension of the proclamation of the Gospel" (JM 6). As a result, we no longer have the option of mouthing declarations of moral principles while avoiding bodily involvement in the restructuring of what have become basically dishonest and less than compassionate social structures. The gospel is not perceived as "good news" if it does not promote genuine humanization. Nor will there be lasting peace without effective justice for all. Structural sin is now to be denounced just as firmly as individual sin. "Prophetic mourning" is the order of the day, as Walter Brueggemann taught us; it is indispensable, absolutely required if we are to lay bare the darkness of evil to the redeeming light of truth.[2]

There are, however, many reasons for hope and rejoicing. Just think of the council's recognition of the universal and foundational baptismal priesthood. Note how we are beginning to move from a "morality of prescriptions to an ethic of co-responsibility," to recall an expression attributed to the late Bernard Häring. See the swelling wave of increasingly mature lay leadership emerging in many parishes and faith communities. Remember key issues like decentralization, subsidiarity, synodality, collegiality, and others. These terms, rarely heard in yesterday's faith communities, are now the objects of serious discussion. Notice the increase in consultations and invitations to communal spiritual discernment.

Many of the above insights stood me in good stead in over thirty-seven years of ministry to the people in the Diocese of Victoria. Several pastoral surveys and a diocesan synod inspired by Vatican II helped greatly to develop the spirit of the council and to strengthen the believing community into a faith family with a clearer sense of purpose.

Many of you rejoice with me at the change of atmosphere and even some structural adjustments brought about by the promising new style of papal governance made manifest by Pope Francis. His fresh approach to church teaching and governance brings back to me memories of hearing Saint John XXIII confidently anticipating the dawning of a New Pentecost. Recall the "medicine of mercy" and the open-arms policies that he advocated in his opening address to the assembled council fathers. Neglected aspects of council teachings are again coming to the fore. I hear widespread rejoicing and a renewed awakening of hope as directives promulgated by Vatican II are increasingly gaining ascendency.

This volume reflects for me a promising array of essays and studies illustrating how the people of God in this part of the church universal are living up to the prophetic calling emanating from Vatican II. I join all of you in prayer and hopeful anticipation of further achievements as we wend our pilgrim way forward to ever-expanding and promising horizons.

NOTES

1 "Message to Humanity" (20 October 1962), in Abbott, *Documents of Vatican II*, 3–5.
2 Brueggemann, *Prophetic Imagination*; Brueggemann, *Reality, Grief, Hope*.

Acknowledgments

We would like to express our sincere gratitude to all those seen and unseen hands who have been part of the creation of this volume. As we have worked through the process of gathering and editing these texts, we have come to an ever-deeper appreciation for the depth of insight offered by each of the contributors.

Their initial papers were offered at the Turning to the World: Social Justice and the Common Good conference held at St Thomas More College, University of Saskatchewan, 8–9 March 2013. That conference was made possible through the generous support of the Social Sciences and Humanities Research Council, the University of Saskatchewan, St Thomas More College, and its Leslie and Irene Dubé Chair for Catholic Studies. We would also like to thank Joanne Illingworth for her exceptional assistance in organizing the conference.

Kyla Madden at McGill-Queen's University Press provided timely and professional guidance for this project. Editorial assistance for the present volume was also contributed by Ursula Acton, Ellie Barton, Jordan Olver, and Don Ward. Normand Breault acted on behalf of the late Gregory Baum's estate when we were preparing our final submission of the manuscript. Our thanks goes to them, as well as to the anonymous peer reviewers whose insightful comments helped shape the chapters into their present form. We are particularly grateful to Bishop Emeritus Remi De Roo and Archbishop Don Bolen, who provided the bookends to the volume and shared their unique perspectives as leaders within the ever-evolving church in which they serve.

Finally, we wish to honour the memory of Gregory Baum, who died on 18 October 2017 as we were preparing to submit the final manuscript. Dr Baum generously participated in the 2013 conference despite his health concerns. His chapter serves as an illustration of his deep commitment to, and advocacy of, the vision of the Second Vatican Council. We are grateful to include his voice as part of this volume.

TURNING TO THE WORLD

Introduction

Carl N. Still and Gertrude Rompré

The Second Vatican Council (1962–65) was unquestionably a watershed in the history of the Catholic Church and arguably the most decisive ecclesial event of the twentieth century. Instead of aiming to resolve a doctrinal crisis as previous councils did, however, this council engaged in a critical examination of the Catholic Church itself. It sought at once to rediscover the most ancient sources of Christian thought and practice and to bring a church steeped in tradition into the modern world. Over the course of four sessions spanning four years, the council spoke in such a different voice on so many issues that many concluded that the council represented a break from the church's past rather than a development of its previous teachings. Yet if the council spoke in a new vein about social justice and the common good, it did not invent either concept. Instead, what the council did was to turn the Catholic Church to the world in a new and decisive way.

The present collection explores the legacy of the council's teachings about social justice and the common good, both in broad theoretical terms and in specific contexts. Fifty years after the council, it is now opportune to reexamine both what the council proposed and what happened to the council's vision over the past half century. To do so, we begin with the council itself, deliberating in the context of the sixties on the pressing social and political issues of a world still in the grip of the Cold War but also peering into the future as far as the bishops could then imagine it. If, for instance, the council fathers were prescient in setting the Catholic Church on a new path to ecumenism, they could not foresee the rise of global capitalism or the emergence of environmentalism. In its dialogue with the

world after the council, the Catholic Church sometimes adopted a
more cautious and limited approach to social issues than the council
had imagined. As we shall see, this led some to question whether
the church was backtracking to a pre-conciliar position where the
Catholic Church stood apart from the world.

Turning from the theoretical to the practical, our authors focus
on a number of specific contexts where engagement with the world
since the council has reshaped the church. For example, dialogue
with Judaism reshaped the church's self-understanding as a faith
community that cannot remain true to itself without recognizing the
integrity of Judaism in its own right. Moreover, the Latin American
church emerged after the council as the crucible where the council's commitment to social justice was deepened into a preferential
option for the poor and a theology of liberation. More recently, the
environmental movement has provided a new, positive source for
broadening theological reflection and action on behalf of a new relationship with the earth. And finally, implicit in all of these contexts
is the Canadian experience, both as Canadian bishops shaped the
council's unfolding in little-known but crucial ways and as Canadian
Catholics have responded to the council. No contextualized survey
of the council's influence could be exhaustive, but these examples
demonstrate that the council's turn to the world has exercised vast
influence on the world and the church in relation to it. At the same
time, these contexts provide ample scope for assessing how robustly
the council's social teaching was applied in the lived circumstances
of the world.

In the opening chapter, Michael Duggan sets the major themes of
the Second Vatican Council – especially conscience, freedom, and
social justice – in the context of the intellectual landscape of the
1960s and the previous teaching of the Catholic Church. He argues
that Vatican II marked the turning point for Catholic social teaching,
which had begun with Pope Leo XIII's encyclical *Rerum Novarum*
(*On the Condition of Labour*) in 1891. Further, Duggan sees the
council as standing out from previous councils in that it articulated
a "new humanism" marked by an appeal to conscience. This new
humanism was also shaped by a commitment to the well-being of all
people and so involved a turning to the world, including to those outside the church. Most importantly, the council identified conscience as
the common ground for dialogue between believers and nonbelievers,
particularly when working for the common good.

The next two chapters explore how faithfully the Catholic Church followed the council's inspiration over the following fifty years and in the face of a rising global neoliberalism. Gregory Baum traces the uneven trajectory of the church's turn to the world from the council to Pope Francis's current pontificate. Despite an exuberant reception of the council in the late sixties and seventies, many have felt that Popes John Paul II and Benedict XVI encouraged a retrenchment of the church's position vis-à-vis the world. Baum's analysis goes further, however, and shows how John Paul and Benedict were themselves agents of their times and represented broader sociohistorical tendencies. Given the challenge of interpreting what it means to live in right relationship with those on the margins, Baum argues that the church must reclaim its prophetic stance in favour of the poor. Indeed, that is exactly the message, Baum claims, that is now being incarnated and proclaimed by Francis.

Anna Blackman then considers the problem from another angle: how can any church turn to the world without obscuring its identity as a distinctive spiritual community? Specifically, she examines the challenge posed by neoliberalism to the principles of subsidiarity and the preferential option for the poor. Central as these principles are to Catholic social teaching, the church's position in relation to capitalism and socialism has fluctuated since the time of *Rerum Novarum*. In light of this ambivalence, John Milbank has characterized Catholic social teaching as a hybrid of incompatible elements and an uncritical capitulation to secular claims. In response, Blackman argues that Benedict XVI's vision in *Caritas in Veritate* (*On Integral Human Development in Charity and Truth*) comprehends and counters such a critique. At the same time she concurs with Rowan Williams's insight that the church must engage in a period of self-reflection focused on how it has sometimes failed to live out its prophetic role as a Christian community called to transform the world.

If the council's turn to the world meant engaging in a new way with secular society, it also meant reconsidering its relationship with other faith traditions. Chapters 4 and 5 explore the Catholic Church's vexed history with Judaism. Alisha Pomazon examines the council's reorientation of the church's relationship with the Jewish people through *Nostra Aetate* (*Declaration on the Relations of the Church to Non-Christian Religions*), which inaugurated a new era of dialogue between Catholics and Jews that continues to be active. *Nostra Aetate* was revolutionary among Catholic documents both in recognizing Judaism as a world religion independent of Christianity and in acknowledging Christian culpability in the Jewish holocaust during the Second World War. At the same time, however, Pomazon notes that Catholic theology has not fully absorbed the implications of the *Declaration*'s recognition of Judaism. Ambiguity remains in the church's acknowledgment of the Jewish covenant with God and simultaneous affirmation of a new covenant in Christ. In subsequent documents, the church has affirmed the need for continuing dialogue between Christians and Jews and joint social action, as well as the rejection of anti-Semitism in all its forms.

Starting from *Nostra Aetate*'s new openness to Judaism, Loren Stuckenbruck turns to Jewish scripture for a critique of the social injustice that influenced Jesus and his early followers and has since been incorporated into Catholic theology. He finds in the little-known text *1 Enoch* – influential during the period of Second Temple Judaism but written in an ancient prophetic voice – a striking condemnation of social injustice practised by social and religious elites of the day. Notwithstanding its apocalyptic tone, *1 Enoch* does not defer justice for the oppressed to a future age, but questions the present world order in terms of a perfected order promised to believers, in which the categories of persecutor and oppressed will no longer hold sway. Its author considers the perennial question of whether violent resistance is warranted among the oppressed faithful and suggests instead that reconciliation will ultimately be achieved with some of their former oppressors. Remarkably, *1 Enoch* projects a final state in which the whole of humanity – Jews and Gentiles alike – will be called into a new pattern of justice, while monstrous evils that were not part of the original created order will be destroyed.

The next two chapters consider the experience of the Latin American church, which serves as a litmus test for the implementation of council teachings about those living in poverty. Does the global church's turn to the world shape, or reflect, the Latin American church's experience of moving to the margins? By examining social justice initiatives in Latin America before and after the council, Eduardo Soto Parra illustrates how the Latin American church's turn to the world is a direct result of the council, and yet also an independent response from the bishops there to the conditions of Latin American life. Remarkably, only three years after the council the Latin American bishops gave a name to the church's "preferential option for the poor" at their conference in Medellín. While subsequent episcopal conferences did not consistently display the boldness of that first conference, Soto Parra shows how the Latin American church has been at the forefront of the church's thinking about social justice over the past half century.

The council also suggested that literature should be recognized as a source of insight into contemporary culture and its social contexts. In this vein, Cynthia Wallace examines Ana Castillo's novel *The Guardians*, which illustrates the church's turn to the world in Latin America. Using *The Guardians* as an example of post-conciliar Catholic literature, Wallace argues that Catholic literature today reflects the shifts that have taken place both in society and in the church over the last fifty years. Through the eyes of its characters, *The Guardians* offers insight into how the spirit of the council has permeated the Catholic imagination in Latin America. Wallace challenges us to look at the contribution of literature, particularly Catholic literature from the Global South, to see how Catholics imagine themselves living out the church's turn to the world in the painfully real circumstances of poverty and injustice.

When the council spoke about the need for peace, it was specifically concerned about the urgent need for geopolitical peace in the context of the Cold War arms race between the United States and the Soviet Union. In chapter 8, Christopher Hrynkow considers the council's turn to the world by locating peace-building as an integral part of Catholic social teaching. In examining this legacy of the council, Hrynkow conceptualizes peace in "eco-ethical" terms, insisting that environmental sustainability must be joined with larger ethical commitments to human dignity. From the council's statements on peace to Benedict XVI's World Day of Peace messages to Francis's encyclical *Laudato Si'*, Hrynkow argues that there is a framework within Catholic teaching that supports the development of a green culture of peace. He posits that the church has moved away from its focus on just-war theory based in natural law to embrace a nonviolent understanding of Jesus and his gospel. However, as Francis has recently emphasized in *Laudato Si'*, a continued commitment is required if the earth and its inhabitants are to live in peaceful and sustainable coexistence in the years ahead.

The last two chapters turn to the context in which the volume arises and consider Canadian contributions to the council as well as the council's impact on Canada. Catherine Clifford documents key ways in which Canadian bishops shaped the council's social justice agenda and Canadian Catholics acted on the conciliar vision after the council. Significantly, Canadian bishops were among the first to call for a more constructive engagement with the world than was appearing in the council's early draft documents. This shift in orientation opened the way for the council's turn to the world and with it the creation of institutional initiatives such as the Pontifical Commission for Justice and Peace, in which Canadians played a leading role. Back on Canadian soil, the council's new commitment to ecumenism inspired the formation of ecumenical coalitions, which in turn paved the way for the Canadian ecumenical justice initiative KAIROS. Similarly, the theme of integral development informed the establishment in 1967 of the Canadian Catholic Organization for Development and Peace, which continues to be active as the official international development organization of the Catholic Church in Canada.

Finally, Mary Jo Leddy offers a reflection on Canada today through the lens of social justice. Inspired by liberation theologians in Latin America, Leddy argues that the Canadian context requires a specifically Canadian response to the council's teaching today. Turning to the world effectively requires a careful analysis of what exactly that part of the world looks like. Drawing on the work of Northrop Frye and Margaret Atwood, Leddy suggests that Canada has been shaped by its colonial history and a concomitant garrison mentality. This worldview even now conditions how we relate to the "other" – from Indigenous peoples to newcomers in our land. Leddy offers as a remedy a practical theology firmly rooted in the "here" of a particular time and place which, in turn, allows the local church to turn authentically toward the world. She cites examples from her work of welcoming refugees at Romero House in Toronto to illustrate how this can be done, even when this means going against the grain of history and the prevailing culture.

As a whole, then, *Turning to the World: Social Justice and the Common Good since Vatican II* tells the story of how the Second Vatican Council has reshaped the Catholic Church in the last half century and up to the present day. The narrative we see depicted here is neither static nor without tension. The church's reception of the council's vision of social justice is unmistakably human, fraught with hesitation and marked by hopeful possibility. It is a vision that is encapsulated in the very first words of *Gaudium et Spes*: "The joys and hopes, the grief and anguish of the people of our time ...

are the joys and hopes, the grief and anguish of the followers of Christ as well" (GS 1). By choosing to stand in solidarity with all of human experience, the Catholic Church has called not only its members but all people of good will to embrace the world in a new way, shedding any tendency to withdraw from it. As Francis compellingly underlines in *Laudato Si'*, the earth is our common home. The social world in which we live is also our common heritage. Vatican II provided some powerful guideposts for the Catholic Church to turn itself more fully to the concerns of social justice and the common good. With a half-century of experience since the council to reflect on, we are now well placed to consider how the church's turn to the world reshaped both the church and the world.

1

Conscience, Freedom, and Humanism: New Foundations for Catholic Social Teaching at Vatican II

Michael W. Duggan

A distinctive feature of the Second Vatican Council was its exploration of the interactions between the interior universe of the person and the external world of society. The council employed the language of evolution and development to express the symbiotic relationship between what is unfolding inside human beings and the dynamics that are shaping the global community. World history may be viewed as the externalization of the energies in the innermost core of every person.

Vatican II identified conscience as the nucleus of the interior life and social justice as the animating force that makes a society healthy. These are foundational principles of the new humanism that the council initiated. The conciliar documents profile the individual conscience and personal freedom as the prerequisites that allow people to be authentically themselves. Such authenticity generates the instincts for practising social justice. One may surmise from these documents that everyone who exercises genuine freedom of conscience works instinctively for justice in the world.

In this chapter, I point out how the focus on personal conscience and freedom supplied the foundations for the social teaching on the common good and social justice in *Gaudium et Spes* (*Pastoral Constitution on the Church in the Modern World*). I begin by locating the Second Vatican Council within its historical context and highlight some features that distinguish this council from the previous twenty ecumenical councils. I then examine the council's expositions on conscience and freedom in *Gaudium et Spes* and related texts: *Lumen Gentium*

(*Dogmatic Constitution on the Church*), *Dei Verbum* (*Dogmatic Constitution on Divine Revelation*), and *Dignitatis Humanae* (*Declaration on Religious Liberty*). I describe how this material provided the ingredients of a new humanism that the council mentioned and that Popes Paul VI, John Paul II, and Benedict XVI developed in the half-century following Vatican II. In conclusion, I offer a reflection on the pastoral humanism of Pope Francis as the embodiment of the Vatican II heritage in the twenty-first century.

DISTINCTIVE FEATURES OF VATICAN II

The Second Vatican Council transformed the consciousness of the Catholic Church. The documents express a new self-awareness of the universal church as standing in relationship to, rather than isolated from, the world. The church emerged from self-imposed isolation and began learning the art of conversation with all people. The assembled bishops came to realize that they had to listen with new ears and see with new eyes what was going on in the world. In their encounters with the world, listening had to precede speaking, and self-critical discernment needed to inform teaching.

The church's discourse had to reflect the church's identity. The council described the church as the people of God journeying through life along with everyone else (LG 7, 9), and as a servant who identifies with those who are poor and suffering on the margins of society (LG 8). Just as the church abandoned its nineteenth-century profile as a perfect society set apart from outsiders, so too it gave up the rhetoric of a disciplinarian addressing a fallen world. The church would articulate its message as a participant in the global conversation on how to enhance the lives of all human beings.

The council acknowledged that, in the second half of the twentieth century, people were acquiring a new global awareness. Astronauts were entering outer space, quantum physicists were disclosing the instability of matter, diplomats were pursuing world peace in the wake of World War II, and human rights activists were demanding an end to discrimination based on race, gender, and religion. Jews who survived the Shoah were constructing the state of Israel, African nations were shedding the heritage of colonialism, and Indigenous peoples across the globe were recovering their languages and cultures.

Historical consciousness delivered the church from a fixation on what is eternal and unchanging and provoked an incipient interest in an evolutionary universe where the only constant is change. The church had to surrender its nostalgia for both the Thomistic synthesis of the thirteenth century, with its foundations in the classical metaphysics of Aristotle, and the Augustinian worldview derived from Plato. Investigation of the real world had to temper speculation about an ideal world. The council redirected its attention from heaven to earth. Historical, critical studies of the Bible were propelling theologians to search for Jesus within history instead of viewing him exclusively as the divine Son eternally with the Father and the Holy Spirit. Philosophical traditions of phenomenology and existentialism redirected attention from the nature of objects to the experiences of the human subject. Freudian analysis exposed the dynamics of the unconscious and subconscious as more profound and determinative than the rational mind. G.W.F. Hegel had described history as unfolding according to the dialectics of the Spirit, whereas Karl Marx attributed the shaping of history to social dialectics stemming from economic disparities. Charles Darwin demonstrated that humans are descendants of animals, and Albert Einstein described matter as a transient crystallization of energy.

Against such a background, the church had to contemplate God within the world. If God was present in the dynamics of history, surely the church had to become a more fully engaged participant in the world. In order to do so the church had to renounce attachments to privilege and status, commit itself to ongoing renewal, and thereby gradually earn the trust of all people (LG 8, 41, 48). The church needed to let go of its residual fear and suspicion of the world. It set about learning the art of relationship, lessening its tendencies to be aloof, cerebral, pretentious, and domineering while cultivating attributes of empathy, compassion, and vulnerability. The church assumed the profile of a prophetic presence – a leaven in the world – that seeks to animate rather than dominate (LG 40; cf. AA 2; AGD 15). As such, it professed a commitment to respect the rightful independence of human enterprises (GS 36).

Aggiornamento and *ressourcement* were the processes that brought the church to a fresh understanding of revelation and tradition at Vatican II. *Aggiornamento* is the name bishops and scholars gave to the church's learning from the contemporary world. An essential element of *aggiornamento* was inculturation, which entailed rethinking theology and representing liturgy within the full span of languages and cultures across the globe. Just as *aggiornamento* brought the church more in sync with modernity, so *ressourcement* grounded the church in its most ancient roots.[1] *Ressourcement* involved the fresh examination of biblical and patristic sources that predated Thomism by more than a millennium. Scholars were freed from slavish attachment to Latin texts and translations, as they now read biblical and early apostolic sources in their original languages against the background of their native cultural settings in order to seek out the message intended by the original authors. These movements enhanced the catholicity of the church insofar as inculturation relocated the church beyond its Eurocentric horizons and *ressourcement* reintroduced the church to its Semitic ancestry in ancient Israel and early Judaism.

CATHOLIC SOCIAL TEACHING AT VATICAN II

Aggiornamento and *ressourcement* were creative intellectual and existential adventures that made Vatican II the turning point in the history of official Catholic social teaching. That history extends from the encyclical *Rerum Novarum* (*On the Condition of Labour*), which Pope Leo XIII issued on 15 May 1891, to *Caritas in Veritate,* which Benedict XVI published on 29 June 2009, and surfaced most recently in *Evangelii Gaudium*, the apostolic exhortation of Francis dated 24 November 2013.[2] Every document of the Magisterium within this tradition addressed contemporary political, economic, and social issues. For example, just as Leo XIII concentrated on the rights of workers in the wake of industrialization at the end of the nineteenth century, so Benedict XVI offered a perceptive critique of the market economy in the wake of the worldwide financial crises at the end of the first decade in the twenty-first century. The documents of Vatican II made a distinctive contribution to the tradition in that they set Catholic social teaching on new theological and philosophical foundations.

   Gaudium et Spes identified seminal concepts in earlier Catholic social teaching and expanded them into a synthesis on the human person, which was unprecedented vis-à-vis the previous twenty ecumenical councils. This was the first "pastoral" constitution in the history of the church and, as such, reoriented the theological enterprise toward the actual life experience of human beings. I examine *Gaudium et Spes* by describing the theme of personalism that runs throughout the document, and then focus on the particular issues of conscience, freedom, social justice, and the common good.

Personalism

Concern for people runs throughout *Gaudium et Spes*. The document begins with a description of the church living in solidarity with every human being and concludes with a profile of the church as an agent of dialogue among all peoples (GS 1, 92). A survey of societal change in the 1960s introduces the two major sections of the document, the first on the human vocation and the second on particular issues related to family life, culture, economic development, political action, and the pursuit of peace (GS 1–10, 11–45, 46–93).

The opening lines of *Gaudium et Spes* highlight affectivity as the energy that generates solidarity between the church and all people. Feelings of joy, hope, grief, and anguish are the experiences that bond the church with everyone else, beginning with those who are on the margins of society.[3] People may have different thoughts but they have common feelings. They may be separated by creeds but they are united by shared intuitions. Ideologies divide but love unites. Ultimately, suffering is the experience that binds each person to every other person and to God insofar as suffering calls forth compassion.

I concentrate on the first major section of *Gaudium et Spes*, which presents a description of the human person that provides the theological bases for the discussion of economics and politics in the second section. The opening section consists of four chapters that contemplate human beings from the inside outward: (a) the interior life of the individual (GS 12–22); (b) the person in community (GS 23–32); (c) human activity that shapes the world (GS 33–9); and (d) a summary reflection on the interaction between the church and society (GS 40–5).

The first chapter elaborates a theological anthropology that serves as the groundwork for the discussion of social justice in the second chapter. It begins by describing human beings as created in the image of God and ends with a description of Christ as the new Adam who reveals most fully what it means to be human (GS 12, 22). The intervening paragraphs describe the human condition under four headings: body-soul unity (14), intellect (15), conscience (16), and freedom (17). Reflections on the human experiences of sin (13) and death (18) frame this material. An extended examination of atheism with an encouragement of dialogue between believers and nonbelievers serves as a coda for the whole chapter (19–21).

The second chapter opens with the proposal that the communitarian nature of human beings demands that each person relate
not just to an immediate circle of friends but also to all humankind
(GS 23–5). The chapter then concentrates on seven principles that
need to inform everyone's decisions and actions so that they benefit
the human family. These principles are the common good (GS 26),
respect for the human person (GS 27), love for one's enemies (GS
28), social justice on the premise of the equality of human beings
(GS 29), the need to transcend an individualistic morality (GS 30),
participation in society (GS 31), and solidarity (GS 32).

Conscience

The council identifies conscience as the source of activity that defines
each person and shapes the world: "Deep within their consciences men and women discover a law which they have not laid upon
themselves and which they must obey. Its voice, ever calling them to
love and to do what is good and to avoid evil, tells them inwardly at
the right moment: do this, shun that. For they have in their hearts a
law inscribed by God. Their dignity rests in observing this law, and
by it they will be judged" (GS 16).[4] The text is suffused with biblical language as it echoes Paul's instruction on conscience (Greek
syneidēsis) with its allusions to Jeremiah and perhaps Second Isaiah
(Rom. 2:14–16; Jer. 31:31–4; cf. Isa. 51:7).[5] Paul asserts that when
Gentiles fulfill the demands of the law they do so by acting "according to nature" (*physei*). Their capacity to behave in conformity to
Torah is evidence that the requirement of the law is written on their
hearts. Their righteous behaviours illustrate a correspondence between the dictates of conscience and the prescriptions of the Torah.

Here Paul elaborates upon Jeremiah's description of the "new covenant" as consisting in YHWH's inscribing the Torah on the hearts of
Judahites during the exile (587–538 BCE; Jer. 31:31–4).[6] The covenant is "new" insofar as the Torah becomes internalized within the
consciousness of every Judahite. Indeed, such consciousness consists
in Torah awareness, which provides an interpretive insight into reality. The old dispensation had centred on the Torah that God had
inscribed on stone tablets and Moses had written on parchment
(Deut. 5:22; 31:24–9). Jeremiah asserted that, since the citizens of
Judah had not aligned their behaviour with these stipulations, the
commandments stood over against them as sources of judgment and

condemnation. The people's refusal to observe the written Torah had provoked YHWH to allow the Babylonians to destroy Jerusalem in 587 BCE (Jer. 25:8–11). Nevertheless, Jeremiah viewed the exile as the period in which the Judean deportees would experience an interior transformation that consisted in Torah instruction moving from outside among the community to reside uniquely within the heart of every Judahite. The Jeremiad tradition envisions the new covenant as being actualized in early Judaism, which began with the restoration of Jerusalem and Judah when the exiles returned to the land in 539 BCE. In this new era, personal consciousness is synonymous with consciousness of Torah, experienced not as an external prescription but as intuitive wisdom. The post-exilic Deuteronomists describe this wisdom reservoir as "the word in your heart for you to observe" (Deut. 30:14). Jeremiah and his associates envisioned the new covenant of Torah consciousness specific to the interior life of the individual as replacing the former dispensation of the external text calling for group conformity. This was a transition from the old era of communal prescription to the new era of personal perception.[7]

The early gospel tradition narrates Jesus bringing the tradition of Jeremiah to new realization in his blessing the cup at the last supper with the words, "This is the new covenant in my blood" (1 Cor. 11:25; Luke 22:20). Paul adopts Jeremiah's language when he speaks of apostles as "ministers of a new covenant" (2 Cor. 3:6) and expands the scope of the new covenant tradition in Second Temple Judaism by applying to the Gentiles what Jeremiah had foreseen for the Jews. He asserts that God has inscribed the Torah on the hearts of Gentiles as the instructive wisdom in their consciences that motivates them to actualize in practice the core virtues of Judaism (Rom. 2:14–16).

Vatican II describes this word of God as resonating in the conscience of every person, in every time and place (GS 16). The council maintains the objective nature of God's law in the heart while emphasizing the unique manner in which each person assimilates and acts upon its content.[8] Adherence to objective norms liberates a person from self-attachment. Truth challenges egotism and beckons an individual toward self-transcendence and community. The dictates of love and justice invite a person out of self-centred isolation and into relationships based on service. Renouncing egocentric ideas and preferences is essential to maturing as a person. At the same time, conscience always belongs to an individual human subject.[9] Everyone hears the commandments and acts on them in a unique

manner. Subjectivity demands that each person take up the primary vocation of becoming oneself, distinct from all other people.
Individuals accomplish this by living out the dialogue with divine
wisdom that takes place in their conscience. As one matures by putting into practice the word in the heart, faithfulness to God becomes
synonymous with loyalty to one's innermost being. Therefore, the
judgment of God concerns the degree to which one has lived according to the demands of a personal conscience and thus has become a
genuine self. This perspective underlies the council's statement that
atheists will experience eternal life by adhering to the dictates of
their consciences (LG 16).

Vatican II describes conscience as the resource of both personal
uniqueness and interpersonal connection because conscience is the
habitation of the divine presence. "Their conscience is people's most
secret core, and their sanctuary. There they are alone with God whose
voice echoes in their depths" (GS 16). This language had originated
in a radio address of Pope Pius XII on the Day of the Family, 23
March 1952.[10] The Holy Father had described conscience under the
metaphor of the *adyton*, the innermost sanctum in Greco-Roman
temples where priests accessed the divine presence. The metaphor
emphasizes that only the individual and no one else has access to
his or her own conscience, the most intimate of all locales where the
most sacred of all encounters – between God and the person – takes
place. The highlighting of secrecy corresponds with Jesus' instruction: "pray to your Father who is in secret; and your Father who sees
in secret will reward you" (Matt. 6:6).

This encounter with God in solitude makes people conscious of
their unique identity with the attendant responsibility to express
that uniqueness in their actions. Personal uniqueness is essential to
relationships, which naturally occur between individuals who celebrate their differences while finding their common ground in shared
intuitions and experiences. Solitude provides the instincts for loving
one's neighbours in ways that set those people free to be themselves.
Awakening to the subjective dimensions of one's inner conscience is
the premise for putting objective moral norms into practice.

This relative priority of the subject in relation to the object is
consistent with the distinctive outlook on revelation and faith at
Vatican II compared with Vatican I. The First Vatican Council (8
December 1869–20 October 1870) described revelation as the
communication of divine truths set forth in scripture and then

handed on in tradition through the teaching of the apostles and bishops.[11] Faith, as the acceptance of revelation, consists in the submission of intellect and will to the truths of scripture and the church's Magisterium. In *Dei Verbum* (*Dogmatic Constitution on Divine Revelation*), Vatican II described revelation as God's communication of divine life in love to human beings, and faith as the receptivity of human beings to this life-giving love (DV 1, 2, 5). Vatican I had described revelation in terms of prescriptive doctrine, whereas Vatican II, while incorporating this content, presented revelation more in the vocabulary of divine self-disclosure that is not reducible to categorical definitions. Vatican I had concentrated on the objective content of faith, "what one believes" (*fides quae*), whereas Vatican II directed attention to the subjective experience of faith, "the act of believing" (*fides qua*). These dimensions of revelation and faith are not mutually exclusive. However, God's personal self-communication of divine life that human beings access through existential trust constitutes the precondition for apprehending doctrine by intellectual assent. Therefore, Vatican II provided the experiential foundations for contemplating the normative formulations of Vatican I. In less benign terms, one may conceive of the movement from Vatican I to Vatican II as a shift in focus from ideology to intuition.

Vatican II exhibited a new-found fascination with interiority. The council directed attention inward in order to disclose the resources within each person that move them to care for all other people. The description of conscience in *Gaudium et Spes* is consistent with the portrayals of revelation and faith in *Dei Verbum*. God communicates divine life in love to all people all the time. The conscience of every person, atheist and believer alike, is the reservoir of truth that informs a person's behaviour. However, consciousness of the divine presence grows according to the measure of one's faith. Such faith is the trust that binds one to God after the model of Abraham, who "trusted YHWH and it was accounted to him as uprightness" (Gen. 15:6; Rom. 4:3). This is also "the faith of Jesus Christ" that brings justification to everyone who actualizes it by personally believing (Rom. 1:17, 3:21–2; Gal. 2:16). Such faith consists in being responsive to the life and love that originate in God and not in the self. This vulnerability to the invasion of God's love into the deepest recesses of one's being culminates finally in one's participating in the divine nature (DV 2). Faith, therefore, acquaints a person with the subtleties of grace and produces the intuitive wisdom that accounts for the development of doctrine. *Dei Verbum* asserts that tradition, as the handing on of divine wisdom from generation to generation, develops insofar as individuals become more attuned to God's presence in their personal experience, contemplation, and study of sacred texts (DV 8).

Freedom

Vatican II emphasized freedom as the single requirement necessary for the operation of conscience. "It is, however, only in freedom that people can turn themselves toward what is good ... [Human] dignity therefore requires [people] to act out of conscious and free choice, as moved and drawn in a personal way from within, and not by their own blind impulses or by external constraint" (GS 17). This positive evaluation of freedom was controversial. For example, Ratzinger argues that the description of the human person in GS 17 lacks a Christological foundation. He states, "The section on freedom, in which the Constitution deliberately takes up a theme of modern thought, is one of the least satisfactory in the whole document" (136–7).[12] As a result, in his opinion, the instruction reflects a natural ethic that is overly optimistic about the capacity of humans to exercise freedom without explicitly relying on grace. The council could have grounded the biblical tradition on freedom more fully in the Torah by pointing to liberation as the defining activity of the God of Israel. In the covenant at Sinai, all commandments are premised on YHWH's self-identification as the one who liberates people from slavery: "I am YHWH your God who brought you ... out of the house of slavery" (Exod. 20:2; see also Exod. 3:7–8). Adherence to YHWH implies commitments to live in personal freedom and to liberate and protect anyone who suffers oppression (e.g., Exod. 22:21–7, 23:1–9).

Nevertheless, Vatican II teaching follows the rationale that, since humans are the image of God (Gen. 1:26–7), the freedom of human beings originates in the freedom of God. Since God does not act by coercion, freedom is essential to an individual's every action. Moreover, everyone is capable of exercising genuine freedom, according to Ben Sira's instruction: "If you choose, you can keep the commandments, and to act faithfully is a matter of your own choice" (Sir. 15:15). This scriptural support provides common ground for dialogue between believers and nonbelievers. The church's contribution to such dialogue consists in its proclaiming

the gospel of freedom in the tradition of Paul, who describes the
spirit of adoption as animating the daughters and sons of God,
thereby liberating them from the controlling power of legal prescriptions (Rom. 8:14–19; Gal. 4:4–7, 5:2).

Gaudium et Spes broke new ground when it linked freedom to
conscience and asserted that the gospel "scrupulously respects the
dignity of conscience and its freedom of choice" (GS 41). Such
words represent the final withdrawal of the opposition to freedom
of conscience that had characterized papal teaching in the nineteenth century. In his denunciation of Félicité de Lammenais and
liberal Catholicism, Pope Gregory XVI had described freedom of
conscience as a principle that undermined society and jeopardized
people's salvation. Pius IX quoted this denunciation in *Quanta
Cura*, the encyclical that accompanied his *Syllabus of Errors*.[13]
Vatican II contradicted these instructions by asserting that freedom
of conscience is actually essential to accomplishing what is good and
therefore most beneficial to society (GS 17).[14]

This discontinuity between the personalism of Vatican II and the
ideological preoccupations that led up to Vatican I becomes more fully
manifest in *Dignitatis Humanae* (*Declaration on Religious Liberty*).
In the *Syllabus of Errors*, Pius IX had denounced freedom of religion
as articulated in these terms: "Every man is free to embrace and pro-
fess that religion which, guided by the light of reason, he shall consider true" (*Syllabus* 15). By contrast, *Dignitatis Humanae* insists on
the moral obligation of each person to adhere to the religious truth
he or she discovers by free inquiry. "Human beings cannot satisfy this
obligation in a way that is in keeping with their own nature unless
they enjoy both psychological freedom and immunity from external
coercion. Therefore, the right to religious freedom is based ... on the
very nature of the individual person" (DH 2).

In the *Syllabus,* Pius IX had decried both the principle of separation between church and state and also opposition to Catholicism's
status as the only legitimate religion in certain countries (*Syllabus* 55,
73). By contrast, *Dignitatis Humanae* implicitly asserts the necessity
of a pluralistic society in which the state functions independently
from the influence of a particular religion. The state guarantees the
individual's right to choose and practise a religion and safeguards
the freedom of religious institutions to function without undue
interference from society or government (DH 13). An indication of
the distinctive emphasis in *Dignitatis Humanae* is its employment of

the Latin term *libertas* (freedom) and its cognates some fifty-three times, in stark contrast to a single occurrence of the term in the documents of Vatican I.[15]

Vatican II grounds religious freedom in the individual's inalienable right to self-determination. Epistemologically, people move toward truth always by attraction and never through coercion (DH 1). Theologically, faith is a free response to the self-disclosure of God, who engages humankind by invitation devoid of manipulation (DH 10). Every person has the single obligation to live and act in fidelity to his or her conscience.[16] This adherence applies even when one's conviction is at odds with church teaching.[17]

The Common Good and Social Justice

Such assertions on the priority of an individual's freedom to act according to conscience are foundational to the reflection on the communitarian dimension of human beings in *Gaudium et Spes* (23–32). Because people are relational by nature, conscience always beckons individuals to love their neighbour.[18] The council implicitly criticizes capitalist individualism by describing social activity as oriented toward community-building rather than as a zero-sum competition that separates the victors from the vanquished. The critique of such individualism is explicit in the council's exhortation for everyone to develop an ethic of social responsibility that extends beyond the confines of private morality (GS 30).[19] Since each person is related to every other person, social justice must be a primary matter of conscience. Individuals express their freedom most fully when they work for justice on behalf of everyone else. Freedom in society originates with individuals courageously exercising freedom of thought, speech, and action to change the social, political, and economic structures that oppress their sisters and brothers locally and globally.

Vatican II calls people to work for the enhancement of the common good rather than the mere advancement of the individual. The council builds on the legacy of John XXIII when it describes the common good as "the sum total of social conditions which allow people, either as groups or as individuals, to reach their fulfillment more fully and more easily" (GS 26; cf. MM 65). The council gives universal extension to the scope of the common good by beckoning everyone to work for the benefit of all human beings across the globe. Individuals must challenge governments, corporate enterprises, and international agencies to provide the basic necessities of food, clothing, and shelter to people struggling for survival and to guarantee the civil rights of all people.

Work on behalf of the common good is always labour in the cause of social justice (GS 29). The pre-conciliar tradition asserted the obligation of the state to practise distributive justice. Leo XIII spoke of justice in the interest of the common good as he addressed the plight of the working poor in Europe at the end of the nineteenth century (RN 27). Pius XI introduced the term "social justice" as the principle that demanded state intervention to prevent the accumulation of wealth in the hands of a few due to an economy that focused only on the individual (QA 88). In *Mater et Magistra*, John XXIII spoke of social justice when addressing the disparities in social and economic development both within and among nations. Social justice entails the reallocation of resources. He stated that "the economic prosperity of any people is to be assessed not so much from the sum total of goods and wealth as from the distribution of goods according to norms of justice, so that everyone in the community can develop and perfect himself or herself" (MM 74).

In the council's call to action, one may detect the influence of the American civil rights movement under the leadership of Dr Martin Luther King Jr. Insofar as *Gaudium et Spes* seeks to awaken people from "indifference" to pressing social issues and "inertia" brought on by acceptance of the status quo in a self-centred conscience, it offers an implicit response to the "Letter from Birmingham Jail" that Dr King wrote to church leaders who had criticized him for causing social unrest. In that letter dated 16 April 1963, Dr King asserted, "Human progress never rolls in on the wheels of inevitability; it comes through the tireless efforts of men willing to be co-workers with God, and without this hard work, time itself becomes an ally of the forces of social stagnation. We must use time creatively, in the knowledge that the time is always ripe to do right."[20]

Dr King stated more than once in his letter, "I have been disappointed with the church," referring to its reluctance to take up the cause of desegregation on behalf of all African Americans. In a lapidary statement on the need for change that many theologians and bishops would contemplate at Vatican II, Dr King wrote, "I have watched many churches commit themselves to a completely otherworldly religion which makes a strange un-Biblical distinction between body and soul, between the sacred and the secular."²¹ By taking up the cause of social justice and portraying the church as the advocate of freedom, Vatican II made a decisive turn toward the world. This reorientation was signalled by the council's adopting the terminology of a "new humanism," which would become a theme in Catholic social teaching for the next fifty years.

HUMANISM AT VATICAN II

The council's descriptions of conscience and advocacy of freedom propel action in the cause of social justice and therefore comprise the core of the new humanism. The council employed the term in its positive evaluation of initiatives to build the world community. "We are witnessing the birth of a new humanism, where people are defined before all else by their responsibility to their sisters and brothers and at the court of history" (GS 55). It is significant that the council ascribes the new humanism to cultural movements that originated in the world at large, independent from the church. In fact, the bishops at Vatican II were ambivalent about the term "humanism." The positive estimation noted here stands in contrast to the two other occurrences of the term, which are comparatively pessimistic: "In the past it was the exception to repudiate God and religion to the point of abandoning them, and then only in individual cases; but nowadays it seems a matter of course to reject them as incompatible with scientific progress and a new kind of humanism" (GS 7); and "Finally, how are we to accept that culture's claim to autonomy is justified, without falling into a humanism which is purely earthbound and even hostile to religion?" (GS 56). In each of these statements, the council was attempting to read "the signs of the times" (GS 4). Its contrasting evaluations of "humanism" indicate this was not an easy task.

In facing the formidable challenge of determining the parameters for dialogue with the world at large, the council employs the language of "autonomy." The council devotes a full paragraph to the topic, in which it asserts that research in the sciences and humanities needs to follow universally accepted methods of inquiry into nature without reference to divinity or religion (GS 36). Similarly, procedures of law and governance that shape societies must derive from research and debate that follow the norms of sound human logic and discourse. The rightful autonomy of humankind consists in people using the gifts of intellect and judgment to advance learning and enhance society. However, autonomy is wrong-headed when human beings do not acknowledge the transcendent source of everything and, instead, make moral judgments on the presupposition that God does not exist. In summary, the council argues that God works within history in a manner that actually confirms the rightful autonomy of human activity (GS 41). Since reason and revelation are complementary to each other, human agency without explicit reference to God is vital to the advancement of humankind.

The unresolved tensions in the council's outlook on humanism reflect a residual dualism that had previously set people of faith in opposition to atheists. The council began to remedy this polarity between believer and nonbeliever when it identified conscience as the common ground for dialogue (LG 16). People with a living faith and atheists with a refined conscience share a commitment to serve humankind. People who act in good conscience without reference to God advance the common good instinctively. This presupposition compelled the council to support the rightful autonomy of the world from the control of any particular religion. People of good conscience without explicit faith in God were creating the new humanism that the council commended (GS 55).

Tensions arise when explicit ideology replaces the instinctive wisdom of sound consciences. The bishops at Vatican II had grown up lamenting the antagonism toward religion that had animated the French Revolution, became a prerequisite for the disciples of Karl Marx, and fuelled the atheism of Friedrich Nietzsche. Therefore the council protested any humanism that derived from nineteenth-century anticlericalism (GS 7, 58). However, this antagonism toward programmatic atheism reflected a clash of ideologies. Ideologues are not given to dialogue. Defenders of nineteenth-century formulations of papal authority and teaching had carried on a century-long combat with purveyors of systematic atheism. Now at Vatican II, bishops who had absorbed a lifetime of prescriptive Catholicism were changing their mode of engagement from adversarial confrontation to sympathetic dialogue on the basis of the interlocutors' shared humanity. The bishops' education in humanity had refocused their understanding of Jesus to the point that they could assert, "To follow Christ the perfect human is to become more human oneself" (GS 41). Experiences of pain and affliction, joy and hope, and the interior voice of conscience provided the meeting ground for engaging people whom the hierarchy had formerly perceived as their adversaries. Becoming conscious of the common ground provided by the experience of being human prompted the bishops to commend people outside the church for giving birth to a new humanism.

THE NEW HUMANISM FROM PAUL VI TO BENEDICT XVI

Following the council, Paul VI, John Paul II, and Benedict XVI furthered this humanism, which they proceeded to qualify with the adjectives "new," "integral," or "transcendental." Paul VI focuses on the theme in his encyclical *Populorum Progressio (On the Development of Peoples)*, which he issued less than two years after the closing of Vatican II. He provides a positive description of "humanism" by tying it to "development," a concept he transferred from the sphere of economics to the process of human maturation. Development is the multifaceted dynamic through which individuals construct their lives by thought, decision, and action. Some of the papal language is surprisingly close to popular speech of the 1960s as the pope declares that each person is responsible for "fulfillment" as "the principal agent of his or her own success or failure" (PP 15).[22] Nevertheless, Paul VI frames these phrases in the discourse of vocation and teleology. Each person is called into being in order to become a unique self. The process culminates in ultimate communion with Christ, which is "a new fulfillment of self."[23] Orientation toward this final self-realization in God is the defining element of the new humanism. However, this perspective is eschatological rather than otherworldly insofar as it describes individuals growing by relating to all other people throughout their personal history rather than living in self-protective isolation in hope of meriting life beyond the grave. Love, service, and action in the cause of social justice are the vital ingredients that lead to maturity (viz., PP 20). Paul VI draws upon the works of Jacques Maritain and Henri de Lubac when he argues that, since every person is oriented toward self-transcendence, openness to God is the necessary premise for a "complete humanism" (PP 42).[24]

John Paul II issued his encyclical *Sollicitudo Rei Socialis (On Social Concern)* as a reflection on the world situation in light of *Populorum Progressio* twenty years later, on 30 December 1987. John Paul laments how that time span was marked by a widening gap between the many nations that suffered underdevelopment and the few that experienced "super-development." The poorest nations were so overwhelmed by debt that they had no hope of recovery from systemic deprivation, whereas the wealthiest nations experienced the excesses of unbridled consumerism. In either case, human beings were diminished by their isolation, whether due to the absence of food, clothing, and shelter on the one hand or to the superfluity of creature comforts on the other. In response to such extreme inequalities, John Paul highlights the interdependence of the human race and calls for an ethic based on solidarity, which he identifies as the virtue essential for the times. He describes solidarity as "a firm and persevering determination to commit oneself to the common good; that is to say to the good of all and of each individual, because we are really responsible for all" (SRS 38).

Solidarity is the antidote to the economic systems based on individualism on the one hand and collectivism on the other. Solidarity expresses the personalism of John Paul II. Everyone becomes uniquely oneself by living in relationship to every other person. Therefore, we must view economic development in a global context and appreciate that it consists not only in the production of goods but also in their distribution according to the requirements of the global common good. Furthermore, economic development is inseparable from personal development just as, in personal and communal living, "having" is inseparable from "being" (SRS 27–9). The headwaters of development reside in the interior life of every person. John Paul portrays human development as emerging from the transcendent origins of humans as created in the image of God to do work that expresses a unique self for the benefit of all other people. One's being becomes productive through work that provides the substance of "having" both for one's self and for others. A person develops him- or herself by contributing to the lives of all other people. Economics is the art of organizing human productivity so that its benefits sustain the lives of everyone. This vision of human development for individuals applies also to nations and ethnic groups. Wealthy nations become more humane as they provide goods and services to enhance the economies of nations mired in poverty. The humanism of John Paul II provided a cohesive vision of the reciprocal relationship between human and economic development.

Just as John Paul II had composed *Solicitudo Rei Socialis* as a reflection on *Populorum Progressio* twenty years hence, so, after approximately the same time span, Benedict XVI adopted both of these documents as the primary sources for his encyclical *Caritas in Veritate* (*On Integral Human Development in Charity and Truth*), which he issued on 29 June 2009. In keeping with the post-Vatican II tradition, Benedict reasserts that openness to God is the essential ingredient of an integral humanism. He advances the tradition by describing this openness as a response to grace that endows an individual with the courage and endurance necessary to persevere in working for justice (CV 78). Benedict calls for a spirituality of justice since the maturity of one's interior life determines the long-term effectiveness of one's actions in the cause of the common good. He contributes to this spirituality by examining social justice within the context of an extended meditation on the reciprocal dynamics of love and knowledge, the essential components of truth. Love orients knowledge toward goodness while knowledge informs love with the insight that cultivates virtue and effective living (CV 3–9). Love is the foundation for justice but expresses a generosity that is greater than justice. Therefore, love is the measure of justice and, at the same time, presumes an unconditional commitment to social justice (CV 6).

THE HERITAGE OF VATICAN II: *EVANGELII GAUDIUM*

Francis issued his apostolic exhortation, *Evangelii Gaudium* (*The Joy of the Gospel*), on 24 November 2013, the Feast of Christ the King. This marked the closing of the Year of Faith that Benedict XVI had inaugurated on 11 October 2012 to celebrate the fiftieth anniversary of the opening of the Second Vatican Council. Throughout the document Francis describes the church's foremost mission as evangelization. This act of proclaiming the Good News is distinct from proselytism in that it wins the attention of people by attraction, not coercion (EG 15). Furthermore, evangelization cannot be reduced to ideological disquisitions on moral or doctrinal precepts (EG 39). Francis describes evangelization as the announcement of God's love that redeems people from slavery to self and liberates them to care for all people. Christians communicate this message primarily by the way they live, and secondarily by conversations that enhance the freedom and well-being of everyone involved. Far from drawing people into a sectarian subgroup, such evangelization aims to break through the walls of elitist associations so that the church becomes, in the words of Vatican II, "a sign and instrument ... of the unity of the entire human race" (LG 1). Francis calls for the adaptation of the gospel to local cultures and encourages interfaith and ecumenical dialogues, conversations between theists and atheists, and deliberations between science and religion.

However, the social implications of the gospel require that it not be confined to the sphere of religion or private spirituality (EG 183). Francis identifies exclusion as a primary offense against the human community. Poverty is the most pervasive force fragmenting humankind today. In light of the prevailing economic disparities in the world, Francis devotes some 30 per cent of *Evangelii Gaudium* to the social implications of the gospel, first in his description of major contemporary tensions in the human race and later in a full chapter on the gospel of social justice (EG 50–75, 176–258). He begins his analysis of the world situation with a pointed criticism of the free market economy that has made outcasts of the poorest people on the globe and reprimands everyone who naively puts faith in this system, which he tags as the golden calf idol of the twenty-first century (EG 53–8; cf. Exod. 32).[25] Subsequently, he calls for a reform of economic theory and practice so that they focus not only on the production but also on the distribution of goods and resources to people who are most in need across the world (EG 204).

Francis follows his post-conciliar predecessors in decrying the individualism that makes people of wealth blind to the plight of their impoverished neighbours.[26] He reviews God's preferential love for the poor in the Hebrew scriptures and the gospels (Exod. 3:7–8, 10; Deut. 15:9; 1 John 3:17). Most emphatically, he exhorts the followers of Jesus to express solidarity in action by actually changing social, government, and business structures in order to provide for a more equitable distribution of goods among all people (EG 188). Francis describes solidarity as a mentality that views goods and resources in terms of their destiny to the human community at large rather than in terms of their ownership by a privileged few. Solidarity provides the standard by which the global village must evaluate the efficacy of private ownership. The right to ownership depends on a person's commitment to transfer the goods and resources that are under his or her control into the hands of the people who most need them. People who accumulate a superfluity of the world's goods are stealing from the poor (EG 189; cf. 57).

Francis mentions a latent Christian humanism among marginalized people in western cultures, which can be awakened to confront the individualism that is fragmenting society (EG 68). He echoes the new humanism, which Paul VI and Benedict XVI had formulated, when he describes openness to God as the element that can provide scholars and leaders with the insight necessary to reconfiguring economics to serve the common good (EG 205). Francis suggests God is practically synonymous with the compassionate freedom that overwhelms the narrow confines of human systems (EG 57).

In his apostolic exhortation, Francis does not employ the vocabulary of conscience and freedom but attends to the dynamics of the interior life that generate works of justice and peace. The hallmarks of anyone who has accepted the *kerygma* of Jesus are a commitment to the common good, a predisposition of preferential love for the poor, instincts of solidarity, and action in the cause of social justice (EG 177–201). In other words, Francis's description of everyone who accepts the Good News accords with the orientation of evangelization in *Justice in the World,* the concluding document of the 1971 Synod of Bishops: "Action on behalf of justice and participation in the transformation of the world fully appear to us as a constitutive dimension of the preaching of the Gospel" (JM, Introduction).[27] If justice is central to the proclamation of the gospel, works of justice are essential evidence of its reception.

Where Paul VI, John Paul II, and Benedict XVI had articulated the intellectual components of the new humanism, Francis now puts this new humanism into practice. Following Vatican II, his predecessors had described the science of transcendent humanism; now he embodies its art. "Realities are more important than ideas" is a principle Francis offers to guide individuals and societies in their work on behalf of peace and justice (EG 231–3). Francis eschews ideologies and formulaic prescriptions for thought and action. In the field of economics, for example, he calls for a "non-ideological ethics" (EG 57). Every particular circumstance requires a creative response marked by unconditional love on the part of the people involved. Generous spontaneity emerges from instincts and intuitions that prompt a person to do what is genuinely good by pushing beyond the confines of convention and predictability.

Anyone who reviews the seminal formulations on conscience, freedom, and social justice in the documents of Vatican II can give thanks that Francis has inaugurated a new era of action. He expands upon what the bishops began at Vatican II as he invites everyone to encounter God and to meet Jesus in their sisters and brothers who are abandoned and excluded (EG 197–8; cf. LG 8; GS 1, 22). Sharing life with every person on the basis of our common vulnerability is what it means for the church to turn to the world in the tradition of Vatican II.

NOTES

1 On the vital role of *ressourcement* in propelling the renewal at Vatican II, see O'Malley, "*Ressourcement*," 47–55.

2 The tradition of Catholic social teaching consists of at least these fourteen essential documents: Leo XIII, *Rerum Novarum* (*On the Condition of Labour*), 1891; Pius XI, *Quadragesimo Anno* (*On Reconstruction of the Social Order*), 1931; John XXIII, *Mater et Magistra* (*On Christianity and Social Progress*), 1961; John XXIII, *Pacem in Terris* (*Peace on Earth*), 1963; *Gaudium et Spes* (*Pastoral Constitution on the Church in the Modern World*), 1965; *Dignitatis Humanae* (*Declaration on Religious Liberty*), 1965; Paul VI, *Populorum Progressio* (*On the Development of Peoples*), 1967; Paul VI, *Octogesima Adveniens* (*A Call to Action on the 80th Anniversary of* Rerum Novarum), 1971; Synod of Bishops, *Justitia in Mundo* (*Justice in the World*), 1971; Paul VI, *Evangelii Nuntiandi* (*Evangelization in the Modern World*), 1975; John Paul II, *Laborem Exercens* (*On Human Work*), 1981; John Paul II, *Sollicitudo Rei Socialis* (*On Social Concern*), 1987; John Paul II, *Centesimus Annus* (*On the One Hundredth Anniversary of* Rerum Novarum), 1991; Benedict XVI, *Caritas in Veritate* (*On Integral Human Development in Charity and Truth*), 2009. See Curran, *Catholic Social Teaching*, 7; and O'Brien and Shannon, *Catholic Social Thought*, v–vi.

3 The opening lines of *Gaudium et Spes* are among the most quoted of Vatican II: "The joys and hopes, the grief and anguish of the people of our time, especially of those who are poor or afflicted, are the joys and hopes, the grief and anguish of the followers of Christ as well" (GS 1).

4 See O'Malley, *What Happened at Vatican II*, 306–11. O'Malley identifies this text as emblematic of a new form of discourse at Vatican II. The rhetoric appeals to common human experience and therefore opens the way to dialogue.

5 See Fitzmyer, *Romans*, 309–12.

6 See Lundbom, *Jeremiah 21–36*, 464–79.

7 The early gospel tradition narrates Jesus bringing the tradition of Jeremiah to new realization in his blessing the cup at the last supper with the words, "This is the new covenant in my blood" (1 Cor. 11:25; cf. Luke 22:20).

8 See Weaver, "Vatican II and Moral Theology," 32–6. Weaver stresses the objective content that informs moral intelligence in the deliberations of conscience according to Vatican II.

9 See Curran, *Catholic Social Teaching*, 75–8. Curran underlines the distinctive emphasis on the subjective dimension of conscience at Vatican II.

10 The original Latin of GS 16 reads: "Conscientia est nucleus secretissimus atque sacrarium hominis, in quo solus est cum Deo, cuius vox resonat in intimo eius." Cf. Pius XII, *Radiomessaggio di sua santità Pio XII in occasione della "Giornata della Famiglia"* (23 March 1952): "La coscienza è quindi, per dirla con una immagine tanto antica quanto degna, un ἄδυτον un santuario, sulla cui soglia tutti debbono arrestarsi. "

11 See "Dogmatic Constitution on the Catholic Faith," section 2, "Of Revelation," in McNabb, *Decrees of the Vatican Council*, 19–21.

12 Ratzinger, "Dignity of the Human Person," 136–40.

13 Gregory XVI, *Mirari Vos* (*On Liberalism and Religious Indifferentism*), 14: "Th[e] shameful font of indifferentism gives rise to that absurd and erroneous proposition which claims that liberty of conscience must be maintained for everyone. It spreads ruin in sacred and civil affairs, though some repeat over and over again with the greatest impudence that some advantage accrues to religion from it ... When all restraints are removed by which men are kept on the narrow path of truth, their nature, which is already inclined to evil, propels them to ruin." Pius IX quoted this text in *Quanta Cura* (*Condemning Current Errors*), 3: "[Our opponents] do not fear to foster that erroneous opinion, most fatal in its effects on the Catholic Church and the salvation of souls, called by Our Predecessor, Gregory XVI, an 'insanity,' viz., that 'liberty of conscience and worship is each man's personal right, which ought to be legally proclaimed and asserted in every rightly constituted society; and that a right resides in the citizens to an absolute liberty, which should be restrained by no authority whether ecclesiastical or civil, whereby they may be able openly and publicly to manifest and declare any of their ideas whatever, either by word of mouth, by the press, or in any other way.'"

14 See O'Malley, "Trent and Vatican II." O'Malley describes how the rhetorical style of the documents of Vatican II represents a marked contrast to that of nineteenth-century papal documents.

15 In delimiting the boundaries of reason in relation to faith, Vatican I asserted that the church upheld the "just freedom" of arts and sciences to follow academic methodology on the condition that "they do not become infected with errors by conflicting with divine teaching, or, by going

beyond their proper limits, intrude upon what belongs to faith and engender confusion" (*Dogmatic Constitution on the Catholic Faith*, IV.12).

16 "All are bound to follow their conscience faithfully in every sphere of activity so that they may come to God, who is their last end" (DH 3).

17 "The right to ... immunity [from coercion] continues to exist even in those who do not live up to their obligation of seeking the truth and adhering to it. The exercise of this right cannot be interfered with as long as the just requirements of public order are observed" (DH 2).

18 Here the council derives its principles on respecting others and loving one's enemies from scripture, notably the Gospel of Matthew (GS 27–8). The judgment scene compels its readers to recognize the poor as Christ's presence in the world (Matt. 25:31–46). Jesus' admonition against judging undergirds the council's appeal for Christians to learn from people who hold different worldviews or social, ethical, and religious convictions (Matt. 7:1–5). Jesus' precept to love one's enemies points to the Sermon on the Mount as an essential resource that guides the practice of social justice (Matt. 5:43–4; see also Matt. 5–7).

19 See Dorr, *Option for the Poor*, 107–10, 127. Dorr describes the controversy John XXIII generated when, in *Mater et Magistra* (59–60), he used vocabulary associated with socialism to outline the intricate network of relationships that define a person. The pontiff's implicit challenge to western individualism carried over to *Gaudium et Spes*.

20 King, "Letter from Birmingham Jail," par. 26; cf. GS 30.

21 King, "Letter from Birmingham Jail," par. 37; cf. GS 33–4.

22 "In the design of God, every individual is called upon to develop and fulfill himself or herself, for every life is vocation" (PP 15). Human beings construct their lives by their personal decisions. Paul VI validates the capability of every person for this task when he says, "By the unaided effort of his or her own intelligence and will, one can grow in humanity, can enhance his or her personal worth, can become more a person" (PP 15).

23 "By reason of union with Christ, the source of life, one attains to a new fulfillment of self, to a transcendent humanism which gives one his or her greatest possible perfection: this is the highest goal of personal development" (PP 16).

24 "What must be aimed at is complete humanism. And what is that if not the fully rounded development of the whole human being and of all people? A humanism closed in on itself and not open to the values of the spirit and to God who is their source, could achieve apparent success. True, human beings can organize the world apart from God, but 'without God human beings can organize it in the end only to peoples' detriment.

An isolated humanism is an inhuman humanism.' There is no true humanism but that which is open to the Absolute and is conscious of a vocation, which gives human life its true meaning" (PP 42). Paul VI quotes de Lubac, *Le drame de l'humanisme athée*, 10, and alludes to Maritain, *L'humanisme integral.*

25 John Paul's concentration on the equality and interdependence of all people had prompted his incipient critique of unfettered global financial markets that are premised on capitalist individualism (SRS 19, 37). Benedict XVI elaborated on this analysis when expressing his disaccord with unfettered free market financial trading (CV 35–6).

26 While Vatican II directed attention to people on the margins, the church's decision to identify itself with the poor took place after Vatican II, beginning with the Second General Conference of Latin American Bishops in Medellín, Colombia, 24 August to 6 September 1968. See Sobrino, "Church of the Poor." For an examination of poverty as a theme at Vatican II from a European perspective at the time of the council, see Dupont, "La Chiesa e la povertà."

27 For a systematic analysis of this document, see Himes, "Commentary on *Justitia in Mundo*."

2

The Social Mission of the Church:
An Issue of Dialogue

Gregory Baum

In 2012 the church celebrated the fiftieth anniversary of the opening of Vatican II, and in 2013 Catholics commemorated the fiftieth anniversary of Pope John XXIII's encyclical *Pacem in Terris*. These were two major ecclesiastical events that turned the Catholic Church to the world. Vatican II and *Pacem in Terris* made Catholics aware of their co-responsibility for their own society and for the common good of the entire human family. The church detects in the world sinful, self-destructive forces that damage human life and the earth itself, yet trusting in Christ's promises, the church also recognizes in the world the work of the Holy Spirit, summoning people to resist evil, to practise the love of God and neighbour, and to stand for justice, peace, and the protection of the earth. Catholics are not a sect that says "no" to the world; we are a church engaged in critical dialogue with humanity.

The turn to the world of Vatican II and *Pacem in Terris* was confirmed by papal and episcopal declarations in the 1970s. Yet in the second part of his pontificate, John Paul II, and after him Benedict XVI, decided to disregard the emphasis of Vatican II on dialogue and pluralism and foster a conservative movement in the church. In an article in *Historical Studies,*[1] I document the measures taken by the two popes to reverse the conciliar promise of collegiality and restore the monarchical idea of the papacy. In the present chapter, concerned with the church's openness to the world, I wish to contrast the conciliar teaching on the church's mission in the world with the more traditional understanding preferred by Pope Benedict XVI and a conservative current in the Catholic Church. Finally, I shall make a few remarks showing that Pope Francis has returned to the orientation of Vatican II, adding to it new vigour.

WORLD AND CHURCH IN THE SIXTIES

To gain a fuller understanding of the church's teaching at a particular time, one must take its social and cultural context into consideration. Allow me, therefore, to contrast today's historical situation with that of the 1960s, when John XXIII convoked Vatican II and published *Pacem in Terris*.

The sixties was a period of cultural optimism in the West. After World War II, a capitalism regulated by government and a labour movement protected by law had produced the welfare state that greatly improved the social and economic conditions of working men and women. Ordinary people came to live in conditions that were better than those experienced by their parents. Reacting to the oppressive dictatorship and the horrors associated with World War II, men and women in the West gave strong support to the UN Universal Declaration of Human Rights and appreciated the freedom and responsibility offered by democratic institutions. The experience of greater wealth and greater freedom produced a cultural optimism that was shared by social and political scientists. Some political thinkers even believed that the system that had made western society wealthy could be exported to the poor countries of the South and allow the people there to thrive economically.

This was the culture in which Vatican II took place. Listening to Catholic thinkers and activists, the bishops at the council wanted the church to be open to the modern world and express its solidarity with men and women who were working for greater social justice. While the bishops warned people of the dehumanizing forces operative in society, they recognized at the same time the action of the Holy Spirit in the striving of men and women for social justice, international peace, human rights, and universal reconciliation.

FAITH AND THE COMMITMENT TO SOCIAL JUSTICE

This critical openness to the world was accompanied by a significant doctrinal evolution. Following the experience of many engaged Catholics, the conciliar bishops heard in the gospel a divine summons to social justice and peace among nations. While, in the past, the church's social teaching was based on natural law and belonged to the order of reason, the church now called for social solidarity and the ethics of citizenship in the name of God's Word revealed in the scriptures. Commitment to social justice was no longer seen as a virtue pertaining to the natural order; it was now recognized as a response to a divine call, a spiritual path guided by faith, the social incarnation of charity. The council acknowledged that the primary message of the gospel in the present age deals with life on this earth, not with the promises of heaven. Jesus taught us to pray that God's reign may come and that God's will be done on earth. God's promised reign, at odds with that of Caesar, will be the victory of love, justice, and peace over the massive evil initiated by humanity. The conditions of modernity have produced great evil, yet they have also provided instruments and institutions that allow people to become co-responsible for their world. This radical change of perspective, transcending centuries of Catholic piety, explains why a good many Catholics joined a conservative current calling for the return of the Catholicism of yesteryear.

The new conciliar teaching had a profound influence on the church's understanding of its mission in the world, the meaning of the liturgy, and the self-understanding of religious orders and congregations. A new spirituality emerged in these communities, generating social concern, solidarity with the poor, and support for the social struggles for greater justice and greater freedom. Since I am associated in Montreal with Le Centre justice et foi, a Jesuit centre for faith and justice, I give as an example of the new spirituality the decision made by the Society of Jesus in 1974 to redefine its mission as the service of faith and the promotion of justice.[2]

The hopeful orientation toward social reform that characterized western societies, including the conciliar document *Gaudium et Spes,* was not shared by critical thinkers in the Third World. The Latin American bishops, meeting at Medellín in 1968, recognized that great masses of people were oppressed and excluded, that capitalism was an economic system that enriched the centre at the expense of the periphery, and that social justice could be brought about only by a structural transformation of society. At Medellín, the bishops introduced a pastoral project called "conscientization,"[3] or the raising of consciousness, a program to help people recognize the institutional causes of their misery, stand against destructive institutions, imagine a more just and humane society, and invent alternative practices that produce greater justice. This pastoral approach was also called "the preferential option for the poor," referring to a twofold commitment in the name of Jesus (a) to look at society from the perspective of the poor, and (b) to give public witness in support of their struggle for greater justice.[4]

The teaching of Medellín influenced several Vatican documents and a number of national episcopal conferences, among them the Canadian bishops. This how the Canadian bishops express "the option for the poor" in their pastoral statement of 1982: "As Christians we are called to follow Jesus by identifying with the victims of injustice, by analyzing the dominant attitudes and structures that cause human suffering, and by actively supporting the poor and oppressed in their struggle to transform society."[5]

This brief historical overview shows that since the 1960s, Catholic social teaching has been read in two different ways. A *reformist* reading urges Catholics to work for the reform of the institutions in which they live and strive for a humane form of social democracy. A *radical* reading of Catholic social teaching reveals the destructive impact of capitalist empire, acknowledges the need for an alternative economic system, and supports community development and the social economy at the base of society. Let me give a concrete example of the two distinct social commitments: a reformist option is embraced by Catholics engaged in the NDP or another political party to foster social democracy in Canada, while a more radical option is pursued by Catholics engaged in the World Social Forum and the social forums in Canada.

We note that in the 1960s and 1970s, Catholic social teaching still ignored the damage to the natural environment caused by the spread of industrial society. The church's ecological concern arrived a decade later.

WORLD AND CHURCH IN THE PRESENT

Society has greatly changed since the 1960s and 1970s, the time of the church's bold social teaching. The Keynesian capitalism that produced the welfare state has been replaced by neoliberalism or the unregulated market system, now on a global scale. Large corporations have become giant international institutions that accumulate wealth and power – a wealth greater than that of many nations and a power capable of obliging national governments to serve the corporations'

economic interests. Neoliberalism is also a culture. It fosters individualism – "each one for himself or herself" – a competitive attitude
that looks upon the neighbour as rival, a serene indifference to social injustices, and the search for happiness in the consumption of
goods. Governments decide or are forced to decide to disregard the
common good, dismantle the welfare state, humiliate labour, declare
war against unions, refuse to protect the natural environment, and
destabilize institutions that foster social solidarity.

This present political trend calls itself conservative – a beautiful
word it does not deserve. For example, in Canada, Stephen Harper's
Conservative government served the interests of the economic elites
and opted for an increasingly narrow understanding of democracy.
That Mr Harper closed the Office for Rights and Democracy and
replaced it with the Office of Religious Freedom is symbolic of his
political orientation. To promote a culture of conformity and respect
for law and order, the government fostered a new militarism, emphasized Canada's monarchical status, and cut the funds of groups and
institutions that promote critical thinking, such as women's groups
and networks, educational and artistic projects, and nongovernmental organizations serving the poor in the Third World. The Christian
institutions, KAIROS[6] and Development and Peace,[7] have each been
affected by this. These groups were deemed dangerous because they
promote critical thinking.

This is the real world in which the church finds itself today. As
the optimistic culture of the 1960s affected the church at Vatican II,
so does the present culture, indifferent to social injustice, affect the
official church. That Development and Peace has been in trouble
with both the Harper government and the Canadian Conference of
Catholic Bishops[8] has symbolic value.

BENEDICT XVI'S PRE-CONCILIAR PERSPECTIVE

Unconvinced by Vatican II's openness to the world, Benedict XVI
chose to return to a pre-conciliar theology of the church's social
mission. Since I do not have the space for a detailed analysis of his
position, I will simply mention three significant instances.

1. In his encyclical *Caritas in Veritate* (2007), Benedict XVI writes
that without faith in God, society is unable to promote integral
human development. The deepest problem of contemporary society
is its secular character, its materialistic culture, its refusal to believe

in God. He writes, "a humanism which excludes God is an inhuman humanism" (CV 78).[9] For Benedict, the first and foremost step to rescue society from its self-destructive orientation is the conversion to God.

That faith in God is a precondition of social justice will not convince North Americans who remember that President George W. Bush, an ardent Christian, was indifferent to justice and peace among the nations. He said that he prayed to God before deciding to launch a military attack on Iraq, justified by information that turned out to be false. In some Latin American countries, Catholic faith has been used as an ideology by the governing authorities to resist all efforts to reform society. In addition to this, fundamentalist currents presently active in all religions are producing believers in God who are intolerant, hate their neighbours and, in some parts of the world, even bless the use of violence. Reflecting on what is happening in the world, I find myself obliged to disagree with Benedict XVI: the source of injustices and wars is not atheism, but the lust for ever-increasing wealth and power, a vice to which believers as well as atheists are vulnerable.

The grain of truth in Benedict's proposal is that God is indeed the origin and source of all justice and peace in the world. Revealed in Jesus Christ is that God's Word addresses all human beings, believers and nonbelievers, calling and enabling them to practise love of neighbour and promote justice and peace.

2. In his first encyclical, *Deus Caritas Est* (2005), Benedict recognizes the practice of charity or *diakonia* as an essential dimension of the church's mission, yet at the same time restricts it to the service offered to people in need. The raising of consciousness is no longer part of it. Practising charity, he writes, "is not a means of changing the world ideologically nor a service of worldly stratagems, but a way of making present ... the love which humans always need."[10] Returning to pre-conciliar Catholic teaching, Benedict XVI makes a clear distinction between the supernatural order of faith, hope, and love and the natural order of social justice and political responsibility. For him, the promotion of justice in society, an essential duty of all citizens, is a secular activity and, as such, not part of the supernatural order of charity. In 1984, Cardinal Ratzinger, as prefect of the Congregation for the Doctrine of the Faith (he became Pope Benedict in 2005), had accused liberation theology of overlooking the distinction between the two

orders and falsely ascribing a political dimension to the church's mission.[11] As pope, he continued to restrict the church's *diakonia* to the practice of charity. He emphasized this again at the end of his pontificate in November 2012 in the canonical document *De Caritate Ministranda*. This legislative text introduces greater ecclesiastical control of Catholic organizations engaged in countries of the Global South, like Caritas Internationalis and its affiliates such as Development and Peace, in order to ensure that the services they offer to the poor remain nonpolitical and do not challenge the established order.

The grain of truth in Benedict's conservative idea of the church's *diakonia* is that Catholics supporting struggles for greater social justice must recognize that their commitment does not dispense them from the practice of charity and compassion. However important social justice is, it is not enough; it must be accompanied by love.

3. In his homily at the mass before the opening of the conclave in 2005, Cardinal Ratzinger said that contemporary society suffers under the "dictatorship of relativism": society no longer recognizes any value as definitive, and the moral norm of people's behaviour has become their self-promotion and their hedonistic desires.[12] Returning to this theme as Benedict XVI, he often presented the church as the pillar of truth surrounded by a world that has lost its moral conscience. Is this perception of the world correct? According to Vatican II, the church has something to learn from the world, despite the sin operative within it (GS 44).

Benedict's theme is invoked by the Canadian bishops in their pastoral letter of April 2012, "On Freedom of Conscience and Religion," which explains to Catholics that their religious liberty is presently threatened in Canada.[13] "Subtle threats to religious freedom arise from the cultural predominance of radical secularism and 'a subliminal relativism that penetrates every area of life'" – a quotation from Benedict's Address to the Central Committee for German Catholics at Freiburg on 24 September 2011. Because of this dominant relativism, argue the Canadian bishops, the conscience of Catholics working in hospitals and pharmacies is not respected. Catholics, they write, "are obliged to express [their] objection with clarity and courage."

It is interesting to note that the Quebec bishops remain unconvinced by Benedict's theme of "the dictatorship of relativism." Their pastoral letter of November 2012, *Catholiques dans un Québec pluraliste*,[14] recognizes that Catholics in Quebec are surrounded by people with a variety of ethical positions: Protestants, Jews, Muslims, the followers of other religions, secular humanists, and relativists. In a pluralistic society, the bishops argue, Catholics must engage in dialogue with the other citizens, explaining their own ethical position and respecting the ethical judgments adopted by others. Catholics want to be faithful to their conscience, but so do many other citizens. The aim of dialogue in a pluralistic society is to uncover values shared by all and to arrive at compromises on issues on which people's consciences are deeply divided.

AN ULTRA-CONSERVATIVE CURRENT

Benedict's theme of "the dictatorship of relativism" has encouraged a reactionary Catholic current that wants the church to turn its back on modern society and Catholics to stop cooperating with secular organizations. In recent years, reactionary Catholic groups have denounced Catholic institutions that cooperate with secular movements, some of whose members disagree with the church's moral teaching. Well known in Canada is the attack against Development and Peace, accusing it of supporting a social justice movement in Central America, some of whose members approve of abortion under certain conditions.[15] In the United States, Catholic Relief Services (CRS), founded by the American bishops, has to defend itself against attacks of reactionary Catholic groups accusing it of supporting and cooperating with secular organizations that advocate contraception and abortion. Defending itself, Catholic Relief Services explains, "We also participate in humanitarian initiatives undertaken by a range of groups, including governments, other faith communities and secular institutions. Although some positions and practices of these institutions are not always consistent with the full range of Catholic teaching, CRS' work with these institutions always focuses only on activities that are fully consistent with Catholic teachings."[16]

Some American bishops even use the Catholic ban on contraception and abortion as an instrument to oppose progressive public policies. They have forbidden Catholics to vote for political candidates who disagree with the church's ban on abortion, even if their social policies aim at creating greater social justice. When in 2009 the University of Notre Dame invited President Obama to deliver the commencement address, many Catholics, including forty bishops, vehemently objected. They indicted the president for supporting contraception and abortion, without admitting that his ideals for a just society were closer to Catholic social teaching than the social vision of the Republican Party. Bishop John M. D'Arcy of South Bend refused to attend the ceremony, accusing the president of "long-stated unwilling-ness to hold human life as sacred" and the University of Notre Dame of choosing "prestige over truth."[17] Bishop Daniel Jenky of Peoria, Illinois, denounced the president for contempt of human life, compar-ing him to Hitler and Stalin.[18]

This ultra-conservative stance is not shared by the Vatican. Even Cardinal Ratzinger recognized that under certain conditions Catholics may vote for political candidates who make allowances for abortion. As prefect of the Congregation for the Doctrine of the Faith he wrote, "When a Catholic does not share a candidate's stand in favor of abortion ... but votes for that candidate for other rea-sons, it is considered [only] remote material cooperation, which can be permitted in the presence of proportionate reasons."[19]

Vatican II had opened a new chapter in the church's history by call-ing upon Catholics to cooperate with "others" in support of justice and peace even if, in addition to common values, others also entertain ideas at odds with Catholic teaching. Catholics are urged to cooper-ate with non-Catholic Christians in the *Decree on Ecumenism* (UR 4, 10, 12), with Jews and the followers of other religions in *Nostra Aetate* (NA 2, 3) and the *Decree on the Church's Missionary Activity* (AGD 12, 15, 36), and with secular people, including atheists, in *Gaudium et Spes*: "Although the church altogether rejects atheism, it nevertheless sincerely proclaims that all men and women, those who believe as well as those who do not, should help to establish right order in this world where all live together" (GS 21; see also 40–2, 55, 74–5). The cooperation of Catholics with others, be they religious or secular, in promoting social justice and human rights was repeatedly recommended by John Paul II. At Assisi, in 1986, he expressed his ardent wish that the world's religions, despite their doctrinal differ-ences, work together for the peace of the world and give a common witness to the invisible mystery they address in their prayers – the mystery that is unrecognized by secular society.[20]

The *Decree on Ecumenism*, calling for cooperation with Protestants, actually alludes to the difficulty created by the dis-agreements over abortion and contraception. Protestants, the decree says, may "not admit the same solutions for the more dif-ficult problems of modern society," yet Catholics should remember that these Protestants "want to cling to Christ's word as the source of Christian virtue" (UR 23). This summons has been largely forgotten. The widespread Catholic rhetoric condemning abortion under all circumstances assumes that people who disagree with this unconditional rejection are relativists, guided by selfish interests and lacking respect for human life. Even the contemporary Magisterium is unwilling to admit that some people who approve of abortion under certain conditions do this on the basis of moral reasoning and in obedience to their carefully formed conscience.

Needless to say, Catholics have the right to advocate their radical opposition to abortion and persuade the government to prohibit abortion or at least legislate to reduce its frequency. At the same time, Catholics must use a respectful discourse, recognizing the rights of other citizens to follow their conscience on this issue and advocate their position, at odds with Catholic teaching, in the public square. The present conflict over abortion is not between people of conscience who totally reject this practice and people without conscience surrendered to relativism. In a pluralistic society, many significant moral debates set conscience against conscience. This is why dialogue is the only way to social peace. This, as we saw, was the position taken by the Quebec bishops.

It is instructive for Catholics to study how the United Church of Canada arrived at a position on abortion that differs from Catholic teaching. In the United Church, doctrinal and ethical issues are settled through a long process that involves pastors, theologians, and lay people – men and women – in fact all the congregations across Canada. A committee appointed by the moderator studies the issue and produces a preliminary text that is distributed and discussed in all local congregations. The reactions of these congregations to the text are brought forward and discussed at the General Council (a church parliament meeting every three years), whereupon a new text is produced, taking into account the responses of the believing community. After discussion of the new text in the local congregations and at a subsequent meeting of the General Council, a definitive text is approved by this ecclesiastical parliament. This extended process shows that the position of the United Church on abortion is not based on value relativism or ethical indifference; it has clearly been produced by a Christian community wrestling with its conscience.

What is the position of the United Church on abortion? Several statements produced by the United Church are found on its website.[21]

According to the United Church, a fundamental principle of the ethics of human procreation is that every child born in the world has the right to be wanted. An unwanted child, a child treated as an inconvenience, suffers profound wounds that affect his or her entire life. The great responsibility of a couple in love is to prevent their sexual life from producing an unwanted child. To achieve this, the couple may practise continence, use various methods of birth control, or, in some cases, even opt for a surgical interruption of the pregnancy. According to the theology of the United Church, abortion is always an evil, the destruction of a human life, yet in certain situations a couple is obliged to choose between two evils, eliminating the fetus or giving birth to an unwanted child. This painful choice must be made by the couple – or in some cases by the mother herself – after careful reflection and prayer before God. In the eyes of the United Church, there are exceptional circumstances that make opting for abortion a moral choice.

The reasoning of Catholic moral theology is quite different. Still, in a society that is pluralistic and democratic, both Catholics and United Church Christians have the right to advocate their position in public and address the government. A pro-life movement must argue against the moral discourse of the United Church, but it may not accuse it of being unconcerned about Christian truth. The great drama in a pluralistic society is that conscience is set against conscience. Here conflicts are often between groups of people holding different ethical values, values to which they are deeply committed and for which they offer rational arguments. Here social peace calls for dialogue, mutual respect, efforts to clarify common values and, if need be, a democratically worked out compromise, demanding of all parties to lower their expectations.

A good example of such compromise is John Paul II's proposal that politicians personally opposed to abortion, yet unable to make the government outlaw this practice, may well support a legal bill that limits access to abortion and thus reduces its evil effects. "When it is not possible to overturn or completely abrogate a pro-abortion law, an elected official, whose absolute personal opposition to procured abortion was well known, could licitly support proposals aimed at limiting the harm done by such a law and at lessening its negative consequences at the level of general opinion and public morality. This does not in fact represent an illicit cooperation with an unjust law, but rather a legitimate and proper attempt to limit its evil aspects."[22]

I conclude that the ethical pluralism in democratic societies is not the manifestation of an underlying ethical relativism. Thoughtful people in modern society, capable of resisting the cultural pressure of liberal capitalism, hold the same humanistic values – justice, freedom, mutual respect, compassion, and honesty – even if the concrete applications they make of these virtues are different and sometimes even incompatible.

In an interview with three Jesuit journalists in August 2013,[23] Francis uttered two sentences subsequently cited in newspapers across the world. "We have been obsessed with abortion, gay marriage and contraception ... We have to find a new balance, otherwise the moral edifice of the church is likely to fall like a house of cards."[24] The new balance assigns priority to God's love made known in Jesus Christ and does not allow issues of personal morality to occupy the centre.

DIALOGUE IN THE CHURCH

The debate over the church's social mission should be seen as part of the ongoing dialogue among Catholics, including popes and bishops. While I am committed to the openness to the world of Vatican II and believe that the gospel summons us to work for a more just and more humane social order, I listen to conservative Catholics and try to learn from what they have to say. Speaking above of Benedict's conservative positions, I always noted the grain of truth I found in them, a truth that demanded that I take a critical look at my own theology. Conservative Catholics fear that the contemporary stress on the this-worldly message of the gospel, the promise of "integral human liberation," will lead to a dangerous "horizontalism" characterized by forgetfulness of God, neglect of divine worship, indifference to prayer, and unbelief in eternal life. This fear deserves to be taken seriously. Liberal or radical Catholics in dialogue with conservative Catholic voices will want to reexamine their reading and their practice of the Christian gospel.

Conversely, conservative Catholics will want to listen carefully to the social concern that has become central in the official teaching of the post-conciliar church. In his exhortation *Evangelii Gaudium* (2013), Francis quotes this sentence from an ecclesiastical document: "Defenders of orthodoxy are sometimes accused of passivity, indulgence, or culpable complicity regarding the intolerable situations of injustice and the political regimes which prolong them" (EG 194). Faith in Jesus Christ demands that Catholics stand for justice and peace in our society.

It is important to distinguish between conservative Catholics with whom dialogue is interesting and fruitful and ultra-conservatives who refuse to engage in dialogue. These latter are called in French *les intégristes* and sometimes in English "Catholic fundamentalists."[25] Ultra-conservative Catholics believe in the unchanging character of Christian doctrine; they interpret doctrines without reference to their historical context; they resist respectful dialogue with other Catholics; and they do not reply to questions raised by philosophical thought. Fundamentalism, a heavy burden in all religious traditions, fosters intolerance, spreads a prejudiced perception of people at odds with it, and creates detrimental conflicts in pluralistic societies.

POPE FRANCIS ON THE CHURCH'S SOCIAL MISSION

In his exhortation *Evangelii Gaudium*, Francis offers the innovative teaching that the church's social mission is part and parcel of its evangelizing mission. He entitles chapter 4 "The Social Dimension of Evangelization." He writes, "The kerygma has a clear social content: at the very heart of the Gospel is life in community and engagement with others" (EG 177). He shows in this chapter that the church's mission to give witness to Jesus Christ is exercised in its preaching, its ecumenical involvement, its interreligious dialogue, and its social engagement for justice and peace, in cooperation with other groups, secular and religious. Like the Latin American bishops at Medellín in 1968, Francis understands the engagement for justice as a "preferential option for the poor." He writes, "Each individual Christian and every community is called to be an instrument of God for the liberation and promotion of the poor, and for enabling them to be fully a part of society ... [This] means working to eliminate the structural causes of poverty and to promote the integral development of the poor, as well as small daily acts of solidarity in meeting the real needs which we encounter" (EG 187–8).

Developing these ideas theologically and politically and remembering the poverty of Jesus, Francis arrives at the bold conclusion, "I want a Church which is poor and for the poor" (EG 198). This theme recurs in many of his speeches. His famous talk at Lampedusa, Sicily, on 8 July 2013 addressed masses of refugees detained in camps, uncertain about their future; his talk in Cagliari, Sardinia, on 22 September 2013 addressed the unemployed, young and old, living in poverty and hopelessness. Francis recognizes that these people – victims of their society – are signs that misery and social exclusion are produced even in Europe, not only in the Global South.[26] Looking at the world from the perspective of the excluded, Francis is keenly aware of the sin of the world, yet believing in Christ as *salvator mundi*, the saviour of the world, he does not despair.

Francis wants the church in the name of Christ to turn to the world, engage in conversation with others, and seek allies in a joint effort to create a society that is more just and more humane and rescues the poor from their exclusion. Already, as archbishop of Buenos Aires, he called upon Catholics to foster "a culture of encounter." This is what he said in an interview:

> A culture of encounter is founded upon the idea that "the other," the other person, has much to give me, that I have to be open to that person and listen without prejudgment. I may not think that because his ideas are different from mine or because he is an atheist, he can't offer me anything. This is not so. Everyone has something to offer, and everyone can receive something. Prejudging someone is like putting up a wall which prevents us from coming together. Argentines are very judgmental. We immediately label people so that, deep down, we can avoid the encounter and the dialogue. So we wind up fostering dissension which, in my opinion, reaches the level of social pathology.[27]

Speaking to the Brazilian bishops during World Youth Day in July 2013, Francis asked them to turn to the world and foster a culture of encounter. He asked himself whether one reason so many people have left the church is that we have been too closed in upon ourselves: "Perhaps the Church appeared too weak, perhaps too distant from their needs, perhaps too poor to respond to their concerns, perhaps too cold, perhaps too caught up with itself, perhaps a prisoner of its own rigid formulas, perhaps the world seems to have made the Church a relic of the past, unfit for new questions; perhaps the Church could speak to people in their infancy but not to those come of age."[28]

Addressing the young people at the same World Youth Day, Francis urged them to turn to the world: "Let me tell you what I hope will be the outcome of World Youth Day: I hope there will be noise … I want you to make yourselves heard in your dioceses, I want the noise to go out, I want the Church to go out onto the streets, I want us to resist everything worldly, everything static, everything comfortable, everything to do with clericalism, everything that might make us closed in on ourselves ... May the bishops and priests forgive me if some of you create a bit of confusion afterwards. That's my advice."[29]

Celebrating the Vigil of Pentecost in May 2013 with the new movements and the new communities, Francis made a vigorous appeal, asking them to step outside their closed circle and start conversations with the world:

> At this time of crisis we cannot be concerned solely with ourselves, withdrawing into loneliness, discouragement and a sense of powerlessness in the face of problems. Please do not withdraw into yourselves! This is a danger: we shut ourselves up in the parish, with our friends, within the movement, with the like-minded ... but do you know what happens? When the Church becomes closed, she becomes an ailing Church, she falls ill! That is a danger. Nevertheless we lock ourselves up in our parish, among our friends, in our movement, with people who think as we do ... but do you know what happens? When the Church is closed, she falls sick ... Think of a room that has been closed for a year. When you go into it there is a smell of damp, many things are wrong with it. A Church closed in on herself is the same, a sick Church.[30]

Francis leaves no one in doubt as to where he stands in the dialogue about the church's social mission.

NOTES

1 Baum, "Forgotten Promises." *Historical Studies* is the review of the Canadian Catholic Historical Association.
2 32nd General Congregation of the Society of Jesus, "Our Mission Today."
3 Medellín Documents, Peace, #18, in Gremillion, *Gospel of Peace and Justice*, 461.
4 See the chapter on the preferential option for the poor in the Final Document of the 1979 Latin American Bishops Conference at Puebla, in Eagelson and Sharper, *Puebla and Beyond*, 264.
5 Qtd in Sheridan, *Do Justice*, 399.

6 KAIROS, "KAIROS and CIDA Funding."

7 Development and Peace, "Funding from CIDA Reduced."

8 Gruending, "Development and Peace."

9 This is a quotation from Henri de Lubac, who wants to show that purely secular societies, not summoned by religion to renew themselves, will in the long run become oppressive. Still, this sentence is arrogant and offensive. It wants the reader to forget that fascism did well in the Catholic societies of Spain, Portugal, Slovenia, and Croatia, and that the Catholic bishops supported Vichy's cooperation with Nazi Germany.

10 *Deus Caritas Est*, 31. See Baum, "Benedict XVI's First Encyclical."

11 Congregation for the Doctrine of the Faith, "Instruction."

12 Ratzinger, Homily on 18 April 2005.

13 Canadian Conference of Catholic Bishops, "Pastoral Letter."

14 Assemblée des évêques catholiques de Québec, "Catholiques dans un Québec pluraliste."

15 Leclerc, "L'angoisse de l'organisme Développement et Paix."

16 Catholic Relief Services, "About."

17 Carroll, "Notre Dame's Stand."

18 Filteau, "Notre Dame Faculty Members."

19 Ratzinger, "Memo," 13. I did not find this text on the website of Congregation for the Doctrine of the Faith.

20 John Paul II, "Address of John Paul II to the Representatives of the Christian Churches."

21 Documents relating to abortion and contraception can be found on the United Church Commons website at http://www.united-church.ca/united-church-commons.

22 John Paul II, *Evangelium Vitae*, 73.

23 Spadaro, "Big Heart Open to God."

24 Goodstein, "Pope Says Church Is 'Obsessed.'"

25 See Ryan, "Catholic Fundamentalism."

26 Francis, "Address to the Workers of Cagliari."

27 Rubin and Ambrogetti, *Pope Francis*, 124.

28 Francis, "Address to the Brazilian Bishops."

29 Francis, "Address to the Young People from Argentina."

30 Francis, "Address to the New Movements."

3

Moralizing Neoliberalism?
An Analysis of the Principle of Subsidiarity in
Catholic Social Teaching

Anna Blackman

This chapter explores how Catholic social teaching[1] has responded to the expansion of both the state and the market into all spheres of human activity through the growth of neoliberalism. As Catholic social teaching is founded on protecting the dignity of the human person, it maintains that human dignity should be preserved above the interests of the state and the market, both of which should function to serve the human person. This priority is demonstrated in Catholic social teaching's deep commitment to the "option for the poor,"[2] which seeks to ensure that those at the lowest levels of society are provided for. A key factor in realizing human dignity lies in assessing when it is necessary and appropriate for the state to intervene; such assessment is guided by the principle of subsidiarity. Yet due to the growth of neoliberalism, faithfully enacting subsidiarity has become problematic. This chapter will explore internal tensions within Catholic social teaching between natural law theories and ecclesial theology in the church's response to neoliberalism that are evident in its teachings on subsidiarity, and question how these tensions have affected the church's commitment to the protection of the human person from the forces of both the state and the market.

Subsidiarity is a founding principle of Catholic social teaching, and yet its practical application has remained ambiguous, especially as it has lent itself to use in secular politics and has become detached from the wider body of teaching. By analyzing the critique of Catholic social teaching by the Radical Orthodoxy Movement in the work of John Milbank, this chapter will question whether Catholic social teaching has failed to be sufficiently critical of neoliberalism and the expansion of the market, perhaps even going so far as to implicitly endorse them.

Do we need to rethink the framework within which subsidiarity is formulated? Can the ecclesial theology of Radical Orthodoxy act as a corrective to Catholic social teaching through a radical rejection of the entire system of capitalism and neoliberalism rather than aiming only to "moralize" its worst excesses, as it criticizes Catholic social teaching for doing? The chapter concludes by suggesting that the theology of Rowan Williams may propose a middle ground between both theologies and a promising way forward.

THE PRINCIPLE OF SUBSIDIARITY IN CATHOLIC SOCIAL TEACHING

Subsidiarity has been implicitly incorporated into Catholic social teaching since its official beginning in 1891 with Pope Leo XIII's encyclical *Rerum Novarum,*[3] and has served as a fundamental tenet, having been addressed in every subsequent papal social document.[4] Arising in response to modern developments in the West,[5] Catholic social teaching was rooted in Aquinas's theology of humans as inherently "social animals" and aimed at opposing political theories that viewed social relations as contractual.[6] This is unsurprising, given that Catholic social teaching arose during the period of neo-scholasticism that developed in reaction to the modernist crisis in the latter half of the nineteenth century.[7] Aquinas's philosophy was seen as a safeguard against modernity,[8] and as Robert Barry states, his "social-ethical doctrines gave the church powerful instruments after the French Revolution to challenge socialism, liberalism, totalitarianism, capitalism, and atheism."[9] All papal social teaching since the late nineteenth century has drawn upon Aquinas's theology to counter all ideologies that present relations existing on a contractual basis, specifically liberalism and socialism.

Catholic social teaching situates itself as neither individualistic nor communalistic;[10] rather, it aims to balance the dignity of each human person with the common good of society. By viewing individuals as social, Catholic social teaching concludes that participation in society is necessary for human flourishing, and it is in this context that subsidiarity was formulated to preserve the right to freely associate.

The influence of Aquinas's theology is particularly noticeable here. As Barry explains, Aquinas's greatest impact on Catholic social teaching can be seen in his expression of natural law.[11] In Aquinas's understanding, humanity finds fulfilment by acting in accordance with its nature as well as with reason, grace, and the virtues.[12] Although grounded in the divine law of God, natural law promotes the good through faithfulness to humanity's true nature as "rational, free, spiritual and intelligent" beings.[13] The virtues serve to perfect this nature.[14] Barry notes that the virtue of justice dominates Aquinas's social, economic, and political thought, with the aim of ensuring just and equal relationships.[15] Aquinas asserts that humans are naturally social,[16] and it is natural for them to associate through society, the family, and the state.[17] Both the family and the state have ends proper to them and therefore must be allowed the freedom needed to meet these ends.[18] However, the state functions to assist citizens in attaining their full development and happiness. Barry notes that in Aquinas's model, as the state is directed toward securing happiness, "it can legitimately assume more functions than can a state that is only responsible for preventing harm to its citizens."[19]

Drawing on this Thomistic natural-law tradition, papal teaching has incorporated subsidiarity to protect the dignity of the human person and to empower people to become active and responsible agents in their own lives. The principle states that it is "a grave evil and disturbance of right order to assign to a greater and higher association what lesser and subordinate organizations can do" (QA 79) and emphasizes the importance of intermediary bodies functioning between the individual and the state. Yet it also insists that when an individual or lesser body is not capable of upholding human dignity, the state should intervene. However, the church's attempt to find a balance between individual responsibility and state intervention has resulted in a fluid and flexible interpretation of subsidiarity.

Therefore, the evolution of subsidiarity in Catholic social teaching needs first to be addressed. The *Compendium of the Social Doctrine of the Church* states that "subsidiarity is among the most constant and characteristic directives of the Church's social doctrine,"[20] as evidenced by its inclusion in the 1983 Code of Canon Law.[21] The 2008 Plenary Meeting of the Pontifical Academy of Sciences, which focused on subsidiarity,[22] testifies to its continuing significance. However, subsidiarity has been subject to constant reevaluation, evidenced through developments in papal teaching in response to historical events and ideological influences. Three distinct historical phases can be traced: from *Rerum Novarum* to John XXIII, from John XXIII to John Paul II, and from John Paul II to Benedict XVI. These phases fluctuate between readings of "negative" and "positive" subsidiarity. Negative subsidiarity asserts that societies should not perform what individuals or smaller groups can do and relies more on programs of self-help through unions, cooperatives, and associations, whereas positive subsidiarity emphasizes the role of the state to achieve those things that individuals and groups cannot do.[23]

The first phase leans toward a negative reading of subsidiarity. Influenced by Wilhelm Emmanuel von Ketteler's liberal nineteenth-century thought,[24] Leo XIII addressed the effects of the Industrial Revolution in *Rerum Novarum*, criticizing both capitalism for its laissez-faire attitude (RN 23–4) and socialism for excessive state interference, and offered an alternative approach found in the Catholic Church. He asserted that "Man precedes the State, and possesses, prior to the formation of any State, the right of providing for the substance of his body" (RN 7), yet state intervention "in due measure" was necessary (RN 16). Despite his critique of both right-wing and leftist ideologies, he did not envisage an overturning of the capitalist system but rather a series of reforms, such as the formation of unions for workers to protect their interests. Pius XI accentuated this negative reading in light of the growth of totalitarian regimes following the First World War. Unlike Leo, Pius XI acknowledged a more moderate strain of socialism (QA 113), but he saw it as fundamentally irreconcilable with Christianity as it has such a different conception of society (QA 117). However, he believed the errors of socialism stemmed from liberalism, which Pius saw as its ideological father (QA 122). He therefore proposed subsidiarity as a solution to the prevailing form of individualism, which had destroyed intermediary associations, leaving only individuals and the state, burdening the state with issues that these associations could once deal with (QA 78).

Considering the context of worldwide depression, which began with the Wall Street stock market crash in October 1929 and lasted until the beginning of the 1940s, Pius envisaged a restructuring of society along economic lines[25] influenced by Heinrich Pesch's theory of solidarism.[26] It has been argued that solidarism was the only real attempt in papal teaching to give practical directives to apply the principle.[27] In Pius's view, the state was freed from economic duties, only overseeing the smooth running of the economy so that it might protect and secure the common good. Pius shifted toward a more negative reading of subsidiarity than Leo had done. As a result, some critics accused him of advocating fascism, yet only weeks after the publication of *Quadragesimo Anno*, Pius issued the encyclical *Non Abbiamo Bisogno*, which condemned fascism.[28]

The second phase witnessed a shift toward a positive reading of subsidiarity, as John XXIII supported a greater level of state intervention to preserve the freedom of citizens. In 1961's *Mater et Magistra*, John asserted that a greater level of intervention was needed owing to scientific and technological developments (MM 54), and his 1963 encyclical *Pacem in Terris*, issued six months after the Cuban missile crisis, extended the principle to the international level (PT 134, 137, 140–1). As Vivian Boland acknowledges, John stretched subsidiarity to cover the political sphere as well as the socioeconomic,[29] leading to discontinuity with earlier teachings, as he seemingly now approved of the welfare state, something that the church had previously opposed.[30]

The Second Vatican Council went on to create significant advances in Catholic social teaching. With the acceptance of religious liberty in *Gaudium et Spes* and equal rights in *Dignitatis Humanae*, the church envisioned further limits on how governments should exercise authority. *Dignitatis Humanae*, for example, reinforced the dignity, individual responsibility, and freedom of the human person, therefore placing limits on the power of the government (DH 1, 11).[31] Importantly, the council reaffirmed the Catholic Church's unique understanding of humanity's situation in light of modern advances and proposed a conscious change in methodology to engage with the modern world (DH 4, 11). This methodology relied on a historically conscious approach that drew more heavily on biblical revelation and human experience (DH 43).[32] While some scholars have seen John's pontificate as marking a shift away from universal and ahistorical principles, marked by natural law, to a more historically conscious approach influenced by the *ressourcement* movement that spanned the 1920s–1950s,[33] universal principles were still offered, despite the acceptance that they may be applied differently to meet differing conditions.

Joan Lockwood O'Donovan attributes this methodological transition to a shift that occurred after the Second World War toward a modernized form of Thomism. Noting the influence of Jacques Maritain, she sees a fusing of Thomistic-Aristotelianism with modern liberal democratic concepts.[34] Rather than neglecting natural law, this union with liberal democracy extends it to cover not only human obligations but also human rights,[35] which gives political society an "increased moral-social importance." The state therefore becomes "merely the highest part of the body politic."[36]

However, Paul VI reiterated that it was the duty of the church to ensure that all people are able to attain the necessary conditions for their "full flowering," and asserted that the state should also act to guarantee such flourishing. Influenced by the Medellín Conference of Latin American Bishops in 1968,[37] his 1971 apostolic letter *Octogesima Adveniens* emphasized the importance of equality, responsibility, and participation of human beings (OA 22, 24), further extending such principles to the political and social sphere (OA 47). He warned of the dangers of the "human sciences" which "isolate ... certain aspects of man," therefore making it impossible to understand him in his totality (OA 38). Turning to the international level, *Populorum Progressio* focused on Third World poverty and criticized the impact that capitalism had on global inequality in its drive for profit while ignoring social obligations (PP 26). Alfred Hennelly claims that Paul VI envisaged a system of moderate socialism,[38] and arguably the whole of this second phase could be characterized in this way.

However, the third phase turned back toward negative subsidiarity with the anti-communism of John Paul II. O'Donovan argues that, while still using the language of natural rights, John Paul resisted identifying the state with the whole of the social body and, like Pius XI, saw subsidiarity as "the negative statement of the principle of solidarity, that counters the state's totalitarian aspirations."[39] *Centesimus Annus*, which marked the hundred-year anniversary of *Rerum Novarum*, was written when the Soviet Union was collapsing at the end of the Cold War, altering the critique of both systems so characteristic of papal teaching. In this encyclical, John Paul clearly criticized the excesses of the "Social Assistance State" (CA 15, 35, 48) and saw subsidiarity as functioning to counter "the state's totalitarian aspirations."[40] Despite this directive, John Paul earlier declared in *Sollicitudo Rei Socialis* that Catholic social teaching was not an ideological third way, but rather represented a moral theology to "guide Christian behaviour" (SRS 41). Taking a more theological approach, he criticized the "structures of sin"[41] (SRS 36) of both Eastern and Western blocs, which impinged upon the autonomy of Third World countries (SRS 21-2, 32). Clifford Longley has argued that the language of "structures of sin" implies that structural change is needed, using a system of solidarity.[42] However, for John Paul these structures were rooted in personal sin, in forms of idolatry based on money, class, technology, and ideology (SRS 37) that oppress humankind through cultures of consumerism and materialism (SRS 28), denying people "authentic [i.e., spiritual] liberation" (SRS 46). Therefore, the perceived problem for John Paul can be more closely described as moral rather than structural. Even though John Paul critiqued the failed system of socialism and acknowledged the failings within the prevailing capitalist system, his emphasis on moral rather than structural change has lent itself to the critique of those such as Patrick McCormick, who questions whether John Paul II in fact endorsed capitalism.[43]

Pope Benedict XVI's 2009 encyclical *Caritas in Veritate*, which addressed economic life and the recent financial crisis, followed in the same vein. Referring to subsidiarity as the "principle of the *centrality of the human person*" (CV 47), he emphasized that it needs to be accompanied by solidarity (CV 47, 58). He described subsidiarity as "an expression of inalienable human freedom" in that it promotes personal dignity, responsibility, and freedom of association by considering the person as an active agent. For Benedict, it is therefore the most useful way to protect against an "all-encompassing welfare state" (CV 57) on the one hand, and "universal power of a tyrannical nature" in globalized society on the other. However, Benedict acknowledged that subsidiarity can function to promote freedom and dignity even through outside assistance, namely, through autonomous "intermediate bodies" between the individual and the state (CV 57), linking to his claim that charity is the foundation for all other principles of Catholic social teaching (CV 2).

While a constant feature of Catholic social teaching, subsidiarity has remained inconsistent and ambiguous, with great flexibility between a negative and positive reading of it. As Catholic social teaching has loosely left open questions as to the practical implementation and the best framework to do this within, subsidiarity has lent itself to a multitude of readings, even among Catholic scholarship.[44] However, the principle of subsidiarity has still proven highly influential within secular politics – seen, for example, in its adoption into the EU's Maastricht Treaty and in former British prime minister David Cameron's concept of the "Big Society." The flexibility of the teaching may certainly account for its popularity and adoption into politics, as it lends itself to both individualistic and collectivist theories.[45] However, such fluidity proves problematic as it allows for subsidiarity to become distorted and disconnected from the wider body of Catholic social teaching. The papal emphasis on negative readings of subsidiarity may be taken by states as permission to devolve responsibility and power without necessarily guaranteeing the other side of subsidiarity in the protection of human dignity, as can be seen with neoliberalism. Since the 1960s, particularly due to the Second Vatican Council, Catholic social teaching has increasingly attempted to engage with the modern world, but in doing so has it adopted liberal values and only tried to moralize the worst excesses of the system? Has Catholic social teaching, therefore, too easily caved in to modern liberal needs rather than preserving the unique teaching and insight of Christianity? What needs to be questioned is how the church can turn to the world, yet also preserve its identity and assess what is the best framework for achieving this.

THE CRITIQUE BY RADICAL ORTHODOXY

The Radical Orthodoxy Movement has criticized papal teaching for adopting liberal values, and especially for failing to envisage significant structural change. The birth of Radical Orthodoxy can be traced to John Milbank's 1990 book, *Theology and Social Theory,* which attempted to "disclose the possibility of a skeptical demolition of modern, secular social theory," offering instead the perspective of an orthodox Christianity.[46] In light of such aims, Radical Orthodoxy criticizes modern society and culture, while offering a rethinking of tradition to do so.[47] Central to this project is the Platonic principle of "participation"[48] and the Thomistic account of the analogy of being.[49] As Phillip Blond appreciates, Radical Orthodoxy's understanding of participation and analogy means that "all reality owes its origin not to itself but to God,"[50] enabling a holistic theology that does not envisage any space that remains independent of God, which would lead to nihilism.[51]

Using the framework of Radical Orthodoxy, Milbank gives his own reading of subsidiarity that, like Catholic social teaching, criticizes both capitalist and communitarian interpretations, both of which exclude genuine community.[52] However, Milbank's argument rests on a rejection of secularism and liberalism and on the fundamental assertion that religion is the only force that can provide the ethos needed to protect both corporatism and distributism, which Milbank advocates as praxis, from the dominance of both the state and the market.[53] Milbank criticizes papal teaching for failing to completely reject false ideologies and sees Catholic social teaching becoming "a grotesque hybrid: liberal, Lockean understandings of property rights, and Smithian construals of the supposed contribution of capital to production are freely incorporated, and yet upon them is superimposed an organicist, patriarchal vision of society." The result is a combination of "formal emptiness and *de facto* rule of coercive power with paternalist sentiment," seen for example in the social market philosophy of John Paul II, which forms a kind of "soft fascism."[54]

Milbank sees the secular as invented, claiming that it is not a neutral ideology.[55] The vacuum left by the rejection of God is filled with a focus on power,[56] and secular reason is therefore built on "an ontology of power and conflict."[57] He is particularly critical of the teachings of John XXIII, Paul VI, and the Second Vatican Council, which he characterizes as having a "tendency to baptize modernity wholesale."[58] Milbank also criticizes the legacy of "neo-scholastic ahistoricism," which led to the belief that there is some form of "natural" social order. This legacy, fused with the church's turn to modernity, leads Catholic social teaching to run "into the contradiction of thinking *both* that liberal capitalism subverts the natural order, and yet that it in some sense still discloses it," culminating in "a doctrine that in the end will only give a sentimental colouring to, and also emotionally reinforce, a culture of *violence*."[59] Milbank argues that, by working within such a framework, Catholic social teaching is necessarily flawed as it remains grounded in a liberal view of society as violent rather than in a Christian notion of peace.[60]

Milbank draws upon *ressourcement* theology and a de Lubacian understanding of "supernaturalizing the natural" and in doing so rejects the notion of "natural law." Nature, he states, has been corrupted by sin, and therefore an ethic is always "a qualified ethic," such as liberal or Christian.[61] Milbank argues that the church should play a vital role, "as an organisation in continuous excess of the state," in the coordination of intermediary bodies to create a "new mass cultural ethos."[62] Milbank dismisses the distinction between theory and praxis, claiming that "there can only be a distinguishable Christian social theory because there is a distinguishable Christian mode of action," and therefore Christian social theory is primarily always an "*ecclesiology.*"[63] James Smith compares this to Hauerwas's claim that "the church does not *have* a social ethic; the church *is* a social ethic."[64] Therefore, like Hauerwas, Smith notes that "the primary site of this renewed sociality is the *ecclesia* – the body of Christ."[65]

What Radical Orthodoxy calls for is a complete transformation of society based on Christian theology, arguing that it is only within a society structured along these lines that subsidiarity can be fully realized. As Simon Oliver notes, Milbank draws upon Neoplatonism, which views the church, society, and cosmos as "a hierarchy of harmonious differences."[66] For Milbank, subsidiarity must be understood within a Neoplatonic-like framework in order to be truly effective. Milbank fundamentally raises the importance of subsidiarity: it becomes a theological principle used in an ordering of the cosmic hierarchy and true participation in the body of Christ, rather than simply a social tool. Essentially, therefore, Milbank's political aims can be read in terms of "reordering the world according to a cosmic hierarchy."[67]

While Milbank validly reminds the Catholic Church not to conform to false values, his critique of natural law rests solely on the period surrounding Vatican II. Radical Orthodoxy certainly offers a robust ecclesiological standpoint from which to criticize neoliberalism, reminding Catholic social teaching that it must be rooted in Christian values and truly bear witness from a Christian standpoint. However, the theology of Benedict XVI somewhat undermines Milbank's criticism, offering a form of grace-infused natural law and an Augustinian theology rooted in *caritas* and hope. Benedict XVI offers an interpretation of natural law that moves very close to Radical Orthodoxy, and his use of an Augustinian theology offers a much more critical view of modernity and capitalism in *Caritas in Veritate* – a view that embraces the civil economy movement, which is close in sympathy Milbank's aims. Crucial here is Benedict's "Neo-Platonist account of natural law that is always already infused by divine grace" and that presents "a powerful repudiation of the dualist separation of 'pure nature' from the supernatural."[68] Indeed, Milbank himself praises *Caritas in Veritate,* stating that "Ratzinger's hope is realistic ... *because* it is a religious and not a secular hope."[69] Adrian Pabst notes also that Benedict sees more structural, practical change. He states that "against apologies of free-market fundamentalism or statist solutions to get us out of the recession, Benedict seeks to chart a Catholic 'third way' that combines strict limits on state and market power with a civil economy" that is "embedded in the reciprocal relations and civic virtues of civil society" and "transcends the old secular dichotomies of state and market, left and right, and the secretly collusive voluntarism of the individual and the collective."[70]

However, questions still remain as to how successfully the church can engage with the world, and there are still problems within the proposed frameworks of both Catholic social teaching and Radical Orthodoxy. The "ecclesiology" of Radical Orthodoxy remains surrounded by questions as to how successfully the model could be practically applied due to its essentially exclusivist nature,[71] and how dialogue with other traditions could be enacted. There are also issues surrounding how the Catholic Church itself is present within a fallen world and how it deals with its own inadequacies, which both Catholic social teaching and Radical Orthodoxy need to consider.

A brief analysis of Rowan Williams's thought will conclude, suggesting that his theology may offer a useful framework in which to move forward.

A WAY FORWARD

Rowan Williams, former archbishop of Canterbury, is acutely aware of the difficulties in relating the church to political action while retaining its specialized role, and the problems of how the church can turn to the world while retaining its identity. Williams's awareness of the tension is shown, for example, in his criticisms of Radical Orthodoxy. His central concern with the movement is that it presents us with "something 'achieved' ... with little account of how it is learned, negotiated, betrayed, inched forward, discerned and risked."[72] For Williams, the church is still evolving, still learning how to bear authentic witness, still learning how to "do" church, "since it has been historically guilty of reverting to pre-conscious patterns of power." It has "failed in its trinitarian witness, remaining at the historical point of Jesus' collision with the power of his day: it treats freedom as interior and spiritual, and so offers no reconciliation with the political; it does not understand its own belief in the resurrection and the Holy Spirit."[73] For Williams, the church must admit its shortcomings, be truly self-reflexive, and recognize that "social unity is not ever something unproblematically given or achieved."[74] He notes "the dangers of reducing that vision to the claim of an institution ... which constantly slips into treating *itself* as one community among others that must struggle to establish its power or supremacy over others,"[75] and he insists that all potential civic voices must be allowed to engage in the dialogue.[76] Williams's conception of church is one that is open to discourse with others who may hold very different views and is willing to allow for the possibility that they may bear witness to something the church does not. Indeed, "the imagining of 'total peace' must somehow be accessible to those whose history is not yet healed or even heard in and by the Church."[77] While acknowledging the need to be open and receptive, Williams also states that the church must remain separate "from all communities and kinships whose limits fall short of the human race. The church's primitive and angular separateness ... is meant to be a protest on behalf of a unified world ... a church which does not at least possess certain features of a 'sect' cannot act as an agent of transformation."[78] Even so, the church must be "challenged to define itself in such a way that its continuity with a global hope can appear."[79]

Theo Hobson perceives a contradiction between "the Gospel as the call to a universal human society" and the rooting of "this vision in the church"[80] as an inherent weakness in Williams's argument, yet perhaps this may actually present its strength, highlighting the question of where the church achieves its peace; is it through the cross and sacraments, or in the peace it lives out? Williams's church retains authentic Christian witness, but aims to act practically and for real, effective change. Williams does not solve the problem of the church interacting in the world, but he is refreshingly honest and certainly more open than either Radical Orthodoxy or the Catholic Church about the realities involved in such a dialogue. While the church needs primarily to bear witness to the social truths of the gospel, Williams's model also allows the church to be open to dialogue with others in order to better work against social injustices, and indeed to discern what these may be. The church must act for real social change and not simply attempt to moralize the worst excesses of injustice. But neither must it assume that it has all the answers and is itself faultless. Williams is also open to the idea that the church can learn from the world, even as the world learns from the church.

Key to Williams's thinking is that the church must be critically aware of its own failings, a message that is important for both Catholic social teaching and Radical Orthodoxy to take on board.

Perhaps then what is needed is a period of reflection where the Catholic Church turns not toward the world, but first toward itself.[81] In light of the recent crises that have affected the Catholic Church – such as sexual abuse and, in certain countries, decline in vocations and Mass attendance– an acknowledgment of failure accompanied by self-contemplation seems to be an absolutely central concern in order for the church to move forward.

Francis's papacy has already begun to show some promising steps in such a direction. This was especially clear in the first stages of the 2014 Synod on the Family in its process of consultation with both clergy and laity and the subsequent period of reflection. Might this demonstrate how subsidiarity might be utilized within the church itself? Perhaps the beginning of Francis's critical shift can be traced to Benedict's unprecedented resignation, an act that fundamentally humanized and humbled the papal role. Still, a period of self-reflection is truly needed in the Catholic Church, in the hope that practices of ecclesial self-examination will become accepted as the norm. Such reflection is essential for the church in order continually to discern what its unique role may be within society, so as to bear to the world a faithful and constant Christian witness.

NOTES

1 This chapter considers the official papal-issued documents, as opposed to the wider body of theological writings known as Catholic social thought.
2 For a good overview, see Dorr, *Option for the Poor.*
3 See RN 7. While it has been argued that the church has had some form of social teaching since the time of St Paul, the beginnings of official Catholic Church teaching are almost unanimously traced to Leo XII's monumental 1891 encyclical, as it marks the first attempt to address the modern world. See Walsh, "Laying the Foundations."
4 Michael Allsopp refers to the principle as "a central norm of 20th-century Roman Catholic social theory." See Allsopp, "Subsidiarity," 927.
5 Schuck, "Modern Catholic Social Thought," 611–12.
6 Curran, *Directions in Catholic Social Ethics*, 22.
7 See Pius IX, *Syllabus Errorum.*
8 Leo XIII, *Aeterni Patris*; see also Pius XII, *Humani Generis.*
9 Barry, "Aquinas," 945.
10 While the origins of subsidiarity have been traced to, among others, Montesquieu, Tocqueville, John Dewey, Abraham Lincoln, and more

commonly Johannes Althusius, within Roman Catholicism it is traced to
Aquinas and through him back to Aristotle. For a summary of this, see
Kohler, "Lessons from the Social Charter," 617–18. Althusius is credited
with the beginnings of federalism; see Althusius, *Politics of Johannes
Althusius*. For Aquinas's influence on the principle, see Aroney,
"Subsidiarity, Federalism and the Best Constitution," 163; Millon-Delsol,
L'État Subsidiaire, chapters 1 and 3; and O'Donovan, "Subsidiarity."

11 Barry, "Aquinas," 940.

12 Ibid., 940–1. See Aquinas, *Summa Theologiae*, 1–2.94.3, 1–2.109.2,
    1–2.63.2.

13 Barry, "Aquinas," 941. See Aquinas, *Summa Theologiae*, 1.18 ad 2, 1.18.3,
    1.19.10, 1.59.3, 1.75.3, 1.76.1, 1.76.4, 1.77.5, 1.78.1, 1.83.1, 1.86.4 ad 3,
    1–2.50.3 ad 2.

14 Barry, "Aquinas," 941. See Aquinas, *Summa Theologiae*, 1–2.55.1.

15 Barry, "Aquinas," 942. See Aquinas, *Summa Theologiae*, 2–2.57.1,
    2–2.58.7, 2–2.58.9.

16 See Aquinas, *Summa Theologiae*, 1–2.61.5.

17 Ibid., 1–2.105.4.

18 Barry, "Aquinas," 943; Aquinas, *Summa Theologiae*, 3.41.1.

19 Barry, "Aquinas," 944.

20 Pontifical Council for Justice and Peace, *Compendium*, 185.

21 For an account of this, see Brown, "The 1983 Code."

22 See the Pontifical Academy of Social Sciences, "Pursuing the Common
    Good."

23 For a discussion of negative and positive subsidiarity, see Kohler, "In
    Praise of Little Platoons," 34–5.

24 Ketteler, *Social Teachings*. Ketteler believed capitalism was the only system
    possible and encouraged a program of self-help through unions,
    cooperatives, and associations. He asserted that societies should not per-
    form what smaller groups or the individual could do. Phillip Brown fur-
    ther identified Kant's discussion on organisms, later applied to the state,
    and Hegel's thought on corporations, as influential. See Brown, "The 1983
    Code," 588–90, 592–3; Leys, *Ecclesiological Impacts*, 26. See also Kant,
    Kritik der Urteilskraft; Hegel, *Grundlinien der Philosophie des Rechts
    oder Naturrecht und Staatwissenschaft im Grundrisse*.

25 Pius XI, *Quadragesimo Anno*. The encyclical was influenced by German
    Jesuit Oswald von Nell-Breuning, who drafted it. Although the writing
    of encyclicals is usually confidential, in 1971 Nell-Breuning told a
    German Jesuit magazine, *Stimmen der Zeit*, how the encyclical was com-
    posed. Here he acknowledges the influence of solidarism (developed by

Heinrich Pesch) through his contact with the German Jesuit Gustav Gundlach, his mentor.

26 Solidarism was based on Catholic philosophy and suggested a middle way between individualism and socialism by proposing that society should be composed of free and voluntary organizations from various professions that have economic freedom and act as intermediary bodies between the individual and the state. The state only acts in overseeing a smooth running of the economy to secure welfare. See Mulcahy, *Economics of Heinrich Pesch*; Giblin, "*Quadragesimo Anno*," 803; Kohler, "In Praise of Little Platoons," 37.

27 However, Kohler, agreeing with Chantal Millon-Delsol, claims that the Catholic Church never seriously promoted corporatism as a political or an economic system, and that the question of how the state should organize itself is actually left open (86). Indeed, Pius actually rejects interpretations that the state has no right to interfere in the market (*Quadragesimo Anno*, 41–58). See also Kohler, "In Praise of Little Platoons," 37–8; Millon-Delsol, *L'État Subsidiaire*, 158–9.

28 Michael Walsh has suggested that Pius's more negative reading of subsidiarity could be seen as a symbolic gesture toward the secular, as he did not want to alienate Italy under Mussolini. See Walsh, "Laying the Foundations," 36. This tactic is itself potentially problematic, though, as it could be argued that Pius was limiting the church's action and message in order to appease, or even collude with, Mussolini and the secular.

29 Boland, "*Mater et Magistra*," 580.

30 Dorr, *Option for the Poor*, 147.

31 *Dignitatis Humanae* therefore advocated religious freedom due to everyone's individual accountability to God (DH 1, 11). Here it draws on Rom. 14:12 and 1 Cor. 8:9–13, 10:23–33.

32 Lorentzen, "*Gaudium et Spes*," 408.

33 Ibid.; Curran, *Directions in Catholic Social Ethics*, 16.

34 O'Donovan, "Subsidiarity," 232. See Maritain, *Man and the State*.

35 O'Donovan, "Subsidiarity," 233.

36 Ibid., 245.

37 Charles, "Christian Social Witness," 2:244.

38 Hennelly, "*Populorum Progressio*," 765–6.

39 O'Donovan, "Subsidiarity," 238.

40 Ibid.

41 Clifford Longley notes that this term had been mentioned at the Puebla Conference of Latin American Bishops in 1979. See Longley, "Structures of Sin," 102–4.

42 Ibid.

43 McCormick, "*Centesimus Annus,*" 135.

44 See, for example, the work of Michael Novak, who advocates a capitalist liberal democracy; Gregory Baum's support for moderate socialism; Paul Vallely, who has argued that Catholic social teaching offers itself as an alternative middle ground; and Charles Curran, who sees it only as a set of guiding principles. Novak, *Catholic Social Thought* and *Spirit of Democratic Capitalism*; Baum, *Priority of Labour*; Vallely, "Introduction," 2; and Curran, *Directions in Catholic Social Ethics*, 30.

45 Kaufmann, "Principle of Subsidiarity," 281.

46 Milbank, *Theology and Social Theory*, 1.

47 Ibid., 2.

48 Ibid., 3.

49 For an account of this in relation to the political, see Davis and Riches, "Metanoia."

50 Blond, "Introduction," 7.

51 Milbank, Ward, and Pickstock, "Introduction," 3.

52 Milbank, *Being Reconciled*, 165–6.

53 Milbank, *Future of Love*, xvii–xviii, xi.

54 Milbank, *Word Made Strange*, 268–9, 283.

55 Oliver, "Introducing Radical Orthodoxy," 6.

56 Ibid.

57 Milbank, *Theology and Social Theory*, 2.

58 Ibid., 270. See also Milbank, *Future of Love*, 243.

59 Milbank, *Word Made Strange*, 268–9, 283.

60 Ibid., 285.

61 Smith, *Introducing Radical Orthodoxy*, 240. See also Hauerwas, *Peaceable Kingdom*, 60–1.

62 Milbank, *Future of Love*, xviii.

63 Milbank, *Theology and Social Theory*, 380.

64 Hauerwas, *Peaceable Kingdom*, 99, which is also cited in Smith, *Introducing Radical Orthodoxy*, 233. Unlike Hauerwas, Milbank does not neglect the role of the state but seeks rather to transform it.

65 Smith, *Introducing Radical Orthodoxy*, 232.

66 Oliver, "Introducing Radical Orthodoxy," 7.

67 Coombs, "Political Theology," 87.

68 Pabst, "Introduction," 9.

69 Milbank, "A Real Third Way," 47.

70 Pabst, "Introduction," 9.

71 Radical Orthodoxy's critique of liberalism has also not gone unchallenged.
    While it is beyond the scope of this chapter, see Hemming, *Radical
    Orthodoxy?*; Hyman, *Predicament of Postmodern Theology*; Crockett,
    Theology of the Sublime; and Insole, "Against Radical Orthodoxy,"
    214–41.
72 Williams, "Saving Time," 321.
73 Williams, "Logic and Spirit in Hegel," 64.
74 Williams, *Lost Icons*, 116.
75 Williams, "Mission and Christology," 12.
76 Williams, *Lost Icons*, 116.
77 Williams, "Saving Time," 323.
78 Williams, *On Christian Theology*, 233–4.
79 Williams, "Mission and Christology," 13.
80 Hobson, *Anarchy, Church and Utopia*, 99.
81 The place of subsidiarity within the church remains an important ongoing
    discussion. For example, Luca Badini Confalonieri presents an excellent
    account in *Democracy in the Christian Church*. See also Komonchak,
    "Subsidiarity in the Church"; Leys, *Ecclesiological Impacts*; and Losada,
    "Subsidiarity from an Ecclesiologist's Point of View."

4

Dialogue and Dignity:
Linking *Nostra Aetate* to Catholic Social
Justice Teachings

Alisha Pomazon

In 1960, when Jules Isaac, a Jewish historian who fought against antisemitic[1] practices in the world, learned that John XXIII had called for an ecumenical council, he asked for an audience with the pope to discuss Catholic teachings on Judaism. This audience took place on 13 June that year. After the meeting, Isaac wrote the following in his journal: "In telling him of all my gratitude for his welcome, I ask if I can carry away a bit of hope. [John XXIII] cries, 'You have a right to more than hope!'"[2]

The pope did not originally intend for the council to focus on the Catholic Church's relationship with Judaism. John XXIII, who stated his intention to call the council in 1959, saw the ecumenical council as a way to engage the church with the world in a vital new way by learning "how to distinguish the 'signs of the times' (Matt. 16:4)."[3] That is, John XXIII thought the church itself also needed much more than hope; it needed to respond to the crises of the world; it needed action; it needed a New Pentecost. In a letter to Giuseppe Piazza, the bishop of Bergamo, John XXIII wrote, "My soul finds comfort in the thought that a new Pentecost can blow through the Church, renewing its head, leading to a new ordering of the ecclesiastical body and bringing fresh vigour in the journey toward truth, goodness and peace."[4] Indeed, John XXIII used his first Pentecost as pope to announce the details of how the preparations for the council would be organized. As he said at the time, "It is from the spirit and doctrine of Pentecost that the great event of

the Ecumenical Council draws its substance and its life."[5] As part
of the planning for the council and as part of his vision for a New
Pentecost, John XXIII decided that the council would indeed look at
the church's teachings on Judaism, and gave Cardinal Augustin Bea
the mandate to do so.

John XXIII was no doubt influenced by Jules Isaac's suggestion
that a subcommittee should be created to study these teachings, but
the pope himself was vitally interested in healing Jewish-Catholic
relations, as he had shown by his actions to save Jews during the
Shoah and by his removal of negative depictions of Jews from the
Good Friday Prayer. Several other groups approached John XXIII
and the council's Central Preparatory Commission with the request
that the church reconsider its teachings on Judaism, including Rome's
Biblical Institute, the US Institute of Judaeo-Christian Studies, and
the Apeldoorn Working Group.[6] When the secretariat began looking at these teachings, Cardinal Bea did not know how to proceed.
However, in consultation with working groups, a text on Judaism
(Decretum de Iudaeis) was produced, and after many revisions and
setbacks, it became the motivating force behind Nostra Aetate.

In October 1965, the bishops of Vatican II passed Nostra Aetate
(Declaration on the Relation of the Church to Non-Christian
Religions). When Pope Paul VI promulgated Nostra Aetate on 28
October 1965, he said, "The Church is alive. Here is proof. Here is
breath, the voice, the song."[7] Paul VI's words resonate with the images
of the New Pentecost with which John XXIII began the council. These
images of life and breath do not just underlie the hopes of the council;
they ultimately underlie the hopes for the future of Jewish-Catholic
relations within the church. Nostra Aetate and the post-conciliar
relationship between Catholics and Jews have, in fact, been seen as
the "'litmus test' for measuring the success of the council's effort as
a whole, since many of the council's major themes flow into it."[8]
Themes such as dialogue, human dignity, religious freedom, relationship, and interaction with the contemporary world play key roles not
only in the theology and history of the Declaration and the council
in general, but also in Catholic teachings on interreligious dialogue
and social justice that have emerged since the conclusion of the council. In what follows, I will analyze Nostra Aetate by looking at how
this document relates to other Vatican II documents such as Gaudium
et Spes and Dignitatis Humanae, as well as the post-conciliar documents Guidelines, Notes, We Remember, and Gifts. In doing so, I will

ask the following: How do the themes of dialogue, human dignity, religious freedom, and relationship interact? How are these themes grounded in interactions with the world? How has the Jewish community responded to these documents and ideas? And finally, how can we see *Nostra Aetate* itself in connection with Catholic and Jewish social justice teachings? In this chapter, I will argue that the principles of dialogue and dignity are foundational to the practices of interreligious dialogue and social justice in the history of Jewish-Catholic relations since Vatican II. In making this argument, I will also assert that the ideas presented in *Nostra Aetate* and subsequently developed by the council, Vatican Commission, and Jewish historians and communities have brought about a transformation of Jewish-Christian relations that can be seen as a moment of social justice itself.

INTERACTING THEMES: CONNECTING DIALOGUE,
DIGNITY, AND SOCIAL JUSTICE IN VATICAN II
DOCUMENTS

In *Gaudium et Spes* (*Pastoral Constitution on the Church in the Modern World*), the Second Vatican Council connects social justice, dialogue, and dignity. *Gaudium et Spes* begins by asserting the need for social action in the world – the church must respond to the crises of the world because Christians are deeply connected to all of humanity and its history (GS 1). As such, the council focuses its attention on "both the daughters and the sons of the church ... [and] the whole of humanity as well" (GS 2) inasmuch as the "joys and hopes, the grief and anguish of the people of our time, especially of those who are poor or afflicted, are the joys and hopes, the grief and anguish of the followers of Christ" (GS 1). In these phrases, the council consciously puts the church at the service of the people of the world. The need for social justice and action is felt throughout the whole world, and because the crises of the world are the crises of the Catholic Church, the council feels it must respond to that need. *Gaudium et Spes* argues further that the service to the world must be done in dialogue with the world because the church does not always have the solutions to particular problems (GS 33). The council calls Christians to enter into dialogue with the world in order to "search for truth and for the right solution to so many moral problems which arise both in the life of individuals and from social relationships" (GS 16). Thus, dialogue is seen as the necessary precursor to social action.

Gaudium et Spes further connects, or perhaps even grounds, the ideas of dialogue and social justice in human dignity. While human dignity is understood as the inherent worth of every human being, the document also sees human dignity as the individual's ability to achieve his or her goal in pursuit of the Good through effective action (GS 17). Thus, human dignity becomes the basis for social justice in the form of social action, both in terms of an individual's motivation for that action and the need for that action in the world in general. That is, the idea of human dignity establishes the basis for fundamental human rights, including "all that is necessary for leading a genuinely human life" (GS 26), and provides the reason for pursuing action in the world. This action then leads to understanding that responsibility and love for one's neighbour are how human rights are realized in society (GS 26–7). In other words, the ability to act in the world and the ability to find solutions for the crises in the world are predicated on the recognition of human dignity (GS 16–17). *Gaudium et Spes* states that human dignity has a very concrete meaning for the church's relation to the wider world: "All we have said up to now about the dignity of the human person, the community of men and women, and the deep significance of human activity, provides a basis for discussing the relationship between the church and the world and the dialogue between them" (GS 40). Such dialogue "heals and elevates the dignity of the human person, in the way it consolidates society, and endows people's daily activity with a deeper sense and meaning. The church, then, believes that through each of its members and its community as a whole it can help to make the human family and its history still more human" (GS 40). In these passages, the council lays the foundation for dialogue with, instead of rejection of or withdrawal from, the world. The church "stands ready to serve humankind and human institutions, humbly conscious of what it can learn from history and from the social context,"[9] precisely because of the "presence of the church in the world, and its life and activity there" (GS 40).

The connection between human dignity, dialogue, and conscious action in the world in the form of social justice is further elucidated in *Dignitatis Humanae (Declaration on Religious Liberty)*. This *Declaration* takes as its starting point the centrality of human dignity and demands that individuals have not only the right, but also the freedom, to act (DH 1). *Dignitatis Humanae* asserts that this freedom should be a civil right, which means that people should be immune from any form of coercion from individuals or society (DH 2). All Christians must respect this freedom because this freedom is based "on the very dignity of the human person as known through the revealed word of God and by reason itself" (DH 2). Practically speaking, religious freedom also means that religious communities have the right to govern their own religious life unhindered by their government (DH 4). Specifically, *Dignitatis Humanae* argues that governments must protect the equality of their citizens for the common good; any violation of equality for "religious reasons" is a violation of the "sacred rights of the individual person" and of "God's will" – that is, of religion in general (DH 6).

Furthermore, *Dignitatus Humanae* states that the Catholic Church must take seriously that governments can still make life dangerous and difficult for religious communities, a practice that must be denounced and deplored (DH 15). Thus, the council "urges Catholics and appeals to all peoples to consider very carefully how necessary religious liberty is, especially in the present condition of the human family" (DH 15). *Dignitatis Humanae* explains that as people from various cultures and religions come to know each other, the personal responsibility of every person to the world and its people grows (DH 15). Consequently, in order for people to be respected and for peace to exist in the world, religious freedom must become a constitutional guarantee within the state structure (DH 15). In these passages of *Dignitatis Humanae*, the church issues a call for all to be globally responsible. The church here also issues a call to pay attention to the world, to listen to the suffering of the world, to end that suffering, and to do so in dialogue with the world's various communities since they too suffer, have inherent human dignity, and have access to solutions.

Moreover, the church actively engages with the world not only because it lives in the world, but also because "the principle [of] religious liberty is in keeping with human dignity and divine revelation" (DH 12). The church therefore has a part to play in defending and securing all earthly things from injury (DH 13). Thus, the call for governments to protect religious freedom and to deplore any discrimination, along with the exhortation for Catholics to understand that this call is in accordance with revelation, means that the council sees the protection of religious freedom as part of its mission in the world, its covenant with God, and the beginning of social justice initiatives.

INTERACTING WITH THE WORLD: THE CHURCH'S
RELATIONSHIP WITH JUDAISM

However, for all that *Dignitatis Humanae* speaks of human suffering, speaks out against discrimination, and deplores and denounces
how some governments make life dangerous for some religious communities (DH 15), there is no mention of any real-world examples.
Perhaps the Shoah is not explicitly mentioned because the Secretariat for Promoting Christian Unity, which helped to prepare *Dignitatis
Humanae*, was also preparing a document that did make explicit
reference to Judaism, a document that would become *Nostra Aetate
(Declaration on the Relation of the Church to Non-Christian Religions)*. While the secretariat was created by John XXIII to look at
the promotion of Christian ecumenism, the pope also asked Cardinal Bea, an ecumenist and biblical scholar, to create a statement that
dealt with the church's relationship with Jews because the "church
was born out of Israel, and with Israel it shared and venerated the
same sacred text."[10] This statement would become *Decretum de Iudaeis (Decree on the Jews)*.

John XXIII wanted the decree to articulate why the church's relationship with Jews was vitally important not only for Christian
values and identity, but also for the church's engagement with the
modern world. That is, John XXIII wanted to denounce "the vicious
outburst of anti-Semitism in the modern world that culminated
with National Socialism in Germany,"[11] and to take into account
Christian culpability in the Shoah.[12] The secretariat therefore
focused on Christian teachings that had played a role in the Shoah,
particularly the charge of deicide.

Throughout the preparation period and the four periods of the
council, the secretariat faced major opposition to the *Decree on the
Jews*. Opponents did not wish for either a stand-alone statement on
Judaism or a statement that repudiated the charge of deicide.[13] One
proposal asserted that portions of the *Decree* should be inserted into
Lumen Gentium (Dogmatic Constitution on the Church). Although
Cardinal Bea was open to such a move, he thought that it would
weaken the text's points.[14] Eventually, however, a revised statement
based on the *Decree* inspired, and was later encompassed within,
*Nostra Aetate (Declaration on the Relation of the Church to Non-
Christian Religions)*. That is, in analyzing the church's relationship with Judaism, the council fathers realized that the church also

needed to address its relationship with other world religions, and *Nostra Aetate* was finally promulgated in October 1965.[15]

Although the *Decree on the Jews* did not remain a stand-alone document, its placement within a document that dealt with non-Christian religions such as Buddhism, Hinduism, and Islam was a "revolutionary" move, as Rabbi David Meyer asserts, because it showed a "radical change in thinking."[16] Meyer contends that by incorporating the *Decree* into *Nostra Aetate*, the council, for all intents and purposes, recognized Judaism as a world religion in its own right and not merely in its relation to Christianity. Thus, he argues that the council showed a major shift in theological thinking concerning the relationship between Judaism and Christianity. To be sure, this shift in theological thinking allowed the shift in the relationship between Jews and Christians as a whole as well.

Nostra Aetate indeed begins by looking at the idea of relationship, and calls for the church to form a new type of relationship with other religions in order to respond to the world: "In our day, when people are drawing more closely together and the bonds of friendship between different peoples are being strengthened, the church examines more carefully its relations with non-Christian religions. Ever aware of its duty to foster unity and charity among individuals, and even among nations, it reflects at the outset on what people have in common and what tends to bring them together. Humanity forms but one community" (NA 1). Thus, in its first paragraph, *Nostra Aetate* recalls the themes of mission and the church's relationship with the world apparent in both *Gaudium et Spes* and *Dignitatis Humanae*. *Nostra Aetate* then asserts that the church, to engage with the world, must be in relation with the world's religions. The church also must look to its commonalities with these religions in order to enter into dialogue with them. To take these points seriously in relation to Judaism, the following questions must be asked: What is common between Christianity and Judaism? On what ground can dialogue between these two religions be built? How can the relationship between Judaism and Christianity move forward?

The answers to these questions rest upon the concepts of relationship that are found within the council's understanding of covenant, revelation, and social action in the world. In *Gaudium et Spes*, for instance, the council asserts that it acts on the basis of revelation through guarding the heritage of God's word, drawing moral and religious principles from revelation, and adding the light

of revealed truth to the world to find solutions to worldly problems
(GS 33). In line with *Gaudium et Spes*, *Nostra Aetate* turns to revelation to find the basis for the relationship between Judaism and
Christianity located within the covenantal relationship between God
and Abraham and subsequently between God and the "stock" of
Abraham, as first seen in God's promise to Abraham in Genesis 12
(NA 4). Further, *Nostra Aetate* asserts that "the church cannot forget that it received the revelation of the Old Testament ... Nor can
it forget that it draws nourishment from that good olive tree onto
which the wild olive branches of the Gentiles have been grafted"
(NA 4). *Nostra Aetate* searches for the relationship's foundation in
the covenant between God and Abraham (otherwise known as the
Abrahamic covenant) for Jews and Christians alike.

RESPONSES TO *NOSTRA AETATE* FROM THE JEWISH COMMUNITY

Although *Nostra Aetate* sees the Abrahamic covenant as the basis for the relationship between Christianity and Judaism, Meyer
points out an inherent problem: *Nostra Aetate*'s Abrahamic understanding of covenant does not take into consideration God's present-day relationship with the Jewish people. Since *Nostra Aetate*
states that "the Jews remain very dear to God, for the sake of the
patriarchs" (NA 4), Meyer argues that there is no acknowledgment
of the relationship between God and Jews now. For him, this omis-
sion indicates that the church continues to abide by the view that
there is no ongoing relationship between God and Jews beyond
that which is seen in the "Old Testament," especially when *Nostra
Aetate* explicitly states that Christians are "the people of the New
Covenant" and that Jews are the people of the "Old Testament." Although many Christians traditionally have interpreted these teachings in terms of replacement theology or supersessionism,[17] Meyer
is not making this argument. Rather, as a Jewish rabbi he critiques
this part of *Nostra Aetate* for negating the relationship between
God and present-day Jews. According to Meyer, these statements,
then, must shock Jewish readers because Jews "do not understand
this theology in which God does not love us as individuals and
human beings, but only because of the merit of our ancestors." As
Meyer asks, "How is it possible that God does not simply love me
as a human being?"[18]

In further analyzing the problems in *Nostra Aetate*, Meyer also wonders why the idea of the Abrahamic covenant should be so prevalent in a Catholic document when it is losing ground in present-day Jewish thought.[19] Meyer asserts that the idea of election is not as prevalent in Jewish thought and tradition as it once was. However, ideas about God's relationship with Abraham often form the basis for Jewish approaches toward interreligious dialogue. For instance, Michael Wyschogrod titles his essays on Judaism and Jewish–Christian relations *Abraham's Promise* to underscore the significance of the Abrahamic covenant in Jewish–Christian relations in general.

Moreover, Rabbi Jonathan Sacks draws upon the Abrahamic covenant as the foundation for his ideas about social justice, the ethics of responsibility, Jewish identity, and interreligious dialogue. In a speech delivered to an Anglican community, Sacks emphasizes the transformative power that covenantal relationships can lead to: "In a covenant, two or more individuals, each respecting the dignity and integrity of the other, come together in a bond of love and trust, to share their interests, sometimes even to share their lives, by pledging our faithfulness to one another, to do together what neither of us can do alone ... a contract is about interests but a covenant is about identity. And that is why contracts benefit, but covenants transform."[20] According to Sacks, if one understands relationship in terms of covenant, a transformation in thinking can occur, thereby changing relationships in turn. Thus, the focus on the Abrahamic covenant in Jewish–Christian relations clearly highlights the significance of relationship as established in the biblical text by both Jewish and Christian traditions.

Additionally, Rabbi David Rosen, the former international director of Interreligious Affairs of the American Jewish Committee, offers a comprehensive reflection about the transformations in relationship and ideas of covenant that have come about since, and because of, *Nostra Aetate*. For instance, he argues that "interreligious relations are a manifestation of the Abrahamic spirit of hospitality for which the Patriarch is renowned in the Hebrew Bible."[21] To illustrate this transformation in relationship, Rosen describes a meeting with Pope John Paul II in January 1993: "In receiving me and my colleague, he declared, 'I have said, you (the Jewish People) are the beloved elder brother of the Church of the original Covenant never broken and never to be broken.'"[22] For Rosen, John Paul II's proclamation "did not just reflect a transformation in attitude and teaching toward the

Jews; it has profound implications for the church in terms of its own theology." During the conference of the Holy See's Commission for Religious Relations with the Jews in Rome on 27 October 2005, Rosen claims that one can indeed see the impact of *Nostra Aetate* as, in the words of Cardinal Walter Kasper, "an astonishing transformation." Rosen states that with "the promulgation of this declaration, a people – formerly viewed at best as a fossil but more often as cursed and condemned to wander and suffer – was now officially portrayed as beloved by God and somehow very much still part of the Divine plan for humankind." Rosen notes that Pope Benedict XVI, Cardinal Bea, and Cardinal Willebrands have all spoken about these implications and affirm their groundbreaking nature. As Rosen quotes Cardinal Willebrands, "Never before had such a systematic, positive, comprehensive, careful and daring presentation on Jews and Judaism been made in the Church by a Pope or a Council."

Although Rosen underlines the positive transformations begun by *Nostra Aetate*, he also critiques the church's inability to implement these changes thoroughly. While the theological implications of *Nostra Aetate* for the understanding of Christian identity, covenant, and conversion of Jews concern several Catholic theologians, including Mary C. Boys and John Pawlikowski,[23] Rosen points out that there is resistance within sectors of the church to undertake a systematic analysis of the meaning of *Nostra Aetate*. Taking the document seriously, he suggests, would require the church as a whole to rethink God's continuing covenant with Jews in both its Christology and ecclesiology.[24] According to Rosen, the reluctance to look at these issues might be an attempt to minimize them and *Nostra Aetate* itself.[25] He gives the following example of the Italian theologian Illana Morelli, who stated that *Nostra Aetate* had no doctrinal authority and that to "attribute such to it would be 'greatly ingenuous' and a 'historical error.'"[26] At stake here is how official documents of the council and the church are understood in relation to each other. *Nostra Aetate*, as a declaration, does not hold the same authority as the documents promulgated as constitutions like *Gaudium et Spes* and *Lumen Gentium*. Although Morelli's point about the differences in authority does explain why *Nostra Aetate* is not given the same weight as the constitutions within the broader perspective of the church,[27] *Nostra Aetate*'s assertions clearly must be seen in congruence with the constitutions because it was written and promulgated with the constitutions in mind.

Rosen further argues that some Christian theologians and clergy from the Holy Land and the Arab world consider *Nostra Aetate* to be a product of European guilt over the Shoah, and thus it does not have the same relevance for them.[28] In this vein, Rosen quotes Cardinal Avery Dulles's opinion that "it is 'an open question whether the Old Covenant remains in force today'" and that "it is still a Catholic duty to invite Jews to receive the Christian faith."[29] Rosen here is referring to a document that the US Conference of Catholic Bishops co-authored in 2002 titled *Reflections on Covenant and Mission*.[30] This document was met with much controversy from Jews and Catholics alike because it called for continued evangelization of Jews. In response to this document and Dulles's comments, Rosen states, "As an outside observer, it would appear to me that these comments categorically contradict the late Pope John Paul II's clearly articulated teachings on the subject, as well as those of the Holy See's Commission for Religious Relations with Jewry and several statements of leading Bishops' Conferences. I must confess to some disappointment that there no refutation, distancing, or at least clarification on this from the Church authorities in Rome."[31] As a result of the lack of clarification on the above issues, and the fact that *Nostra Aetate* itself is often unknown to Catholic leaders and laity, Rosen continues, "there will remain not only an unhealthy ambiguity in our relationship, but we will continue to have to deal with unfortunate and unnecessary tensions regarding motives."[32] At the same time, while Catholic understanding of covenant, which includes both the Catholic and Jewish covenants with God, remains a critical component for the wider implications of *Nostra Aetate* for both Jews and Catholics, Rosen asserts that the foremost challenge for the Catholic Church is to ensure that "the fruits of *Nostra Aetate* are more firmly embedded in the formal fabric of the Church."[33] Later, as part of this process, the US Conference of Catholic Bishops tried to clarify their position in response to the Jewish community's concerns by issuing another document, "A Note on Ambiguities Contained in *Reflections on Covenant and Mission*,"[34] and then further amended that document in consultation with Jewish voices by removing several objectionable sentences.[35]

Significantly, in 2015, the theological reflection that was issued by the Vatican on the occasion of *Nostra Aetate*'s fiftieth anniversary, *The Gifts and the Calling of God Are Irrevocable (Gifts)*, takes its name from Paul's understanding of God's covenantal relationship with Jews in Romans 11:29. The document unequivocally states, "God's covenant with Abraham proves to be constitutive, as he is not only the father of Israel but also the father of the faith of Christians. In this covenant community it should be evident for Christians that the covenant that God concluded with Israel has never been revoked but remains valid on the basis of God's unfailing faithfulness to his people."[36] The language of this statement illustrates a change from *Nostra Aetate*'s understanding of covenant. For instance, the phrase "the Jews remain very dear to God, for the sake of the patriarchs" (NA 4) is no longer evident in the text's discussion of the covenant. Now, the document displays a view of covenant that underlines the importance of God's continuing covenant with Jews, and not just God's past covenant with the patriarchs. One can also see Meyer's criticism of *Nostra Aetate* reflected here. The phrasing is consistent with Jewish self-understanding, and reflects Jewish and Catholic engagement with *Nostra Aetate* and the further documents issued by the Commission of the Holy See for Religious Relations with the Jews.

POST-CONCILIAR DEVELOPMENTS: THE CHURCH'S NEED FOR DIALOGUE WITH JUDAISM

In 1974, the Year of Reconciliation for the Catholic Church, Paul VI instituted the Commission of the Holy See for Religious Relations with the Jews to develop further the orientation that section four of *Nostra Aetate* had given for the Catholic Church.[37] As part of this endeavour, the commission published four documents explicating and expanding upon the ideas and significance of *Nostra Aetate*: (1) *Guidelines and Suggestions for Implementing the Conciliar Declaration* "Nostra Aetate (n.4)" in 1974, (2) *Notes on the Correct Way to Present the Jews and Judaism in Preaching and Catechesis in the Roman Catholic Church* in 1985, (3) *We Remember: A Reflection on the Shoah* in 1998, and (4) *The Gifts and the Calling of God Are Irrevocable* in 2015 to celebrate the fiftieth anniversary of *Nostra Aetate*. These documents demonstrate that as the Catholic Church works through the implications of *Nostra Aetate*, it also focuses on the key themes of relationship, dialogue, dignity, and social justice.

The purpose of *Guidelines*, the first of these documents written after *Nostra Aetate*, is to offer practical advice for Catholics for developing sound relations with Jews. *Nostra Aetate* provided "an opportunity to open or to continue a dialogue with a view to better mutual understanding" and "mutual esteem."[38] To do so, *Guidelines* proposes to "distinguish the conditions under which a new relationship with Jews and Christians may be worked out and developed."[39] *Guidelines* argues that "Christians must therefore strive to acquire a better knowledge of the basic components of the religious tradition of Judaism; they must strive to learn by what essential traits the Jews define themselves in the light of their own religious experience."[40] Dialogue must be a priority, since it "presupposes that each side wishes to know the other, and wishes to increase and deepen its knowledge of the other."[41] *Guidelines* also points out that dialogue requires respect for people's faith and religious conditions, a teaching that is in line with the ideas of religious freedom and human dignity as set forth in *Dignitatis Humanae*.[42] In these statements, *Guidelines* proposes that dialogue is deepened through the acknowledgment of the dignity inherent in both dialogue partners.

Furthermore, *Guidelines* links dialogue to social justice. The document encourages openness and knowledge of oneself and others in a common meeting before God, both in terms of prayer and the struggle for peace and justice.[43] Here, *Guidelines* argues that dialogue between Jews and Christians can take place on two fronts: liturgy and social justice. Both Jewish and Christian liturgies emphasize that living in the service and love of God means living in community and in the service of humanity.[44] Accordingly, *Guidelines* points out that collaboration between Jews and Christians in these endeavours can foster mutual understanding and esteem,[45] thereby further facilitating service to the world through joint social action. Specifically, with regard to the connection to dignity, *Guidelines* mentions the council's condemnation of antisemitism and discrimination, stating that the idea of dignity alone is enough to condemn all forms of antisemitism and discrimination, which thus leads again to social action.[46]

The connections between a common spiritual background, dialogue, dignity, and social justice are further explicated in *Notes*[47] and *We Remember: A Reflection on the Shoah*.[48] These two documents focus on these themes by pointing to the practical applications and ramifications of dialogue between Jews and Christians. Specifically, these documents call for education initiatives in order to heal the relationship between Jews and Christians, expressing the fervent hope that, in the words of John Paul II about *We Remember*, these initiatives "will help to heal the wounds of past misunderstandings and injustices."[49]

Notes accentuates the need for Christians to learn about Judaism and the Jewish background of Christianity, as the full title reveals: *Notes on the Correct Way to Present the Jews and Judaism in Preaching and Catechesis in the Roman Catholic Church*. From the shared history of Jews and Christians in the "same promise made to Abraham" (*Notes*, II:10) and attentiveness "to the same God who has spoken" (*Notes*, II:11), Jews and Christians must go beyond simple dialogue and work for social justice, respecting the rights of all persons and nations (*Notes*, II:11). Working together for social justice builds upon dialogue and dignity, which in turn fosters education and mutual understanding and leads to further action. In this endeavour, *Notes* emphasizes in section VI (Judaism and Christianity in History) *Nostra Aetate*'s role in the establishment of education and joint social justice initiatives.

We Remember builds upon the call for education in *Notes* and *Guidelines* by acknowledging that Christians have perpetuated anti-Jewish teachings.[50] Accordingly, *We Remember* calls the Catholic Church to express its sorrow for the failures of its followers, and to make "an act of repentance (*teshuva*)," a binding commitment for all Christians to build a future of mutual respect rather than anti-Christian or anti-Jewish sentiments.[51] *We Remember*, then, further expands upon the commitment of the Catholic Church to promote education, dialogue, and joint social action, because respect for the dignity of people should entail protecting them from misinformation, misunderstandings, and any element of injustice. By looking at Christian anti-Jewish teachings and antisemitism, *We Remember* shows that any recognition of injustice is seen by the Catholic Church as a call to fight against that injustice. Adding these points from *We Remember* to the call for joint social action found in *Notes* and *Guidelines* reveals the further connection between dialogue, dignity, and social justice.

Several members of the Jewish community, however, spoke out against certain aspects of *We Remember*. In particular, the International Jewish Committee on Interreligious Consultations (IJCIC), in "Response to Vatican Document 'We Remember: A Reflection on the Shoah,'" pointed out several historical problems. In their view, *We Remember* glosses over, or even completely overlooks, the systematic persecution of Jews by the Catholic Church. The silence of church leaders, particularly that of Pope Pius XII, is one of the most contentious issues for the IJCIC. The authors compare the pope's silence to a

1997 statement by the French bishops in which they take responsibility for their mistaken silence during the Shoah: "The Document could well have spoken out against the silence of the hierarchies ... We do miss the simple statement that the earthly Church as a whole erred during this period and we see the refusal to assign any blame to it as an institution a step backward from the position of the German and French bishops."[52] The authors argue that *We Remember* generalizes the historical record of the church's actions and teachings, and the actions of its individual members, and that doing so may cause further harm. The IJCIC claims that the document, rather than directly dealing with the culpability of the church in the persecutions leading up to and during the Shoah, takes a convoluted approach that sidesteps the issues that matter to the Jewish community.

Nevertheless, the authors acknowledge that *We Remember* does provide steps forward in the context of the ongoing dialogues between Christianity and Judaism. They conclude,

> Our critique of the Document is not meant with any negative intent but as a pointer to the guidelines which we think should be adopted in Catholic teaching of the Shoah. It is in the spirit of Cardinal Cassidy's comment that the Document is not a conclusion but rather a step for further development, and that in the words of Pope John Paul II's covering letter, we will "work together for a world of true respect for the life and dignity of every human being." Indeed "We Remember" is not only an indictment of the past but, in its condemnation of antisemitism, a milestone-guideline for the future.[53]

The connections between dialogue, dignity, and social justice in Jewish-Christian relations are made explicit by two additional examples. First, John Paul II, in his Letter to the Latin-Rite Diocese of Jerusalem, dated 28 November 1997, asserts that the relationship between Jews and Christians is to be a blessing for the world through their shared heritage, duty, and desire to work together.[54] Second, the collaboration of which John Paul writes had already become grounded in the creation of the International Catholic-Jewish Liaison Committee (ILC), the official forum for dialogue between the Holy See's Commission for Religious Relations with the Jews and the International Jewish Committee for Interreligious Consultations.[55] The ILC issued a joint statement from its twenty-second annual meeting in 2013 that both recalls the language of *Nostra Aetate* and expresses the ongoing commitment to Jewish-Catholic dialogue, reaffirming the unique relationship and common spiritual legacy between Catholics and Jews, as well as their shared responsibility to defend the dignity of humanity.

> As Catholics and Jews we strive to build a world in which human rights are recognized and respected and where all peoples and societies can flourish in peace and freedom. We commit ourselves to strengthen our collaboration in the pursuit of an ever more just and equitable distribution of resources, so that all may benefit from advances in science, medicine, education and economic development. We see ourselves as partners in healing our created world so that it may reflect ever more brightly the original biblical vision: "And God saw all that God had made, and behold it was very good" (Gen. 1:31).[56]

In this passage, the ILC understands itself as a body that can create healing in the world by coming together as Jews and Catholics, working together to fulfill a biblical vision of social justice. The ILC thus makes recommendations for the protection of religious freedom, the fight against the persecution of Christians and the rise of antisemitism, and the furthering of Catholic education in seminaries on *Nostra Aetate* and its subsequent documents. According to the ILC, Jewish and Catholic leaders must embrace these teachings and continue to educate the world concerning the ways that *Nostra Aetate* fundamentally changed the relationship between Catholics and Jews. As the statement affirms, "We Catholics and Jews renew our commitment to educate our own respective communities in the knowledge of and respect for each other. We agree to cooperate to improve the lives of those on the margins of society, the poor, the sick, refugees, victims of human trafficking, and to protect God's creation from the dangers posed by climate change. We cannot do this alone; we call on all those in positions of authority and influence to join in serving the common good so that all may live in dignity and security, and so that justice and peace may prevail."[57] Thus, the ILC sees itself as a conduit for social justice, and the defence of human dignity is one of the major outcomes of Jewish-Christian dialogue.

In December 2015, the Commission for Religious Relations with the Jews issued a reflection on the fifty years since the promulgation of

Nostra Aetate. The document, *The Gifts and the Calling of God Are Irrevocable*, focuses on *Nostra Aetate*'s impact on Jewish-Catholic dialogue, the church's understanding of covenant, and the relationship between Judaism and Christianity. As such, this document "is intended to be a starting point for further theological thought with a view to enriching and intensifying the theological dimension of Jewish-Catholic dialogue."[58] Specifically, *Gifts* highlights the shift in the Jewish-Catholic relationship that was only possible because of *Nostra Aetate* and the later founding of the International Catholic-Jewish Liaison Committee. Accordingly, *Gifts* reaffirms that much "has developed over the past 40 years; the former confrontation has turned into successful cooperation, the previous potential for conflict has become positive conflict management, and the past co-existence marked by tension has been replaced by resilient and fruitful mutuality."[59] Moreover, as *Gifts* continues, the "bonds of friendship forged in the meantime have proved to be stable, so that it has become possible to address even controversial subjects together without the danger of permanent damage being done to the dialogue ... [and to address them] in such a way that mutual relations have become stronger."[60]

Indeed, *Gifts* emphasizes the several levels on which dialogue between Jews and Catholics takes place, stressing that each level of dialogue enhances and strengthens the other. The official dialogue organization (ILC), Jewish audiences with the pope, and local-level dialogues have "led with increasing clarity to the awareness that Christians and Jews are irrevocably interdependent, and that the dialogue between the two is not a matter of choice but of duty ... [enriching] one another in mutual friendship."[61]

As a reflection on the theological issues, *Gifts* considers the changes in theology that have come about because of *Nostra Aetate*. In particular, *Gifts* traces how the Catholic understanding of the Abrahamic covenant has developed since *Nostra Aetate*. Although this conciliar text was "a theological breakthrough," *Gifts* acknowledges that it has been

> over-interpreted, and things ... read into it which it does not in fact contain. An important example of over-interpretation would be the following: that the covenant that God made with his people Israel perdures and is never invalidated. Although this statement is true, it cannot be explicitly ready into "Nostra

aetate" (No.4). This statement was instead first made with full
clarity by Saint Pope John Paul II when he said during a meeting
with Jewish representatives in Mainz on 17 November 1980 that
the Old Covenant had never been revoked by God: "The first
dimension of this dialogue, that is, the meeting between the people of God of the Old Covenant, never revoked by God ... and
that of the New Covenant, is at the same time a dialogue within
our Church, that is to say, between the first and the second part
of her Bible" (No.3). The same conviction is stated also in the
Catechism of the Church in 1993: "The Old Covenant has never
been revoked."[62]

The changes evidenced in *Gifts*, which are also apparent in
Guidelines and *Notes*, have come about through the education initiatives of the Commission for Religious Relations with the Jews.
Gifts emphasizes the relationship between education and dialogue
in building on the spiritual bond with which *Nostra Aetate* 4 begins.
That is, *Gifts* asserts that the "first goal of the dialogue is to add
depth to the reciprocal knowledge of Jews and Christians. One can
only learn to love what one has gradually come to know, and one
can only know truly and profoundly what one loves. This profound
knowledge is accompanied by a mutual enrichment whereby the
dialogue partners become the recipients of gifts."[63] That *Gifts* can
speak of love and mutual enrichment with regard to the relationship
between Jews and Christians illustrates how profoundly this relationship has changed since *Nostra Aetate* from the Catholic perspective. At the same time, *Gifts* notes that what its text presents is still
only a "starting point" for further discussion,[64] thus reflecting the
desire for continual dialogue with Jews and the Jewish concern for
the lack of theological reflection on *Nostra Aetate* that David Rosen
pointed out earlier.

Furthermore, Jewish responses to the fiftieth anniversary of
Nostra Aetate call for more work to be done. Rosen continues to
stress the roles of Catholic education and formation in this process and applauds the work done by the Sisters of Sion in the
church in this regard.[65] *To Do the Will of Our Father in Heaven:
Toward a Partnership between Jews and Christians*, written by the
International Group of Orthodox Rabbis, recognizes "that since the
Second Vatican Council the official teachings of the Catholic Church
about Judaism have changed fundamentally and irrevocably." As a

result of these changes, this document continues, "Catholics and other Christian officials started an honest dialogue with Jews that has grown during the last five decades. We appreciate the Church's affirmation of Israel's unique place in sacred history and the ultimate world redemption. Today Jews have experienced sincere love and respect from many Christians that have been expressed in many dialogue initiatives, meetings and conferences around the world."[66] The authors of this document, then, also stress that dialogue and education are key to continued good relations between Judaism and Christianity, especially since "Jews and Christians have more in common than what divides."[67]

CONCLUSION: *NOSTRA AETATE* AS A SOCIAL JUSTICE MOVEMENT

Finally, how then do we see *Nostra Aetate* and subsequent Jewish–Christian relations as moments of social justice themselves?

According to John Paul II in his 1999 apostolic exhortation, *Ecclesia in America*, the foundation of Catholic social teaching "rests on the threefold cornerstones of human dignity, solidarity and subsidiarity."[68] Two of these cornerstones, as we have seen, are present in Jewish-Christian relations. Dignity is evident in the Vatican II documents and the Holy See's Commission for Religious Relations with the Jews, and in the resulting work to establish religious freedom and dialogue with Judaism. Solidarity is clearly present in Jewish and Christian commitments to joint social action, especially in the work of the ILC.

Furthermore, the principles of dignity and solidarity, which infused the creation of *Nostra Aetate* and its subsequent development, transformed the relationship between Judaism and Christianity. As the church focused on its broader relationship with the world, it realized that it must transform its vision of Judaism, which then enabled a new type of relationship between Jews and Christians to begin. While *Nostra Aetate* itself has been criticized by Jews and Catholics, this document has allowed both Jews and Catholics to engage with each other to create moments of healing that should be continually announced and, in the words of John Paul II quoting Paul on the subject of God's covenant with Judaism, "never revoked."[69] A deeper understanding between Jews and Christians has emerged as the church sought to rectify the problems that Jews pointed out in the documents. Thus, the changes that appear from document to document show the results of this dialogue between Christians and Jews, and can be seen as dialogue in action.

In a very real sense, then, Jonathan Sacks's idea of covenant describes Jewish-Christian relations after *Nostra Aetate*. The Catholic Church participated in a transformation of Jewish-Christian relations by focusing on the Abrahamic covenant as seen by both Jews and Christians. We can see this in terms of theology – as Catholic teachings about Judaism were transformed through the further explanation of *Nostra Aetate* in *Guidelines*, *Notes*, *We Remember*, and *Gifts*. We can also see this in the joint initiatives between the Catholic Church and the Jewish community that focus on doing together what neither can do alone – initiatives that work toward the elimination of antisemitism, the establishment of human rights, and the encouragement of other forms of social justice and care for the planet. In fact, Sacks's ideas on Judaism's responsibility for society mirror the language of Vatican II: "There is the common ground of the common good, and there are the semi-private domains of our diverse religious traditions. We are responsible to society for the former, to our own community for the latter. That is, I believe, as it should be. No one should seek to impose his or her religious convictions on society, but we should seek to bring the insights of our respective faiths to the public conversation about the principles for which we stand and the values that we share."[70]

In trying to foster dialogue and understanding between Judaism and the Catholic Church, both Jews and Christians work with the same foundations of dignity and social justice as they do when seeking to eliminate suffering in the world. In the oft-repeated words of John Paul II on the fiftieth anniversary of the Warsaw Ghetto uprising, "As Christians and Jews, following the example of the faith of Abraham, we are called to be a blessing to the world. This is the common task awaiting us. It is therefore necessary for us, Christians and Jews, to first be a blessing to one another."[71] In the words of Sacks, John Paul II, and John XXIII, we can see how *Nostra Aetate* facilitated the fostering of a new relationship between Jews and Christians as people who do much more than hope: they work together for the good of the world. As *Gifts* states, when "Jews and Christians make a joint contribution through concrete humanitarian aid for justice and peace in the world, they bear witness to the loving care of God. No longer in confrontational opposition but cooperating side by side, Jews and

Christians should seek to strive for a better world."[72] Reflecting this statement, *To Do the Will of Our Father in Heaven* further asserts, "In imitating G-d, Jews and Christians must offer models of service, unconditional love and holiness. We are all created in G-d's Holy Image, and Jews and Christians will remain dedicated to the Covenant by playing an active role together in redeeming the world."[73] In these statements, then, we can see that in turning to the world, and acting in it, Jews and Christians alike work for the betterment of all, which in turn allows for authentic healing of the world to take place.

Dialogue and dignity are central concepts for understanding *Nostra Aetate*'s significance because in the history of Jewish-Christian relations, one cannot have dialogue when dignity is missing. For much of the history of Jewish-Christian relations, dignity has been denied to Jewish people by Christians. The focus on dignity in the Vatican II documents has revolutionized Jewish-Christian dialogue. In an address to Pope Francis during his visit to Rome Synagogue, Renzo Gattegna makes precisely this point: "In their diversity, in the mutual respect of different traditions, in the acceptance of equal dignity, the relationship between the Catholic Church and Judaism has since [*Nostra Aetate*] been experiencing a period of great progress, which we can certainly define as one of historic significance."[74] When dialogue and dignity are linked to ideals of social justice and turning to the world as seen above, the actions that ensue can change relationships, and perhaps even the world, which is precisely the point of social justice.

In as much as *Nostra Aetate* became a catalyst for a revolution in Jewish-Christian relations, it fulfilled John XXIII's vision of Vatican II as a New Pentecost.

NOTES

1 Unless included in a direct quote, this chapter will use the term "antisemitism" instead of "anti-Semitism." Anti-Semitism is based on a racial definition of the Jewish people. In contrast, antisemitism refers to the systematic hatred of the Jewish people. Although these terms are often used interchangeably, antisemitism is the proper term for what I will discuss here because it rejects the racial ideas and background implied in anti-Semitism.

2 Isaac, *Crucial Meeting.*

3 John XXIII, *Humanae Salutis,* 704.

4 Hebblethwaite, "John XXIII," 28.

5 Ibid.

6 See Oesterreicher, "Declaration."

7 Qtd in Oesterreicher, "New Beginning," 44.

8 Fisher, "Evolution of a Tradition," 32.

9 Kavunkal, D'Lima, and Monteiro, *Vatican II*, 120.

10 O'Malley, *What Happened at Vatican II*, 195.

11 Ibid.

12 Ibid., 220.

13 Ibid., 221.

14 Ibid., 225.

15 See Oesterreicher, "Declaration," 94–7, and Commission of the Holy See for Religious Relations with the Jews, *Gifts*, 19. Additional information on the council's preparation of *Nostra Aetate* also can be found in Lamberigts and Declerck, "Vatican II on the Jews." The role that the Sisters of Our Lady of Sion played in the preparation and acceptance of *Nostra Aetate* is becoming of great interest to *Nostra Aetate* historians; see Deutsch, "Journey to Dialogue."

16 Meyer, "*Nostra Aetate*," 117.

17 Commission of the Holy See for Religious Relations with the Jews, *Gifts*, 17.

18 Meyer, "*Nostra Aetate*," 125. *Gifts* addresses these criticisms, as discussed below in "Post-conciliar Documents."

19 Meyer, "*Nostra Aetate*," 125.

20 Sacks, "Address to the Anglican Communion Conference 2008," qtd in Kessler, *Introduction to Jewish-Christian Relations*, 171.

21 Rosen, "Jerusalem," 3.

22 The remaining quotations in this paragraph are from Rosen, "*Nostra Aetate*."

23 Boys, "*Nostra Aetate* Trajectory"; Pawlikowski, "Reflections on Covenant and Mission."

24 Rosen, "*Nostra Aetate*."

25 Ibid.

26 Ibid.

27 This point became paramount when *The Gifts and the Calling of God Are Irrevocable* was published, as this document asserts that its "text is not a magisterial document or doctrinal teaching of the Catholic Church, but is a reflection prepared by the Commission for Religious Relations with the Jews on current theological questions that have developed since the Second Vatican Council" (Preface). That is, this document clearly states its status and intention as a reflection.

28 Rosen, "*Nostra Aetate*."

29 Dulles, "Covenant and Mission," qtd in Rosen, "*Nostra Aetate*."

30 Consultation of the National Council of Synagogues and US Conference of Catholic Bishops, *Reflections on Covenant and Mission*.

31 Rosen, "*Nostra Aetate*."

32 Ibid.

33 Ibid.

34 Committee on Doctrine and Committee on Ecumenical and Interreligious Affairs, "A Note on Ambiguities."

35 George, "U.S. Bishops' Reply."

36 Commission of the Holy See for Religious Relations with the Jews, *Gifts*, 33.

37 Commission of the Holy See for Religious Relations with the Jews, *Relations with the Jews*.

38 Commission of the Holy See for Religious Relations with the Jews, *Guidelines*, Preamble.

39 Ibid.

40 Ibid.

41 *Guidelines*, I.

42 Ibid.

43 Ibid.

44 *Guidelines*, II.

45 *Guidelines*, IV.

46 *Guidelines*, Preamble.

47 Commission of the Holy See for Religious Relations with the Jews, *Notes*.

48 Commission of the Holy See for Religious Relations with the Jews, *We Remember*.

49 Cassidy, "Presentation of *We Remember*." John Paul II further outlines his hopes for *We Remember* in a letter written to Cardinal Edward Idris Cassidy dated 12 March 1998: "May it enable memory to play its necessary part in the process of shaping a future in which the unspeakable iniquity of the Shoah will never again be possible. May the Lord of history guide the efforts of Catholics and Jews and all men and women of good will as they work together for a world of true respect for the life and dignity of every human being, for all have been created in the image and likeness of God."

50 *We Remember*, IV.

51 *We Remember*, V.

52 International Jewish Committee on Interreligious Consultations, "Response to Vatican Document 'We Remember.'"

53 Ibid.

54 John Paul II, "Letter to the Latin-Rite Diocese of Jerusalem."

55 See *Gifts* 9–10 for information on the history of this relationship.

56 International Catholic-Jewish Liaison Committee, "Joint Statement."

57 Ibid.

58 Commission of the Holy See for Religious Relations with the Jews, *Gifts*, Preface.

59 Ibid., 10. *Gifts* notes that the original occasion for these statements was the ILC's look back on the relationship between IJCIC and the Commission in Paris, February 2011.

60 Ibid.

61 Ibid., 13.

62 Ibid., 39.

63 Ibid., 44.

64 Ibid., Preface.

65 Rosen, "Fifty Years since Nostra Aetate," 7.

66 International Group of Orthodox Rabbis, *To Do the Will of Our Father*, par. 2.

67 Ibid., par. 5.

68 John Paul II, *Ecclesia in America*, 55.

69 John Paul II, "Address to the Jewish Central Council in Germany," qtd in Henrix, "The Covenant Has Never Been Revoked"; cf. Rom. 11:29.

70 Sacks, *To Heal a Fractured World*, 124.

71 John Paul II, "Address on the 50th Anniversary of the Warsaw Ghetto Uprising."

72 Commission of the Holy See for Religious Relations with the Jews, *Gifts*, 49.

73 International Group of Orthodox Rabbis, *To Do the Will of Our Father*, 7.

74 Gattegna, "Importance of Symbolic Gestures."

5

Images of Dealing with Social Injustice from Jewish Apocalyptic Tradition: A Resource for Renewed Reflection

Loren T. Stuckenbruck

Social injustice is reprehensible. This truism, however, is complex; almost no one, even those in positions of power who are often accused of carrying out or colluding with forms of oppression, openly claims that injustice is a good thing. Indeed, discourse about justice can be a matter of perception and socially constructed rhetoric. How can one convey a prophetic message that challenges power structures without being caught up in making things worse or being entangled in the messiness of ambiguity and even self-doubt? Apart from adopting or finding a lifestyle that openly resists the unjust exercise of privilege and power at the expense of others, how can one agitate for change in society on socioreligious and theological grounds that, at the same time, are not open to misinterpretation and to subversion in the hands of others who have a different perspective? In relation to the theme of social justice, one of our common tasks is to search for new language and fresh ways to innovate change that are not easily domesticated by routinized and well-worn habits of thought and practice. While I can make no claim to come up with such language, it is nonetheless possible to draw attention to a resource for thinking, reflection, and activity that the Second Vatican Council and follow-up documents have encouraged the Christian religious community to engage with.

I am referring to *Nostra Aetate* and subsequent elaborative statements[1] in which the Roman Catholic Church has expressed the need for religious tolerance within the current world climate, while at the

same time standing firm in its commitment to a doctrinally faithful
position based on the gospel as entrusted to the church. While *Nostra
Aetate* is, in principle, a statement broadly concerned with the relation of Christianity to other major world religions, its sharpest edge is
nowhere more apparent than in the question of how the church relates
to Judaism (NA 4) and Jewish tradition. One might acknowledge that
this particular front is the result of the untold tragedies of human suffering linked to the rise of national socialism in Germany during the
twentieth century; however, the statement on religious tolerance and
interfaith dialogue and understanding runs deeper. When raising the
question of Judaism in relation to Christian faith, the church is fundamentally engaging in an inquiry into the origins of its existence, especially as its roots are inseparably bound to Jewish tradition. Indeed,
one of the sections of the *Notes* arising out of *Nostra Aetate* affirms
the "Jewish Roots of Christianity."[2] I am not concerned with problem
of religious tolerance per se; nevertheless, the issue of respect among
different religious traditions is significant for the ways we deal with
conditions in society that lead to oppressive behaviour among individuals and to the economic and sociopolitical downgrading of others
based on ethnic and/or religious values. Interfaith dialogue involves
more, however, than the mere recognition of obvious and profound
differences of identity by people who share social space. In a constructive vein, sometimes language used by "the other," in this case by
representatives of a sister (or, as in relation to Judaism, a "mother")
religion, can serve to re-enliven the language we use to approach
problems we have in common, not least that of social justice.

In order to address injustice theologically, the church may instinctively wish to draw on her own time-worn teachings as traditions
that set her apart from perspectives espoused by other religious traditions. However, the interfaith links with Judaism recognized during
and since Vatican II show that what constitutes one's *own tradition*
is not straightforward. Not only the Hebrew Bible (called the Old
Testament by most Christians), but also Jewish tradition that emerged
during the Second Temple period before and during the inception
of earliest Christianity, had a lot to say about social justice. Indeed,
Judaism around the turn of the Common Era, in all its bewildering
variety,[3] not only provided a framework within which and in response
to which Jesus and his followers could challenge a religious establishment; it also supplied the very conceptual basis upon which to
articulate their critiques. Thus, while acknowledging the significant

steps of openness articulated in *Nostra Aetate* toward a recognition of Judaism as a faith with an integrity of its own, I would argue that perhaps the best effect of such a statement is not simply the advocacy of religious tolerance per se, but the *theologically constructive* learning that may take place within the church when it adopts such a stance.

If we acknowledge that the prophetic messages of Amos (4:1, 5:11, 6:4–6, 8:3–5), Habakkuk (2:9, 3:13–15, 12, 19), Isaiah (10:1–2, 22:12–14, 32:7, 58:7), and Jeremiah (2:34, 17:11, 22:13), or the sayings and activities of Jesus in the Gospels (e.g., Matt. 19:21; Mark 10:21; Luke 14:15–23, 16:19–31, 18:22, 19:1–10), should occupy a prominent place in theological critiques of oppressive activity by the privileged, we are at the same time laying claim to the fact that such critiques are essentially Jewish. It is well known that over against a religious establishment in which sociopolitical structures and discourse about God were intertwined with one another, writings attributed to the Hebrew prophets and the proclamation of Jesus attempted to paint a portrait of life as God would have it to be, whether such was to be realized through a transformation of the world as we know it or through an eschatological event that introduces a new order of existence that altogether dispenses with the present order of things.[4] Both alternatives would play a role in shaping early Christian perspectives and, ultimately, the theology of the church as a whole. Both envisioned the world, whether transformed or as a new creation, in which people who have been robbed of dignity have an integral place. If, in particular, we are to understand the more immediate background to Jesus' message to his contemporaries about the kingdom of God, then it was an apocalyptic orientation that provided the most immediate matrix that made it possible for people to understand or at least imagine that Jesus advocated for something essentially new. Apocalyptic thought, which had begun to take shape in the late fourth century BCE, not only on occasion anticipated a new beginning at the end of history; it also engaged in a discourse of resistance that hoped for and welcomed any alleviation of suffering that might take place in the meantime.[5] Contrary to what many specialists of "apocalyptic" have maintained in the past and continue to argue,[6] social justice was not simply a matter of postponing much-longed-for justice, but rather a program for change through resistance that can already operate in the present.

The prophetic tradition anticipated (and Jesus and his followers reflected) a world order in which people who have been taken advantage of and robbed of their human dignity have a place – even a central place – in the establishment of something new. Most commonly at the time of Jesus, it would be the apocalyptic tradition that expressed and described a vision of the world under God's control in response to hostile circumstances that had become part of the experience of the socially underprivileged who claimed at the same time to be religiously faithful. Apocalyptic thought not only looked forward to a new world in an eschatological future at the end of history; it could also attempt to put persistent suffering and societal injustice into perspective.

In what follows, I would like to draw attention to three different models for advocating social justice in a tradition that may have wielded more influence on Jesus and the structures of early Christian thought than any other religious source from several centuries leading up to the Common Era. I am referring to a web of traditions composed over a period of 400 years and collected within a document known as *1 Enoch*, which today belongs to the sacred scriptures of the Ethiopian Orthodox Tewahedo Church.[7] Consisting of 108 chapters composed of five major sections[8] and two appendices (*Birth of Noah* in chapters 106–7 and *Eschatological Admonition* in chapter 108), the work is largely attributed to the patriarch figure of Enoch (Gen. 5:21–24), who, according to biblical tradition, lived before the time of the Great Flood (Gen. 6–9). Writing in the name of Enoch, the anonymous authors behind *1 Enoch* were appealing to an exemplary figure (a) who "walked with God" during a time of increasing evil (Gen. 5:22, 24), (b) who was supposed to have been given revelations about the secrets of the universe and the ultimate fates of the righteous and the wicked, and (c) who supposedly did not meet death (see Gen. 5:24; and, e.g., Heb. 11:5).[9] During the Second Temple period leading up to the time of the New Testament, *1 Enoch* became an influential text with a remarkably broad range of ideas written from the perspective of groups who regarded themselves as oppressed by their contemporaries in positions of sociopolitical and religious power.[10]

THE MODELLING OF SOCIAL JUSTICE IN AN ANCIENT JEWISH TRADITION

The first model for envisioning and advocating for social justice occurs in the so-called *Epistle of Enoch* (*1 En.* 92:1–5 and 93:11–105:2), composed around 175–170 BCE, just prior to the great Maccabean

Revolt against both the Seleucids (who were heirs of Alexander the Great's conquests in a region extending from Anatolia to Afghanistan and the Indus River) and other Jews who were colluding with them in imposing Hellenistic culture in Jerusalem and its environs.[11] In its approach to social inequity and persecution, the *Epistle* conforms in large part to what is often associated with apocalyptic thought from the Second Temple period. Its writer denounces injustices being carried out by the rich and social (even religious) elite against a seemingly helpless community of people trying to be faithful to God; this message is communicated in the *Epistle* with an intensity greater than that of any other document from the ancient world, including the Hebrew Bible, Second Temple Jewish writings, and early Christian literature.[12] Here an author, who models himself on the prophets of the Hebrew Bible and writes in the name of Enoch,[13] lays blame for the destitute conditions of "the righteous" – their hunger and poverty, along with forms of social, material, and corporeal enslavement – at the feet of a group that he most often designates as "rich" or "wicked." Since the writer does not harbour any hope that the wicked will change their ways and because he does not expect the socioeconomic well-being of the righteous to improve, divine justice is not to be anticipated within the cosmos as it now exists. Only an eschatological reordering of things, a final judgment, will bring about conditions as they were meant to be. The anticipated future world is not in itself described in much detail; the author's statements, which make no mention of a messianic figure playing any role, assume that a just world will in effect take shape as a theocracy in which the righteous, disinherited in the present age, will enjoy the status of an angelic existence and be rewarded with a wealth that is only possible in the next age.[14]

The anticipation of such a future in the *Epistle of Enoch* is not in itself unusual for apocalyptic literature composed from around the Common Era.[15] It is also picked up in parts of the New Testament (with the addition of a messiah), as for example in Matthew's Gospel,[16] the letters of the Apostle Paul,[17] and the Book of Revelation.[18] There are, however, two things to note about the message of the *Epistle* itself. First, its writer is not merely denouncing the wicked and predicting their ultimate downfall. The repeated denunciations are couched in such juridical language that they are intended to function as formal testimony at the time of the final judgment itself. In other words, *these words* are being formalized in writing now because *they* will be brought before God when the time of reckoning comes. The writer states on a number of occasions that the misdeeds of the privileged wicked and the suffering of the righteous will herewith be brought as a "memorial" before God.[19] Unjust acts that have devalued and maligned those without privilege will not be forgotten.

The second thing to notice is the role the writer assigns himself: he regards his indictment against the wicked as formal testimony that will be decisive in the divine court of justice at the end of time. In this role, he acts as a witness on behalf of the oppressed, who, on account of the magnitude of their suffering, are unable to speak for themselves. In other words, in the *Epistle* the writer is giving those who suffer oppression a stronger voice to ensure that the unjust will be held responsible for what they have done. He does this by drawing on and reinterpreting tradition from the Hebrew Bible that both he and the religious elite he criticizes hold sacred.[20] This advocacy on behalf of the righteous is not as straightforward as it might initially appear; at least some of the oppressors, also Jews, seem to justify their well-being on the basis of the covenant blessings described in Deuteronomy 28. In a beautiful poetic speech near the end of the *Epistle* (1 *En.* 103:9–15), the author puts into the mouths of the righteous a lament that admits as much: the blessings that should be theirs are actually being experienced by the wicked, while the curses that are supposed to happen to those who disobey the covenant have been theirs to experience.[21] This problem is resolved not by rejecting the message of Deuteronomy, as such, but by postponing the blessings to the afterlife (1 *En.* 104:1–6). Rather than allow the wicked to control the interpretation of the Deuteronomistic theological tradition to justify the social and economic abuse of others, the writer of the *Epistle* offers a counterinterpretation in order to secure a way for the righteous to hope for salvation while assuring them that the wicked, who are socially privileged, will be held responsible and punished. He reconnects the marginalized community with the Pentateuch, and prophetic and wisdom books of the Hebrew Bible, so that this tradition no longer remains the domain of the advantaged.

One may ask whether the message of the *Epistle*, which focuses on reward and punishment in the afterlife, actually offers a vision of social justice. In one sense, of course, the answer is negative. It is not, however, a matter of throwing up one's hands to imagine a future reality that is utterly different from the present. Rather than simply waiting for justice or suffering passively, the recipients of the *Epistle* are invited to invest themselves in a perspective that is not fooled by appearances, and so to be confident as they continue to choose "an acceptable life" and to follow "the ways of peace so that you may live and flourish" (*1 En.* 94:4). Though the terms "an acceptable life" and "flourish" are subjected to reinterpretation, the *Epistle* exhorts its audience to activity in this world, regardless of whether they are going to be visibly rewarded in the way biblical tradition specifies.

The second model for advocating social justice in *1 Enoch* can be found in chapters 85–90, a section of the book frequently referred to as the *Animal Vision* or *Animal Apocalypse*.[22] In this work, another writer, composing in the name of Enoch during the Maccabean Revolt (mid-160s BCE), takes up the imagery of animals to tell his version of the sacred history of Israel from the time of the creation of Adam all the way down to his own time, when he expects God to restore the world to justice. According to the vision narrated in the text, the prominent characters from Israel's past and present are each depicted with symbolic animal imagery: so, for example, Israel's enemies are depicted as various wild animals while the people of Israel are most commonly referred to as "sheep." The sheep are alternately described as "blinded" when unfaithful[23] and "sheep whose eyes have been opened"[24] when faithful (as a small community in the author's day). The writer of the *Animal Apocalypse* shares the *Epistle*'s emphasis on and anticipation of a coming world order in which the religiously faithful will be rewarded and in which judgment will be meted out, at least in principle, to the wicked (90:17–27). Unlike the *Epistle*, however, a messianic figure – who is called a "white bull" – is expected to act as an agent in bringing the new world about (90:37–8).

Two points arising from the *Animal Apocalypse* are noteworthy in relation to social justice. The first has to do with the end result. Readers of the vision learn that the "sheep," with whom the author identifies, are being oppressed by "eagles, ravens, vultures and kites."[25] These birds of prey symbolize the Hellenistic Seleucid overlords who persecute, bear down, and "devour" faithful Jews (90:2–4, 11). In the judgment scene to follow (*1 En.* 90:20–36), the text delivers what one who anticipates divine justice is led to expect: figures who have acted wickedly in the narrative are punished (vv. 20–7, with the "sinners" burned [v. 27]), while the righteous are rewarded (vv. 28–36); in addition, the writer anticipates that the wicked will throw themselves in submission before the very ones they have previously oppressed (v. 30). Not unlike the general perspective of the *Epistle*, the tables are turned.

The text then offers a surprise. Once the judgment and subjugation of the Gentiles have taken place, the writer speaks of a certain *transformation* of "the wild beasts and birds of heaven" into
white bulls, with the result that they are brought into the fold of the
new world order as those who along with Israel belong to God (*1
En.* 90:37–8). This change, the means to which is not described, is
nothing less than remarkable. Despite all the vilification devoted in
the foregoing lengthy narrative to disparaging the Gentile holders
of sociopolitical power, the author actually holds out for a salvific
overhaul that includes at least some of them. Unlike the *Epistle*, the
oppressors will not simply be annihilated, not even at the conclusion
of history. Even they can be given a place in the future world among
the people of God.

The second point to notice in the *Animal Apocalypse* is the way
the resistance against sociopolitical persecution is allowed to manifest itself. The writer's community is but one of a number of groups
being oppressed by the Seleucids. Another group led by "a big horn,"
who may be identified as Judas Maccabeus (*1 En.* 90:9), takes up
arms. In the first phase of the resistance against the Seleucids, the
writer's community is not involved in the military struggle that the
text describes. However, once the "horn" is established and appeals
for others to join, the community of sheep "whose eyes have been
opened" joins him in battle. An apparently initial hesitance gives
way to armed defiance (90:10). Without regarding military activity
as the means by which to resolve the sociopolitical and religious
persecution of the Jews, the writer nonetheless is able to sanction
participation in the Maccabean Revolt by those who have otherwise
been placed at the margins of Jewish religious life and who may not
even have participated in the Jerusalem Temple cult. This Enochic
text thus allows for the possibility of violent resistance, in exceptional circumstances, on the part of the pious and oppressed faithful.

The third model in *1 Enoch* that relates to social justice overlaps
in part with that of both the *Epistle* and the *Animal Apocalypse*, but
does so in a somewhat surprising way. It is found in the earlier *Book
of Watchers* (*1 En.* 1–36), one of the oldest sections of *1 Enoch* that
exercised considerable influence on the later Enochic traditions as
they were added to the collection. Again, the context in which the
earliest part of the *Book of Watchers* was composed is that of sociocultural oppression and persecution, this time in the more immediate wake of the military conquest of the eastern Mediterranean

world by Alexander the Great during political and military instability brought about by his successors (called Diadochi) during the late fourth and early third centuries BCE. Alexander's successors had not only enslaved some of those they had conquered, but also attempted to impose Greek culture, ideals, and practices onto Jews and other ethnic groups in the region. The Enochic text, similar to its later counterparts in the *Epistle* and *Animal Apocalypse*, offers a voice of protest and resistance, couching its message in the form of a myth.[26]

In an adaptation of tradition known from Genesis 6:1–4, the text of the *Book of Watchers* (*1 En.* 6–11) attributes the beginnings of evil in the world to a group of rebellious angels who, impressed by the beauty of the women on earth, decide to commit a sin by mating with them and siring children as humans do (*1 En.* 6:1–8). As in the biblical story, the children born to this prohibited sexual union are called "Nephilim" (see Gen. 6:4; *1 En.* 7:2);[27] they are further described as giants who reach a height of 3,000 cubits (*1 En.* 7:1–2, the Ethiopic text). On account of their size, the giants have an insatiable appetite; they enslave humans to grow food for them and, when this is not enough, turn to eating humans themselves, in addition to creatures of the land, sea, and air (7:35).[28] The rebellious angels are blamed for introducing all sorts of unwanted cultural habits and practices: they teach people the making of weapons, the fashioning of jewelry, techniques of makeup on the face, beautification of the eyelids, the use of herbs as medicine, astrology, and "magical" practices (8:1–3). In economic terms, these teachings might have been considered a "good" thing for Jews, creating industries from which the more progressive sectors of society would have benefited. This storyline, then, was not simply myth but mirrored to some extent the incursions of Hellenistic culture in Judea[29] – incursions that the text held to be reprehensible forms of culture being imposed by oppressors who had no respect for the religious sensibilities and indigenous values of their Jewish subjects.

This combination of activities from the giants, on the one hand, and their angelic progenitors, on the other, produces such a crisis that it threatens the very survival of the environment and of humanity itself. How does the text expect this crisis to be resolved? How will God hold perpetrators of sociopolitical violence and enforced cultural dominance responsible? The answer comes in several stages. First, the text draws on the story of the Great Flood to insist that in the sacred past, God has already taken action against such powers.

Unlike the biblical story, the reason given in the *Book of Watchers* for the Flood in the time of Noah was less those sins committed by humanity than it was the need for divine activity to save humans from being oppressed and, indeed, annihilated. The Flood and related events function as punishment for the bearers of Hellenistic culture. The story is told with a view both to what happened in the past during the time of Noah and to what the writer anticipates will happen when the oppressors of faithful Jews are held to account. Thus, those who exercise cultural influence without regard for the sociocultural and religious norms of the weak (faithful Jews) have, in effect, already been defeated in the sacred past (i.e., through the Flood associated with Noah). Since they are already defeated in the past, the text claims that any such activity in the present is like-wise ultimately doomed to failure and will undergo divine judgment. Second, the text states that humans whose existence was threatened by oppression not only emerged intact as a part of the created order in the past (i.e., through Noah) but will also emerge intact in the future. Those who initially survive the divine judgment will be "a plant of truth and righteousness" (*1 En.* 10:16; cf. 10:3). That is, a group of Jews who, in the face of adversity, remain uncompromising in their faithfulness to God (e.g., by not participating in the repre-hensible misdeeds of the giants and angels) are rewarded by survival, while the wicked have been, and presumably will be, punished.

   This, however, is not the end. The final outcome in the future is envisioned as a time when, according to the text (at *1 En.* 10:21–2),

> (21) All the children of men will become righteous,
> and all the peoples will serve
> and bless me,
> and they will all worship me.
> (22) And the entire earth will be cleansed
> from all defilement and all uncleanness.
> And no wrath or torment
> will I ever again send upon them,
> for all the generations of eternity.[30]

The question from this text arises: How does one get from the survival of a small group of faithful Jews to a scenario in which God will be worshipped by "all the peoples" of the earth, not only Jews but Gen-tiles? If Gentiles, precisely whom does the phrase "all people" include?

Are these simply Gentiles who in the future are expected to recognize that Israel's God is the only legitimate God and creator of the world, or is there something particular going on in the literary context that tells us more? For example, how is this expectation shaped by the preceding story in the *Book of Watchers*, chapters 6–8, about the rebellious angels and their gigantic offspring? This is a fair question to ask, since at first there might not seem to be any relationship at all. How can a mythic story about angelic rebellion in heaven and social injustice out of control on earth have anything to do with a story whose outcome involves the globalization of faith and worship? On what grounds can someone expect this to happen?

To the extent that the angels and giants in the previous storyline are symbols for oppressive regimes of power, the claim that "all people" will worship God, not just as an act of submission but as a genuine participation in the new world order that God will set up, is anything but casual. The texts may reflect Jewish protest against a culturally and militarily repressive regime that treated the ancient covenant between God and Israel with contempt. However, does this mean that the angels and giants are *simply* this and nothing more? I think the power of the story lies in its essentially *mythic* character. Social injustice is mythologized. The story is one that is essentially concerned with *demonic* origins of evil – of evil wherever, whenever, and however it occurs. Demonic beings who have violated the created order not only are at work among and within Jews who are prepared to compromise their cultural and religious heritage; they also work *behind* those powerful regimes that have introduced reprehensible and objectionable practices and beliefs in the first place.

For all the Enochic text's rejection of oppressive forms of culture and of the tyrannical rule that characterizes these regimes, this story's *essentially mythic character* ends up being remarkably open: it not only acknowledges the existence of a repressed community of obedient Jews, but also shows awareness of a troubled humanity who, although they are largely aligned with the demonic world, are nevertheless created by God and, as such, have not *in themselves* set the world down the wrong path. They have been taught wicked deeds by the angels and it is *these deeds*, not the humanity that commits them, that will be wiped away (10:16, 20). By contrast, the angels did not merely do bad things; they are *by their very nature* breaching the boundaries between heaven and earth (implied here and explicated in 15:7–10), while the giants they produced are a hybrid combination that ought to have remained separate and likewise have no place in the created order.[31] The humans, like the giants, are a similar combination of the flesh and the soul. However, there is a difference. The combination of body and soul in humans is one that is sanctioned by God as part of the created order, while the giants, by their very nature, are not part of the way God set things up to be. Hence, human beings as a whole, Gentiles included, remain the target of God's salvific activity while, as far as creation is concerned, the giants – from whom demons eventually have their origin – are not authentically part of the world and are doomed. In underlining the participation of all peoples in the worship of God, the text envisions a recreated humanity that operates according to the exercise of sociopolitical and religious justice throughout the world.

In short, the *Book of Watchers* from *1 Enoch* offers a vision of hope for a just world that, in principle, involves everyone. While this may be a controversial idea, the basis for it is especially interesting: the distinction, in principle, between what people *do* and what people *are*. Although humans have engaged in activities that have taken on demonic proportions to the degree that others are made to suffer, and although they will be held responsible for what they have done, they still have an integrity before God, and it is *in and among them* that God's design for the world is to be realized. One can thus see how this text may have inspired the writing of the *Animal Apocalypse* to anticipate a transformation of "the wild beasts and the birds of heaven" into white bulls that participate in the economy of salvation at the end of time.

CONCLUSION

We have reviewed several ways a select group of Jewish authors from the Second Temple period tackled the sociopolitical and even religious injustices of their day. In particular, the authors of the Enochic literature raised voices of resistance "from below" – the level of society where people were suffering physically, socially, and culturally – as they attempted to retain a measure of religious identity in the face of overwhelming challenges. Their *theological accounts of misdeeds and suffering* were attempting to address a question being raised by many Jews: Where is God in all the suffering, especially if there is no apparent reason to hope that things will get better? The Enoch authors wanted their communities to know that their suffering was being heard and would be remembered. Furthermore, the insistence on human dignity – not merely the dignity of those who suffer but also and ultimately that of those who oppress (so in the *Book of Watchers* and, possibly, in the *Animal Apocalypse*) – is remarkable and runs counter to what one might otherwise have expected of such texts. It is possible to see "the enemy" with new eyes as, in some sense, redeemable, though not without their responsibility being taken into account.

Even though they do not form part of most canons of scripture, the texts that we have reviewed in this chapter are being discussed by increasing numbers of Jews and Christians alike, and not merely in the classroom of academic institutions. These texts belong to a heritage shared by Jewish and Christian co-religionists,[32] and they offer grounds for reflection on what such shared traditions may contribute constructively, first, to what it means to suffer, and second, to what it means to advocate on behalf of those who do.

The foregoing discussion, drawing as it does on Jewish literature not included in the Bible of any western tradition, represents a kind of treatment that would hardly have been possible within the church before the Second World War in the twentieth century. Since then we have seen unanticipated discoveries, not least the Dead Sea Scrolls and huge numbers of manuscripts from Africa and the Middle East, that leave us with less doubt than ever before how much Jewish and Christian traditions are wedded and, in not a small number of cases, cannot be distinguished from one another. The church's statements, made possible through the Second Vatican Council, have opened up avenues of mutual understanding between Jews and Christians, whose faith perspectives, in all their diversity, can be informed through the shared study of sources that not only reflected and inspired religious ideas and practices in antiquity but provide grounds for new reflection today. Voices of the poor and the cry for justice form a deep part of tradition within the Hebrew Bible, early Christianity, and ancient and contemporary Judaism. This tradition provides a context within and in relation to which the church finds ways to engage with emerging challenges of the present. As Pope Francis draws the church's attention to the plight of the poor,[33] it is hoped that perspectives found in the rich heritage of Christianity and Judaism will continue to provide constructive insights in the search for social justice, both within the church and in the world at large.

NOTES

1 I am thinking in particular about the *Guidelines and Suggestions for Implementing the Conciliar Declaration* "Nostra Aetate" (1 December 1974), which *inter alia* even calls for "joint social action" (*Guidelines*, IV) among Jews and Christians, and the *Notes on the Correct Way to Present the Jews and Judaism in Preaching and Catechesis in the Roman Catholic Church* (24 June 1985) by the Commission of the Holy See for Religious Relations with the Jews. See also the Pontifical Biblical Commission's "The Jewish People and Their Sacred Scriptures in the Christian Bible" and, for example, the assessment by David Rosen in his "Jewish and Israeli Perspectives 40 Years after Vatican II."

2 Commission of the Holy See for Religious Relations with the Jews, *Notes*, III.

3 As is apparent, for example, through the works of Hengel, *Judaism and Hellenism*; Schürer, *History of the Jewish People*; and Nickelsburg, *Jewish Literature between the Bible and the Mishnah*.

4 For a still-useful account of both these perspectives, see Hanson, *Dawn of Apocalyptic*, although it is misleading to posit a development in which an eschatological solution to the world's problems grew out of a disillusionment through failed attempts at reform; cf. e.g. the essays in Collins, *Apocalypse*.

5 See Portier-Young, *Apocalypse against Empire*.

6 See Stuckenbruck, *Myth of the Rebellious Angels*, 240–56, esp.·243–55.

7 See Stuckenbruck, "Book of Enoch." Officially, the Ethiopian Tewahedo Orthodox Church does not refer to its sacred tradition as "canon" or "Bible," but rather thinks in terms of which books can be "counted" among a fluid tradition of eighty-one books.

8 Namely, *Book of Watchers* (chs 1–36); *Book of Parables* (37–71); *Astronomical Book* (72–82); *Book of Dreams* (83–90, including the *Animal Apocalypse*); and *Epistle of Enoch* (91–105).

9 This detail regarding Enoch is debated. For example, in contrast to most of the ancient traditions, the early Aramaic translation of Gen. 5:24 known as Targum Onqelos insists that Enoch actually died.

10 See the claim made by the great Irish scholar R.H. Charles just over 100 years ago in *The Book of Enoch or 1 Enoch*, xcv (see further ix–xii): "The influence of 1 Enoch on the New Testament has been greater than that of all the other apocryphal and pseudepigraphal books taken together."

11 The date of the *Epistle* is debated. For extensive treatments of the work, see Nickelsburg, *1 Enoch 1*, 409–535; and Stuckenbruck, *1 Enoch 91–108*, 185–605 (with a discussion of the date on pp. 211–15.)

12 The *Epistle* contains no less than eight sets of woe oracles against the
"rich" and the "wicked" (*1 En.* 94:6–95:2, 95:4–7, 96:4–8, 97:7–10, 98:9–
99:2, 99:11–16, 100:7–9, 103:5–8).

13 On the writer's self-presentation under the name of Enoch, see
Stuckenbruck, "Epistle of Enoch."

14 See *1 En.* 104:1–6 and, in the closely related composition, *Apocalypse of
Weeks*, at *1 En.* 91:13 (the promise of possessions to the righteous). See
Stuckenbruck, *1 Enoch 91–108*, 131–9.

15 This is especially true among contemporary and later apocalyptic texts
such as Daniel 12, the Enochic *Book of Parables* (*1 En.* 37–71), *4 Ezra*,
and *2 Baruch*.

16 See, for example, Matt. 13:24–30, 36–43, and 24:1–25:46.

17 See, for example, 1 Thess. 4:13–5:11; 1 Cor. 15:20–58; Rom. 2:1–16.

18 See especially Rev. 6:1–11:19, 14:6–20, 15:5–18:24, 19:11–22:5.

19 *1 En.* 96:4, 96:7, 99:3; cf. 97:2, 104:1.

20 See, for example, Deut. 28; Isa. 10:3; Jer. 5:22, 5:25, 17:11, 22:5; Amos
5:11, 6:6.

21 Deut. 28:7, 13, 26, 29, 33, 44, 48, 62, 65–6.

22 On the present discussion, see Tiller, *Commentary on the Animal
Apocalypse*; Stuckenbruck, "Reading the Present"; and Herms,
Apocalypse for the Church, 120–35.

23 *1 En.* 89:32, 41, 54, 73, 90:7.

24 *1 En.* 89:28, 41, 44, 90:6, 90:9, 90:35.

25 *1 En.* 90:2, 4–5, 11, 13, and 16; these characters are later referred to as
"the wild beasts and the birds of heaven" (90:18–19, 30, 37).

26 On the *Book of Watchers* as resistance literature, see Portier-Young,
Apocalypse against Empire, 3–45.

27 So the text according to the Greek version attested in Syncellus 1 (preferred by Nickelsburg and VanderKam, *1 Enoch 1*, 24): "And they [the
women] conceived from them [the disobedient angels] and bore to them
great giants. And the giants begot Nephilim, and to the Nephilim were
born Elioud. And they were growing in accordance with their greatness."

28 For discussions of the giants and their function in the *Book of Watchers*
and the closely associated tradition in the *Book of Giants*, see
Stuckenbruck, *Book of Giants from Qumran*; "Origins of Evil"; and Goff,
"Monstrous Appetites."

29 On the background to the mythical language in the storyline, see the still
useful publications by Hanson, "Rebellion in Heaven"; Nickelsburg,
"Apocalyptic and Myth in 1 Enoch 6–11"; Collins, "Methodological

Issues"; Dimant, "1 Enoch 6–11"; Newsom, "Development of 1 Enoch 6–19"; and Nickelsburg, *1 Enoch 1*, 171–2.

30 The translation of the Ethiopic text (the only complete version preserved for *1 Enoch*) is my own.

31 See Stuckenbruck, "Giant Mythology and Demonology."

32 In addition to Stuckenbruck, "Book of Enoch," see Reed, *Fallen Angels*.

33 See Pope Francis, *Church of Mercy*, especially 23–42 ("A Poor Church for. the Poor") and 99–110 ("The Choice of the Last").

6

A Voice from the South: Social Justice in the Latin American Church after Vatican II

Eduardo Soto Parra

Suppose that a devout Catholic woman working within the church in a Latin American city in 1960 fell into a deep sleep and woke up thirty years later, in 1990. She probably wouldn't recognize the Catholic Church as the same church in which she grew up. Why? Not only because the liturgy was now being celebrated in the vernacular, but also because social justice, liberation, oppression, base communities, and the option for the poor were the topics being highlighted by church representatives. Moreover, if she looked for the nuns who ran the school where her daughters had been educated, she would probably find that most of the nuns had moved to the slums, far away from the convents that used to stand beside the well-established educational institutions.

This exercise of imagination allows us to skip a treatment of the statistics and explanations we could use to prove that the Catholic Church in Latin America, especially during the 1970s and 1980s, shifted in how it addressed social and moral issues and where many religious women and men undertook their apostolic work. An example of this shift can be found in the work of Fe y Alegría (Faith and Joy) Schools, a "Movement for Integral Popular Education and Social Development" whose activities are directed toward the most impoverished and excluded sectors of the population. This network of schools was founded in Venezuela by the Chilean Jesuit José María Vélaz and the layman Abraham Reyes. Vélaz began with one school in the slums of Caracas in 1960. By 1964 Fe y Alegría boasted 10,000 students, and that number grew continuously because many women's congregations found in this movement a way to provide education and formation to impoverished communities. Since then, Fe y Alegría has opened schools in most Latin American countries and now serves more than 1.4 million students.[1]

Change occurred not only in the education process and the location of schools, but also in the way people were evangelized. The focus shifted from evangelization as something that was received to an activity that could lead to martyrdom. Students, catechists, and those in the slums and marginalized areas who worked in the church often talked about their Latin American "martyrdom."[2] In fact, many members of religious communities, both men and women, were targeted and killed in the past fifty years, including the Jesuits in the Central American University in El Salvador, and Monsignor Óscar Romero,[3] Monsignor Gerardi, and the anthropologist Myrna Mack in Guatemala. In this last case, the responsibility of the Guatemalan government was established by an international human rights court.[4]

As a result of the "martyrdom" of so many priests, nuns, and catechists, a particular notion of social justice developed in Latin American Christian communities. Social justice came to be understood as action to lessen existing economic inequalities in society and to bring opportunities such as education, access to information, human rights, and political participation in society to everyone. As we shall see, this understanding of social justice became central to the mission of the worldwide church thanks to how the council fathers addressed it in the document *Gaudium et Spes*.

This move toward explicitly addressing social justice issues is reflected also in the official documents of the South American church. The most important documents are the conclusions of the various Conferences of Latin American Bishops (CELAM) held after Vatican II,[5] each named after the city in which the bishops held their meeting: Medellín (1968), Puebla (1979), Santo Domingo (1992), and Aparecida (2007). In all these documents, although with different levels of importance, social justice is addressed in a new way, launched at Vatican II and further developed in the Latin American context.

So how does the unique experience of the church in Latin America shape its reception of Vatican II's teaching on social justice? To answer this question, it is necessary to study the references to Vatican II in the main documents of the Latin American Catholic Church, but also to see how the issue of social justice had already been present in that church even before Vatican II. In fact, it is precisely this history that shapes the interpretation of Vatican II in this region. At the same time, Vatican II opened possibilities for a new articulation of the commitment to social justice in Latin America. This commitment, while voiced in different ways, continues to play an important role in shaping the identity of Catholics in Latin American countries today.

SOCIAL JUSTICE IN LATIN AMERICA BEFORE VATICAN II

Long before Vatican II, there were Catholics who raised their voices against social injustices in Latin America. Their history is entangled with the history of the Catholic Church in the region. Since the beginning of colonization, *conquistadores* and missionaries shared the novelty and beauty of the so-called New World.[6] However, their interests in coming to the continent and their perceptions of their roles quickly began to diverge.

Even during the first years of the conquest, there is evidence that church representatives protested and acted against the violent ways in which Spanish expeditions had sought to subdue the Indigenous population.[7] Even though the cultural mainstream in this period embraced the hierarchical structure of colonial society in which injustices were often overlooked, accounts of the conquest and colonization were nevertheless studded with powerful stories about rebel missionaries who fought for the dignity of the Indigenous population and slaves in fidelity to the gospel and the church. In light of the less hierarchical understanding of church brought by Vatican II, such historical movements can now rightly be regarded as the church's struggle for social justice.

For example, from the late fifteenth century, the Dominican Order in La Española Island (now known as Haiti and the Dominican Republic) had a community committed to social justice in the sense in which it is understood by the church today.[8] The sermons of the Dominicans captured this perspective by highlighting the disparities between individuals and within communities in the early stages of colonization. While their words caused discomfort to the masters and commanders in the settlements, they inspired others. One such sermon, given in 1511 by Antonio de Montesinos (1475–1545), struck a chord with the young Bartolomé de Las Casas (1484–1566), a brilliant *encomendero* priest whose prospects were rich because of his many well-treated slaves in Cuba and Santo Domingo. But once he came to see owning slaves as a betrayal of the gospel, he quit his job, joined the Dominicans, and started to study and write about the unjust oppression suffered by many in the lands of the New World.[9]

Las Casas's work, moreover, did not happen in isolation. Moved by their consciences, many Catholics followed his ideas and had a sense that the things in the New World could not be approached exactly in the same way as in the old world. They realized that solutions brought with the colonizers from Europe only worked through the oppression and subjugation of people who could not raise their voices. Another remarkable example of the concern for social justice during colonization is found in the letters of the Capuchin friars Francisco José de Jaca (1645–1690) and Epifanio de Moirans (1644–1689). These religious men of the seventeenth century started writing about the unjust situation of the slaves in the New World and illustrating how dangerous it was to condemn the many church members who had slaves.[10]

From these examples we can see that the Latin American church, even though it enjoyed the peace provided by an unjust colonial order for the spreading of the gospel, tolerated alternative voices within and highlighted the responsibility of church members to be faithful in a coherent way to the message of Jesus Christ during the processes of social transformation of those centuries.[11] Thanks to this particular way of thinking, which was clear to those who struggled for independence from Spain, the church would survive under post-independence regimes. These independence movements, which started after the French Revolution, drew their inspiration from ideas of the Enlightenment and spoke openly against the clergy in the beginning. But in Latin America, this antagonism did not last long.[12]

From the beginning of the independence movement, many priests – including Miguel Hidalgo (1753–1811) and José María Morelos (1765–1815) in Mexico – joined these struggles for independence, motivated by what we would call today a concern for social justice.[13] Bishops, too, supported this movement, as exemplified in the writings and actions of the archbishop of Caracas, Ramón Ignacio Méndez (1761–1834). He explained in his writings to the faithful the compatibility of being Christian and, at the same time, rejecting the sovereignty of European kings in the lands of the New World.[14] Such moral arguments became pervasive in the first states of Latin America when discussing the patronage rights of the king and remained part of the discourse in later interactions between the modern states and the church.[15]

In these new modern states of Latin America, the church stood against foreign modernist and positivist ideas that spread once the struggle for national independence was over.[16] Poverty and unstable government were also common aspects of the post-independence period in Latin American states. Papal documents invited Christian intellectuals in Latin American countries to address the social injustices caused by incipient industrialization in the region. Only at the end of the nineteenth century, however, did the Catholic Church begin to articulate its official teachings about social justice, criticizing both capitalism and socialism while providing a moral framework for political and social action.[17]

As a result, social ethics became a highly promoted discipline in Catholic circles in the twentieth century. This new discipline counteracted a passive image of the church in the midst of the violent struggles of political actors for power and social control while positivism, fascism, anarchism, and communism began to take hold.[18] While the development of social ethics was happening throughout the Catholic world, in Latin America it presented some specific nuances due to the region's particular history and social reality. In fact, in this region intellectual elites still identified themselves as "Catholics" instead of abandoning faith, as was happening in Europe. However, they had to engage with European ideas about ethics and politics in the midst of pervasive injustices from different sources: some coming from inherited colonization, and others from recent populism and aggressive industrialization. We see this reflected particularly well in the work of the Chilean Jesuit lawyer and priest Alberto Hurtado (1901–1952), now a recognized saint.

Hurtado addressed the oppression suffered by many in his native Chile and called for an active response from all Catholics. The theoretical foundations for his controversial involvement in social action were based on the church's authorized documents on social justice coming from Europe. However, Hurtado's writings were also influenced by his own particular experience in social work while a student and later by his accompaniment of the Young Catholic Worker Union in Chile. In *Moral Social – Acción Social*, a collection of writings compiled after his death on 18 August 1952, Hurtado wrote:

> In the light of social justice, a legal order enabling countries to achieve a high standard of living cannot be consolidated at the expense of others less fortunate who have a low standard of

living: they will need cultural and technical education so that they can obtain at least the minimum of goods necessary to the dignity of the human person.

The concrete way to realize these principles must be illuminated by the virtue of prudence, which will employ the means which circumstances require, and which for its full implementation will involve the formation of a universal social mentality. The Christian conscience will be the leaven that will lift the population. What social justice won't do will be done by Christian charity, which will mean seeing in fellow human beings the giver of all good.[19]

Hurtado then elaborates the relationship between justice and society:

Rights are reciprocal: if others must respect my right, I have to respect theirs. Justice is, therefore, this stable provision of respect for the rights of others in all its manifestations: material and spiritual property, health, honor, wealth, freedom, partnership, etc. The right of others creates a corresponding obligation on us. Those who have been injured in their rights may claim them, demand them – to the degree that is possible, given human imperfection – with compensation for the damage caused.

Justice is an essential virtue, but unpopular. It does not shine out because its requirements are very modest at first sight, and therefore [the search for justice] does not generate enthusiasm, nor does its implementation lead to glory. One may boast of one's charity, but not of not killing someone: one must practice justice and that's all. However, it is a very difficult virtue in practice and requires a great deal of righteousness. There are many who are willing to do charity, but not resign themselves to comply with the law; they are willing to give alms, but not to pay fair wages. Although it may seem strange, it is easier to be charitable (clearly only in appearance) than fair. This is a false charity, because true charity begins where there is justice. Charity without justice will not save us from the social abyss; rather, it will lead to a deep resentment. Injustice causes vastly more evils that can be repaired by charity.[20]

In 1944, Hurtado founded El Hogar de Cristo (Christ's Home), which after his death became the most important charitable organization in Chile for addressing homelessness. Ahead of his time,

Hurtado called for change in how wealth is distributed and justice is implemented in society. Only when this change is complete will works of charity have their proper place in the Christian community.

Hurtado, who died ten years before the first session of Vatican II, spent his life responding in his own way to the injustices that were produced by industrialization and later worsened by US interventions in the region.[21] The virtue of prudence that Hurtado highlighted likely influenced the church's approach in addressing Marxist social analysis and colonialist theory, both of which were proposing violent action to establish a new social order, as actually happened with the Cuban Revolution. As we shall see, that revolution and other revolts by students in many cities in the region during the twentieth century were addressed by the Latin American bishops in their conferences, albeit through an evolving process that took time.

The first meeting of the Conference of Latin American Bishops (CELAM) took place in Rio de Janeiro in 1955, seven years before Vatican II. The conclusions of that conference show a church worried about insufficient clergy, fearing communism, and seeing the struggle for social justice as a cover for the implementation of scientific materialism.[22] The bishops' stance at Rio proved to be a great disappointment, even to the point of despair, to many committed laypeople in Latin America. In their desire to resist injustices, they felt trapped between two extremes: oppressive dictatorships on the one hand and, on the other, non-church-authorized liberation approaches, such as colonialist theory and Marxism.[23]

Dictatorships plagued most Latin American countries in the twentieth century. The response of the church varied depending on the context and the sense of belonging of some church leaders to political factions. Sometimes for the sake of peace and order, church leaders fell into the same paternalistic approaches adopted by many of the dictators,[24] but in most cases they opposed those authoritarian rulers.[25] For this reason, the Rio conference disappointed many who had expected the bishops to explicitly address the political and social injustices of the region from a Christian perspective. The most important document from the conference failed to do so; instead it was very much church-centred, concerned with the role of priests in society and worried about the decreasing numbers of ordained men and seminarians. It made no reference to dictatorship, militarism, or human rights violations. Even when social justice was mentioned as

a general orientation of the church, there was no mention of what
"social justice" was or how it could be achieved.

SOCIAL JUSTICE AND THE RECEPTION OF VATICAN II IN LATIN AMERICA

Vatican II represented an *aggiornamiento* of the church. In *Gaudium et
Spes* (*Pastoral Constitution on the Church in the Modern World*), the
council recognized that "ours is a new age of history with profound and
rapid changes spreading gradually to all corners of the earth. They are
products of people's intelligence and creative activity, but they [these
changes] recoil upon them, upon their judgments and desires, both individual and collective, and upon their ways of thinking and acting in
regard to people and things" (GS 4). This wake-up call evoked a theoretical and practical awareness of the need to find a "fresher" way for
the church to understand itself and its role in the world. Nevertheless,
the novelty has to be found by returning to the sources of the gospel,
instead of repeating the past in a manner devoid of creativity and orig-
inality. In fidelity to Christ and the people of today, the church has
to be in the present, without transmuting or abandoning its perennial
elements. What is required is adaptation to new historical situations.

As we have seen in relation to Latin America, by the time of the
council, the church there required a new approach to address social
issues. Demands for social justice became a prophetic attitude
toward huge economic and social injustices. The council fathers
noted the disparities in this new stage of history: "In no other age
has humanity enjoyed such an abundance of wealth, resources and
economic well-being, and yet a huge proportion of the people of
the world is plagued by hunger and extreme need, while countless
numbers are totally illiterate. At no time have people had such a
keen sense of freedom, only to be faced by new forms of social and
psychological slavery." (GS 4) These inequalities are not caused by
nature or by an "act of God," but by people in society. Therefore,
the call to social justice is a response to inequalities and divisions
caused by people's actions, social movements, or ideas. *Gaudium et
Spes* defines social justice as being at the core of the church's mission in the world and invites local church hierarchies to develop
and promote this mission, on their own terms. The only proviso
was that every action toward social justice be rooted in respect for
the dignity of every human being.

Gaudium et Spes articulates human dignity – a notion taken from a long tradition within the church – as a fundamental human right. Respect for the differences among diverse groups of people throughout the world becomes the way to exercise human dignity:

> Undoubtedly not all people are alike as regards to physical capacity and intellectual and moral powers. But any kind of social or cultural discrimination in basic personal rights on the grounds of sex, race, color, social conditions, language or religion, must be curbed and eradicated as incompatible with God's design ...
>
> Furthermore, while there are just differences between people, their equal dignity as persons demands that we strive for fairer and more humane conditions. Excessive economic and social disparity between individuals and peoples of the one human race is a source of scandal and militates against social justice, equity, human dignity, as well as social and international peace. (GS 29)

Therefore, the achievement of social justice demands a redistribution of material wealth, as well as intellectual and moral resources, in the world. Social justice, then, is based on a conviction that humanity can establish a political, social, and economic order that will increasingly serve to help individuals and groups affirm and develop their inherent dignity (GS 4). The dedication of the people of God to this activity is a moral obligation. These activities, although they can be seen as an "earthly affair," find no contradiction with what religious life implies.

In fact, the council fathers make clear the false opposition between professional and social activities on the one hand, and religious life on the other. This false opposition "is one of the gravest errors of our time," not only because it is a denial of the moral obligation of believers to build a better and more just world for everyone, but also because "Christians who shirk their temporal duties, shirk their duties toward [their] neighbour, neglect God himself, and endanger their eternal salvation" (GS 43). With this statement, *Gaudium et Spes* places social justice at the core of the church's mission in the world.

After underlining the church's need to address social inequalities, the council fathers warn of some urgent problems in the second part of the *Pastoral Constitution*. The church will need to protect marriage and family, promote widespread education that fully respects every culture, and engage in dialogue with society and political institutions. These "universal matters" will become avenues for the pastoral work of the church.[26] In addition, in a chapter dedicated to economic and social differences, the council insists that we "meet the requirements of justice and equity" in the removal "as soon as possible [of] the immense economic inequalities which exist in the world, which increase daily and which go hand in hand with individual and social discrimination" (GS 66).

The council fathers also provide a framework to implement these teachings globally. In *Christus Dominus*, the council recognizes the pastoral role of bishops in applying conciliar teachings to the realities of their local churches. Proclaimed by Pope Paul VI on 28 October 1965, *Christus Dominus* signalled an opportunity for entire regions of the world to see themselves as churches in communion with Rome, and at the same time to address local issues collectively through the bishops' conferences. These conferences sought to ensure that all the changes proposed at Vatican II were assimilated and adapted to the different cultures and localities in the various dioceses around the world. This process of "reception" would prove to be particularly important in the vast Catholic region of Latin America.[27]

The 1968 Conference of Latin American Bishops in Medellín was the first to take place after Vatican II. In their concluding document, the Latin American bishops propose the paradigm by which all the documents must be read and interpreted. They do so by quoting Paul VI's words in his closing speech of the council that "to know Christ it is necessary to know humankind."[28] In other words, the Latin American church must know the particularities of Latin American humanity in order to truly worship and serve Christ there. Furthermore, the document takes up *Gaudium et Spes*, which states that "it is only in the mystery of the Word made flesh that the mystery of humanity truly becomes clear" (GS 22). To know the people of our time, we must know the "joys and hopes, the grief and anguish ... especially [of] those who are poor or afflicted" (GS 1). Thus, an attitude of inquiry is required first about the situation of the Latin American people if the Latin American church is to respond to the direction of Vatican II with creativity and fidelity.

Vatican II's adoption of the language of rights to uphold the dignity of every human being[29] encouraged the Latin American bishops to use contemporary terminology and frameworks to address local situations in a novel way. Following the insights of *Gaudium et Spes*, the bishops turned their attention to social injustice, institutionalized violence, and the church's commitment to addressing these issues. In fact, social justice has been a constant theme in CELAM's recommendations since 1965, even though – as we shall see – the treatment of social justice differs in each document.

SOCIAL JUSTICE AND THE CELAM DOCUMENTS AFTER VATICAN II

Medellín

Medellín can be described as the watershed of the post-Vatican II church in Latin America. It proved "surprisingly good" for many who had been calling for a "transformation in society based upon Gospel principles"[30] and in line with the methodology of Vatican II. The bishops in Medellín understood that Vatican II had overcome the world/church dichotomy and concluded that a greater presence of faith values was needed in contemporary society, which in turn would require the adoption of new forms of spirituality.[31]

The second great influence on the bishops of Latin America was Paul VI's encyclical *Populorum Progressio,* which quotes *Gaudium et Spes,* especially those parts related to the concepts of peace, justice, and respect for every human being.[32] The bishops at Medellín applied an inductive method of analysis: see – judge – act.[33] In their judgments, they affirmed that the oppression suffered by many in Latin America sows the seed for the absence of peace. Given that, the people of God should be committed, following the example of Christ who calls them to work for peace, to oppose any form of oppression. As a result, in their final document, the bishops at Medellín deliberately and explicitly instituted a "preferential option for the poor."[34]

One of the most important shifts in this document in regard to social justice is that it not only denounces the social injustices of the time, but also sets out a program to overcome them. In the words of the Latin American bishops, the church is called to stand in solidarity with grassroots organizations working for justice. In their opinion, only when people develop a certain level of organizational skill can they really participate in bringing about a different distribution of wealth and opportunity. This change – that is, encouraging church involvement in workers' and peasants' associations[35] – had already been anticipated by many priests in the Latin American region, among them Hurtado.

In order to produce this change, the bishops distinguished the church's work with elites (*pastoral de élites*) from its work with the people (*pastoral popular*). Medellín identifies elite groups within Latin American society as "the leading, more advanced and dominant groups in terms of culture, of profession, of the economy and power ... Within these groups [are] committed minorities who have a current or potential influence on different levels of cultural, professional, economic, social, and political decision."[36] This distinction between the elites and the people would orient the work of the whole church, which in 1968 was omnipresent in Latin American society but no longer in the same way. To work toward the establishment of a political, social, and economic order in the terms desired by Vatican II required that the church accompany these two groups in different ways. The accent among the elites is on promoting awareness of cultural and ideological discrimination, while in the popular realm it is on establishing grassroots organizations and associations. The church's work with both groups, the bishops believed, would ultimately bring change to Latin American society.

This spark of commitment from the South American bishops lit a fire throughout the continent. Medellín established the struggle for liberation as a Christian commitment, recognized the fierce division among those who belong to the same church, and thereby created a different kind of pastoral approach for each group. This differentiation had many consequences, including the development of the theology of liberation within the Catholic Church. It also provoked a change in the locus of evangelization in the region.[37] As a result of this encouragement, many Christian intellectuals and religious institutions shifted their focus from the "elites" to "popular" pastoral work and expanded their mission to the poor of Latin America.

Puebla

Eleven years later, in 1979, the bishops met again, in Puebla de Los Ángeles, Mexico. Using the same inductive method of analysis, they addressed the impact of Medellín's conclusions both within the church and in Latin American society. At Puebla, the bishops took particular ownership of the struggle for human dignity and social justice in the Latin American church.[38] In spite of the distortions and hostility of some who vitiated the spirit of Puebla, the bishops recognized and addressed the "preferential option for the poor" prophetically adopted in Medellín.[39] These doctrinal reflections continued to be based on Vatican II documents and also on Paul VI's apostolic exhortation *Evangelii Nuntiandi*, launched ten years after the close of Vatican II, and between the conferences of Medellín and Puebla. *Evangelii Nuntiandi* set forth a "new evangelization of the Catholic Church" based on the awakening brought by Vatican II. Clearly, the teachings of Vatican II influenced the bishops as they considered the role of the poor in their struggle for justice.[40]

However, the bishops at Puebla moved away from the distinction between elites and the people in the pastoral work of the church.[41] Further, in the context of its focus on youth, the conference in Puebla warned that some minorities using Marxist approaches to societal inequalities could manipulate committed youth in the church.[42] The bishops repeated the same argument of the Rio conference, complaining that Marxist ideologies had spread promises and expectations of greater social justice among workers and students; but in pursuing these utopian expectations, many Christian and human values had been sacrificed, as evidenced by the escalating spiral of violence.[43] At the same time, they also critiqued consumer society and economic liberalism for promoting an individualistic view of the human being.[44]

Instead of ideologies, the situation required personal conversion and profound structural changes if society was to respond to the legitimate aspirations of the people for authentic social justice. These necessary changes had either failed to materialize or had been too slow to affect the daily lives of Latin American people.[45] In contrast to Medellín, Puebla no longer encouraged church members to accompany grassroots organizations as the way to reduce inequalities in society. This caution would be justified during the following decades, when increasing numbers of Catholic activists were killed by state forces or migrated to other churches or religious groups. This social and political reality would be reflected in the documents of future CELAM conferences.

Santo Domingo and Aparecida

Social justice issues received less prominence in the last two bishops' conferences. The documents issued at Santo Domingo (1992) and Aparecida (2007) preferred to talk about human promotion rather than social justice, and they began to show renewed concern about the need for a "new period of evangelization." This task of "new evangelization," highly promoted by Pope John Paul II, has since become the main task of the Latin American church and entails consciously addressing cultural differences. In fact, the bishops have come to see a re-Christianization of society as the way to overcome all the problems in Latin American society. For this reason, a new proclamation of the gospel under current realities is needed.

At Santo Domingo, Vatican II was mentioned to highlight its pastoral and ecumenical intention, its ecclesiological vision, and its promotion of liturgical and religious life renewal. But the call for social justice in Vatican II was downplayed. Indeed, social justice is mentioned only as a dimension of the prophetic mission of the church[46] and as one of the principles that should guide legislation as the influence of the private sector increases in society.[47] So, in contrast to both Medellín and Puebla, the Santo Domingo document lacks a program to overcome social injustices.

Santo Domingo even lacks any mention of the struggle for social justice as part of the common heritage in the religiosity of Latin American people. Instead of analyzing that reality and using an inductive approach as Medellín and Puebla did, Santo Domingo applies a deductive approach to social issues. The conference document frequently quotes the ideas developed by John Paul II in the years of his pontificate without a rigorous analysis of the diverse circumstances and contradictions present in Latin American society.

Remarkably, the bishops' conference in Aparecida, held during the pontificate of Benedict XVI, gave more importance than Santo Domingo to social justice and the role of Vatican II in developing the Latin American church's particular response to injustice and poverty. The Aparecida document innovatively addresses social justice as a commitment arising from two sources: popular mysticism or popular religiosity,[48] and the example of Jesus Christ in the gospels.[49] By referencing the work of Bartolomé de Las Casas and Alberto Hurtado, the bishops in Aparecida accepted as background how the struggle for social justice and human dignity in Latin America has always been present in the Latin American church.[50]

The bishops addressed the complex phenomenon of globalization as a source of new forms of poverty in the Latin American region.[51] They called for a transformation of society in line with the requirements of the kingdom of God and Christian charity. In this case, the document follows the doctrine of Benedict XVI in his encyclical *Deus Caritas Est*, in which charity cannot indulge injustices because "true charity begins where there is justice," as we saw stated by Hurtado. For example, racially discriminatory policies should be banned and social justice promoted because these are conditions necessary for the stability of democratic states.[52] However, Aparecida addresses the reality of the church and its challenges from the perspective of "discipleship," with an overall concern for fidelity in following Christ in the midst of a global culture and society that praises and rewards values and "goods" different from those promoted by the church. Unlike Medellín, no change in pastoral structures is proposed. Rather, in continuity with Santo Domingo and the social doctrine of the church, Aparecida repeats the call for "solidarity and human promotion" through social pastoral units that should be present in all ecclesial structures.[53]

CONCLUSION

The CELAM conferences showed the Latin American church's diverse approaches to addressing social issues. Medellín stated the "preferential option for the poor" and designed a pastoral plan to overcome social inequalities in Latin America. Puebla followed Medellín in its inspiration and insights, but not in proposing a plan. Indeed, social injustices were highlighted at Medellín and Puebla, almost disappeared from the discussions at Santo Domingo, but came back into focus at Aparecida. However, we must recall that social justice has been present as a concern of the Latin American church both before and after Vatican II. The most recent Bishops' Conference at Aparecida recognized this yearning for social justice and the need for a preferential option for the poor, even if it addressed the topic through the lens of popular religiosity and deep religious desires. This latest conference stands in continuity with the long journey of development in social teaching in the past.

Vatican II defined social justice as being at the core of the church's mission in the world and empowered local hierarchies to develop and promote this mission. This development ended the dichotomy between the church and the world, a dichotomy exemplified in documents of the Rio conference of 1955. The council's orientation illumined the interpretation of events and situations in the region and resulted in a remodelling of the Latin American church. After fifty years, the Catholic Church in Latin America is still united, and even emboldened by Pope Francis, whose Magisterium seems highly committed to addressing social justice issues. That the Latin American bishops could deeply engage with questions of social justice in their documents is in part due to the window of creativity that Vatican II opened for the whole church. This window has always been somewhat open in Latin America; as we have seen in this chapter, the Latin American church, throughout its history, has always had a voice against social injustices.

Returning to the imaginary woman with whom we began, we saw her surprised by the turn of events during her thirty-year sleep. As her eyes get used to the new light, she will gradually begin to recognize continuity with the tradition of popular religiosity that she had known before. Social justice – in the sense of working for a less unequal world and respecting the dignity of every human being – is deeply at the core of the popular religiosity of the region,[54] in a way that complements and even inspires the documents coming from the hierarchy of the church.[55]

Examples of Latin American "saints" such as Bartolomé de las Casas, Alberto Hurtado, and more recently Óscar Romero and Hélder Câmara resonate deeply in the hearts of many conscientious and intellectual Catholics in Latin America, including the anonymous faithful such as our imaginary woman. The option for the poor in this region comes about as a result of the process encouraged by Vatican II to find the region's own ecclesial identity, but this option is not primarily for counteracting current doctrines such as Marxism or capitalism. As I have argued, the option for the poor is rather an attitude of the church nurtured since the beginning of evangelization, as the documents of Aparecida pointed out when they called for a renewal of such evangelization in 2007. However, living out these teachings has often been problematic for the hierarchy, who were often tempted to side with ruling elites during both the establishment of the colonial state and the later transition to a democratic state. In Latin America, a church committed to the poor is a consistent thread running through the centuries to the present day, always in process and therefore always tentative, precarious, and ever-learning, and yet steadfast.

Rooted both in Latin American popular religiosity and in *Gaudium et Spes*, the struggle continues to find the best way for Catholics in Latin America to creatively and faithfully participate in the necessary changes to build a society in which all may enjoy social justice. This struggle for justice and the "preferential option for the poor" strongly motivates Pope Francis, himself a son of Latin America and a father of the faith, who has lived through and been nurtured by many of the developments I have described. Indeed, he has not just lived through them, but has shown himself as a strong actor in the growth of Catholic social teaching in Latin América. As pope, he now emphasizes that social justice and the preferential option for the poor should be a concern not only for Latin Americans, but for the universal church.

NOTES

1 Fe y Alegría, "Cuantos Somos."
2 Cleary, *How Latin America Saved*, 159.
3 Schwaller, *History of the Catholic Church*, 254.
4 Inter-American Human Rights Court, *Sentencia del Caso Myrna Mack Chang vs. Guatemala*.
5 Cleary, *How Latin America Saved*, 99.
6 Schwaller, *History of the Catholic Church*, 12.
7 Ibid., 43.
8 See *Catechism of the Catholic Church*, 1938, referring to GS 29: "Their equal dignity as persons demands that we strive for fairer and more humane conditions. Excessive economic and social disparity between individuals and peoples of the one human race is a source of scandal and militates against social justice."
9 Losada, *Fray Bartolomé de Las Casas*, 99.
10 Lopez García, *Dos defensores de los esclavos negros en el siglo XVII*, 1.
11 Cleary, *How Latin America Saved*, 17.
12 Schwaller, *History of the Catholic Church*, 119.
13 Ibid., 124.
14 Méndez, *Reflexiones que el Arzobispo de Caracas y Venezuela*, 1.
15 Schwaller, *History of the Catholic Church*, 165.
16 Ibid., 186.
17 McBrien, *Catholicism*, 913.
18 Schwaller, *History of the Catholic Church*, 197.
19 Hurtado, *Moral Social – Acción Social*, 126. The translation is my own.
20 Ibid., 128.
21 Schwaller, *History of the Catholic Church*, 251.
22 Conference of Latin American Bishops (CELAM), *I Conferencia General*, 11.
23 Freire, *Pedagogy of the Oppressed*, 10.

24 Schwaller, *History of the Catholic Church*, 204.

25 Hagopian, *Religious Pluralism*, 43.

26 Leal, "La Noción de Justicia Social en la *Gaudium et Spes*."

27 Schwaller, *History of the Catholic Church*, 232. See also Valiente, "Reception of Vatican II."

28 Conference of Latin American Bishops (CELAM), *II Conferencia General* .

29 See, e.g., GS 21, 25–6, 29, 41–2, 59, 65–6, 68, 71, 73–4, 76, 78, 81, 87.

30 Schwaller, *History of the Catholic Church*, 247.

31 CELAM, *II Conferencia General*, no. 13.

32 Ibid., no. 9.

33 Cleary, *How Latin America Saved*, 108.

34 CELAM, *II Conferencia General*, chapter II.

35 Ibid., chapter III.

36 CELAM, *II Conferencia General*, nos. 6, 7.

37 Claffey and Egan, *Movement or Moment*, 18.

38 Conference of Latin American Bishops (CELAM), *III General Conference*, no. 8.

39 CELAM, *III General Conference*, nos. 1134–5.

40 Cleary, *How Latin America Saved*, 109.

41 CELAM, *III General Conference*, no. 1215.

42 CELAM, *III General Conference*, nos. 181–6.

43 Ibid., no. 44.

44 Ibid., no. 80.

45 Ibid., no. 42.

46 Conference of Latin American Bishops (CELAM), *IV Conferencia General*, no. 33.

47 Ibid., no. 203.

48 Dawson, "Concept of Popular Religion," 107.

49 Conference of Latin American Bishops (CELAM), *V Conferencia General*, nos. 262, 363.

50 Ibid., nos. 4–5.

51 Valiente, "Reception of Vatican II," 818.

52 CELAM, *V Conferencia General*, nos. 76, 385, 533.

53 Ibid., nos. 399–405.

54 Ibid., no. 262.

55 Dawson, "Concept of Popular Religion," 105.

7

To the World: Ana Castillo's *The Guardians* and Literature after Vatican II

Cynthia R. Wallace

The joys and hopes, the grief and anguish of the people of our time, especially those who are poor or afflicted, are the joys and hopes, the grief and anguish of the followers of Christ as well. Nothing that is genuinely human fails to find an echo in their hearts. (G S 1)

These familiar opening words from the Second Vatican Council's document *Gaudium et Spes,* or the *Pastoral Constitution on the Church in the Modern World*, unequivocally turn the church to the world. Repeatedly, the document asserts a vision of the Catholic Church's *service* to the world, its need to understand and participate in responding to the contemporary challenges of globalization, rapid changes in community structures, radical social and economic inequalities, and the ongoing threat of war. Again and again, the document names the value of dialogue, not only within the church but between the church and the rest of the world, holding in tension the need for partnership with those outside the church and its belief that it has a unique "key" to offer to the world's problems in its vision of human dignity rooted in God's desire for relationship and in the person of Christ. Ultimately, *Gaudium et Spes*, as the Second Vatican Council's most explicit comment on the church's need to turn to the world, suggests an acute attentiveness to the world itself, to its unfolding paradoxes of progress and struggle, as the foundation for a spiritually motivated yet humble activism. Such activism is rooted in a cultural moment of widening responsibility within globalization, a "new humanism" (GS 55), as well as the Christian call to love: it implies an ethics of responsibility that implicates both institution and individual.

Understanding must precede response in this ethics – one must *recognize* the state of the world before knowing how to respond with love in pursuit of justice. Early in the document, its authors assert, "In every age, the church carries the responsibility of reading the signs of the times and of interpreting them in light of the Gospel" (GS 4). This language of *reading* and *interpretation* is hardly inconsequential: it highlights the work of attention required as part of the church's ethical endeavour. The language might also be said to imply the value of the more typical objects of reading and interpretation in this ethical project of responding to the world's joys and hopes, grief and anguish. Indeed, while *Gaudium et Spes* does not dwell at length on imaginative literature, it does recognize literature as a source of cultural insight: first, as evidence of the widespread rejection of religion (GS 7) and, later, as a site of struggle for human meaning and understanding (GS 62). In the section on the "Proper Development of Culture," the authors claim, "In their own way literature and art are very important in the life of the church. They seek to penetrate our nature, our problems and experience as we endeavour to discover and perfect ourselves and the world in which we live; they try to discover our place in history and in the universe, to throw light on our suffering and joy, our needs and potentialities, and to outline a happier destiny in store for us. Hence they can elevate human life, which they express under many forms according to various times and places" (GS 62). In other words, literature and art are expressions of contemporary culture and sources of relevance: as such, the argument continues, they should be supported by the church and even integrated into liturgical spaces.

Thus, *Gaudium et Spes* could be said to turn us to literary texts which themselves turn us back to the world. Implicitly, the document suggests the value of texts that can spur the faithful on to the sort of active love to which it calls them. If the stated purpose of *Gaudium et Spes* is to "set down how [the Second Vatican Council] understands the presence and function of the church in the world of today" (GS 2), the purpose of this chapter is to set down an understanding of the presence and function of literature in the ongoing project of Vatican II's turn to the world.

One provocative text in this conversation is Ana Castillo's 2007 novel *The Guardians*, which I choose to consider here – from among many possible options – because it exemplifies the best of Catholic literature after Vatican II, literature wrapped up in the joys and hopes, griefs and anguish of the people of our time. In an irrevocable echo of the Second Vatican Council, and the *Pastoral Constitution on the Church in the Modern World* in particular, *The Guardians* challenges readers' complacency through its representation of the suffering and faith of our global neighbours, emphasizing the difficulties of modern migration and globalization, social and economic disparities, and crises in political and familial realms, as well as the need for community. Ultimately, like *Gaudium et Spes*, *The Guardians* is an invitation to dialogue and responsibility, incarnating a vision of the mutual and active love to which the pilgrim church is called.

But Castillo's novel is not widely known among those who are interested in Catholic literature.[1] The bulk of this chapter will explicate the significance of *The Guardians* as a text that carries on the spirit of Vatican II in its content, style, and ethical appeal, but first I must explore why we have not already been turning, in discussions of contemporary Catholic literature, to this novel and others like it.

AFTER THE REVIVAL

Twentieth-century Catholic writing is often discussed in terms of a "literary revival": this language is debated, but appears repeatedly – for instance, in the title of Ian Ker's *Catholic Revival in English Literature, 1945–1961*. By many accounts, the Second Vatican Council undermined the strong, coherent worldview that so appealed to early and mid-century writers who embraced Catholicism. Evelyn Waugh was famously disgusted by many of the council's changes, including vernacular mass and a broader role for the laity,[2] and scholars continue to disagree on Graham Greene's view.[3] More than one commentator has described the "decline and fall" of the Catholic novel in the second half of the twentieth century.[4] And this decline-and-fall theory is not just prevalent among academics; it also bears out in the general public's view. I tell people I teach Catholic literature, and their eyes light up, and they reference Flannery O'Connor or Gerard Manley Hopkins, almost never living writers. My experience parallels that of Mary Reichardt, who in the introduction to *Between Human and Divine: The Catholic Vision in Contemporary Literature* claims, "I find few readers, Catholic or not, who can name contemporary authors or texts in this tradition."[5]

A broad unfamiliarity with contemporary Catholic literature is also traceable to wider social forces of secularization and literary trends. In 2012, Paul Elie published a piece in *The New York Times* titled, "Has Fiction Lost Its Faith?" In this influential essay, Elie claims that contemporary writing offers few compelling portraits of belief after the high point of books by Flannery O'Connor, Thomas Merton, Walker Percy, and Dorothy Day. (Incidentally, these four are the subject of Elie's 2003 monograph *The Life You Save May Be Your Own*.) Echoing *Gaudium et Spes*'s claim that literature evinces widespread atheism, Elie asserts, "if any patch of our culture can be said to be post-Christian, it is literature."[6] His point in the article seems to be primarily that characters' *belief* is no longer a central feature of the fiction that is being published.

In a high-profile response to Elie in the *Wall Street Journal*, *Image* journal editor Gregory Wolfe contends that "the myth of secularism triumphant in the literary arts is just that – a myth." Citing Elie's appeal to Flannery O'Connor's famous claim, "For the hard of hearing you shout, and for the almost-blind you draw large and startling figures," Wolfe argues that the postmodern scene requires less shouting. Instead, it demands more of a whisper – a subtle exploration of belief and readers who are willing to listen "more closely to the still, small voice."[7] I tend to agree with Wolfe, whose argument dovetails nicely with Reichardt's claim that post-Vatican II Catholic literature is often less distinguished by its subject matter than by a shared vision that is incarnational and sacramental, fascinated by the "mystery of the cross," "intense encounters with suffering and evil," openness to the "existence of another world beyond the senses," even hope.[8] I find all these characteristics in *The Guardians*.

Yet one striking feature of the various conversations that do acknowledge contemporary Catholic writing, including Wolfe's article and Reichardt's book, is their overwhelming focus on texts by white authors – David Lodge, Mary Gordon, Alice McDermott – to the exclusion of works of Catholic literature in English that are being published by, for example, Nigerian, Indigenous North American, and Latino writers. Again, one can trace myriad reasons for these oversights. For one, geographic divisions in literary scholarship lead many studies to be divided by the Atlantic Ocean: our genealogies of English-language Catholic literature are distinctively British and American. They tend to trace their contemporary origins to nineteenth-century aristocrats, Oxford-movement converts, and later Irish immigration to the United States. The grandchildren of evangelized tribes of the Americas or former British colonies in Africa do not fit neatly into these genealogies. The situation is further complicated for texts by Latina/Latino writers, as the situation of Latinos in the United States – and Latino Catholics in the US church – is marked by a forgotten history of centuries-old presence, blurred in more recent associations of Mexican-Americans with contemporary immigration. Indeed, as Julia G. Young notes in her review of Timothy Matovina's book *Latino Catholicism: Transformation in America's Largest Church*, pictures of "American Catholicism" seldom fully address the fact that Latinos do "make up some 35 percent of the U.S. Catholic population."[9]

So we should not be surprised that invoking the label "contemporary Catholic literature in English" does not tend to bring to mind Louise Erdrich, Chimamanda Ngozi Adichie, Cherríe Moraga, or Ana Castillo. However, these writers are vital for our understanding of the vibrancy of post-Vatican II Catholic literature. These writers engage the church with as much critical ambivalence as a Mary Gordon or a David Lodge while also reminding readers of the increasingly global, mosaical face of contemporary Catholicism.[10] They confront us, as well, with narratives of the faithful around the world who struggle daily not only with questions of faith in a postmodern world but with questions of survival, justice, and dignity. In other words, they help us exercise the discipline to which *Gaudium et Spes* calls the faithful, to "look upon [one's] neighbor (without any exception) as another self, bearing in mind especially [one's] neighbor's life and the means needed for a dignified way of life" (GS 27). The neighbour, in texts like Castillo's, may not look like us or live next door: the world to which these texts encourage us to turn is not a tiny sliver of human life mirroring our own, but a vibrant and throbbing globe.

THE GUARDIANS: REPRESENTING THE NEIGHBOUR IN NEED

The Guardians is a complicated novel. Set in the first decade of the twenty-first century in the borderlands between Mexico, Texas, and New Mexico, its narration is shared by four characters: Regina, the middle-aged virgin widow whose brother Rafael has gone missing in an attempt to cross the desert border; Gabriel (or Gabo), Rafael's teenage son and Regina's nephew and charge, whose narration takes the shape of letters to twentieth-century saint Padre Pío; Miguel, a thirty-something history teacher and social activist; and El Abuelo Milton, Miguel's mostly blind grandfather who ends up involved in the quest to find Rafael.

The novel is painfully realist in its engagement with injustice at the Mexican-American border. Its characters are migrants, and while Milton and Miguel have a heritage of American citizenship – Regina and her mother had to struggle for their papers – Gabo is undocumented, and his missing father is at the mercy of the inconsistent border guards and the "coyotes" who charge exorbitant fees to smuggle Mexicans through the desert into the United States. Gabriel himself has suffered during numerous border crossings; we learn early on that his mother died during one such crossing, and a scene later in the novel reveals the extent of Gabo's trauma as he compares his suffering to Christ's on the cross, recalling hiding perfectly still in the desert as "helicopters were hovering over" his family (85), or another time when the family had to drink their own urine to stay alive (87).

But the list of horrors Castillo's novel addresses extends beyond migrant labour and border-crossing; it also includes the all-too-real associated dynamics of trafficking in drugs, body parts, and sex. Not only was Gabriel's mother's body found in the desert with three others, all "mutilated for their organs" (4), his father is ultimately discovered to have been held hostage to work in a meth lab, and several of the novel's women characters are kidnapped, drugged, and held as ransom and sex-slaves. The documentary realism of these injustices is increased by Miguel's own research as an activist: accounts of the notes he compiles for a book he plans to call *The Dirty Wars of Latin America: Building Drug Empires* (32) appear in the text, so that Castillo's fiction writing is woven through with her character's nonfiction writing. Readers of Castillo's novel are confronted not just with the story of imagined situations, but with an uncomfortable picture of reality, even culpability, as the North American Free Trade Agreement (NAFTA), the School of the Americas, disproportionate pollution of the natural resources available to the lower classes and marginalized races, and the economies of contemporary agricultural practices each get their mention.

If the Second Vatican Council encouraged the church to turn to the world as a network of global neighbours, *The Guardians* opens its readers' eyes to the griefs and anguish that should find an echo in our hearts, that should compel us to work, unflaggingly, for the common good of the world, particularly as we recognize our culpability in North America. In the words of *Gaudium et Spes*, "The pace of change is so far-reaching and rapid nowadays that it is imperative that no one, out of indifference to the course of events or because of inertia, would indulge in a merely individualistic morality. The best way to fulfill one's obligations of justice and love is to contribute to the common good according to one's means and the needs of others, and also to promote and help public and private organizations devoted to bettering the conditions of life" (GS 30). *The Guardians* confronts readers with realities of "the needs of others" that demand response, against the temptations of indifference and inertia.

I refer to this sort of literary consciousness-raising as the *ethics of textual representation*.[11] By this phrase I mean the function of the literary text to represent reality both in the sense of mimesis – aesthetically figuring a material, real-world phenomenon – and also in the sense of legal advocacy. While language certainly never straightforwardly reflects reality, it can point to, and even implicitly plead for, some recognition of suffering or injustice. Literature is distinctively textual, but it is also "truly human," and thus capable of raising an echo in readers' hearts. This feature is especially important to remember as we approach literary texts written from the margins, texts written with an eye toward advocacy, with a sense of justice. Such an understanding of literature is not anti-postmodern; indeed, as Linda Hutcheon argues in her *Poetics of Postmodernism*, postmodern fiction often both invokes and problematizes mimesis, both participating in a tradition of apparent realism and undermining it with magic, fragmentation, or other disruptions.[12] Such realism threaded through with the marvelous is also a characteristic Reichardt attributes to contemporary Catholic literature in particular.[13] And it is a feature of *The Guardians*.

"ANOTHER WORLD BEYOND THE SENSES"

For all its near-documentary realism, *The Guardians* is also tinged with the supernatural. Even listing the characters' names highlights an uncanny prevalence of allusions to angels – Rafael, Gabriel, Michael. Abuelo Milton's name and blindness likewise suggest a hard-to-miss allusion to John Milton, that literary giant who wrote his own share of angels in *Paradise Lost*. Regina's full name is Regina Ana: she is named after both the Queen of Heaven and the patron saint of late-in-life mothers, and she is herself an improbably virginal surrogate mother, widow of a soldier killed in Vietnam, her marriage never consummated. The text is densely allusive, suggestive of realities beyond flesh and blood.

It is also riddled with miracles. The profoundly devout Gabo has visions; he prays for – and apparently receives – the gift of stigmata. Late in the novel, he also recounts his experience, as a child, of seeing with his aunt Regina the miracle of the Dancing of the Sun, famous for its earlier occurrence in Fátima, Portugal, in 1917. Some critics have discussed Castillo's novel in terms of the Latin-American prevalence of magic realism, that genre in which the fantastical breaks into worlds thick with suffering and injustice when realism becomes inadequate, but Castillo herself resists the label. Instead, she insists, the magic in her novels is specifically *miracle*: characters accept it because they have faith.[14] Some characters do question Gabo's experience – especially the priest Juan Bosco – but those who believe him do so with a quiet reverence born of religious devotion.

Not that such devotion is unmixed with doubt. Regina prays, worries over purgatory, and wraps her nephew's bleeding hands with apparent faith, but she also avoids church and openly criticizes the local priest. She disapproves of Gabriel's religious fervour and desire for the religious life, thinking in terms of his father's adamant Marxism (7, 21). Gabo's devotion sets him apart even from Father Bosco, who is an almost ancillary character in the novel. Far from acting as a figure of consistent wisdom or guidance, Juan Bosco claims in the narrative's middle that he is leaving the priesthood to marry his housekeeper; he is called to Rome; and eventually he returns, somehow newly committed to his vocation and also *conscientized*, working for the well-being of the migrant labourers against the explicit instructions of the American bishops. The priest's experiences are as dynamic and unfolding as everyone else's. But Bosco's story is emphatically secondary in the novel – it takes place primarily behind the scenes. In a perhaps fitting nod toward the Second Vatican Council's expanded attention to the role of the laity – and contra the literary heritage of novels like Graham Greene's *The Power and the Glory* or Georges Bernanos's *Diary of a Country Priest* – Castillo's primary characters are laypeople, in various stages of communion with the church. Their joys and sorrows beat at the heart of the narrative, and their differing stances of devotion, skepticism, and ambivalence toward the institution suggest a thoroughly post-Vatican II attitude that the church is not immune to challenge, even as it continues to inspire devotion.

Doubt of another sort may enter into readers' experiences of the text, as their own assumptions about the church and the miraculous colour their responses to the text's representations. Some devout readers might find the novel offensive in its implicit critique of the clergy or the institution's blindness to the struggles of migrant labourers. In a certain sense, *The Guardians* is an imaginative exposé of the church's *failure* to serve the international community despite its repeated naming of the need for such service, and even particular concern for migrant workers, in *Gaudium et Spes*. On the other hand, skeptical readers might find characters' apparent acceptance of miracles – not to mention Gabriel's fervent religiosity – off-putting, to say the least. How, one might wonder, does Regina – otherwise so rational, so tough – reconcile her nephew's wounded hands and her own earlier experience of the Dancing of the Sun with the daily struggle to make ends meet and with her open avoidance of Mass? More broadly, how does the novel's ethically weighty and realistic representation of injustice at the border square with its richly allusive nods to heavenly beings and fanciful literature?

The disjunctions are also stylistic: Castillo's novel undermines easy assumptions of realism not only through its matter-of-fact inclusion of miracles and allusions to another reality, but also through its four-narrator format. The cacophony of these voices, which do not always agree with one another, highlights the partial nature of any telling. It disallows readers from settling into the tale as a trustworthy single narration, emphasizing instead the complexity, incompleteness, and need for ongoing struggle and interpretation in approaching *any* narrative. Ultimately, this style serves as a reminder of the need for interpretive humility and a stance of keen focus – a stance I call the *ethics of readerly attention*. Readers' responsibility is both a sort of receptive acceptance of what the text has to offer and an active struggle to understand, not just in their own terms but in the text's. A text that, in its form and in its content, sets readers a bit off-balance is particularly well suited to teaching this lesson of readerly humility and attention.

Such a stance compels even the skeptical reader to recognize the possibility that the answer to the sufferings and injustices represented by *The Guardians* may not simply be a materialist one. In other words – and this is a key point in *Gaudium et Spes* – a practical, on-the-ground responsiveness to the world's needs must be balanced and enlivened by a robust spirituality (166, 182, 209). Awareness of a "world beyond the senses," another of Reichardt's characteristics of contemporary Catholic literature, is also needed to engender and empower the kind of responsiveness invited by the novel's ethical call.

"COMPLETELY IN NEED OF SOCIETY"

The Guardians, for all its sorrow, does not leave us without a vision of ethical responsiveness, and that ethical responsiveness aligns beautifully with the sort of responsibility described by *Gaudium et Spes*. Nor is the novel simply a dourly realist list of major sufferings injected with off-putting instances of the miraculous. It is a compelling human tale on a smaller scale: characters struggle not just with border trafficking but also with the challenges of getting by day-to-day, with religious questions, with family histories leading to self-doubt, with divorce, with body image, with love. The novel is funny in parts, particularly in collisions between the characters' incomplete and unreliable narrations. The awkward romance that develops between Regina and Miguel is one example: she drops a pie in a parking lot in front of him and becomes irrationally angry; she is embarrassed when he arrives at her house and catches her wearing boxer shorts; he does the chicken dance at a church fair to get her attention.

Even more beautiful than the budding romance, though, is the story's development of a community of a mutual aid. The novel's title invites the question, Who are "the guardians"? Early on, Regina speaks of *los Franklins*, the mountains that hover over her life and all the book's events, as self-giving "guardians between the two countries" (5). Yet other options soon arise, as Regina speaks of both guardian angels and her own role as possible legal guardian to her nephew (27). Further, she persists in comparing Miguel to her favourite archangel, implying that perhaps the extremely helpful man is a "guardian" (57, 66). And the possibilities extend, as we see Gabriel, Miguel, and Milton join forces to gift Regina, so used to caring for others, with the best day of her life (147). Indeed, the guardianship is expansive: Milton actively cares on numerous occasions for both Gabo and Miguel. And Gabo cares not only for his father and a young woman nicknamed Tiny Tears, but also for his aunt, whose feet, swollen from years of work, he soaks and rubs (137). These various, intercrossing relations of guardianship exemplify the mutual aid called for by Vatican II: "Life in society is not something accessory to humanity: through their dealings with others, through mutual service, and through fraternal and sororal dialogue, men and women develop all their talents and become able to rise to their destiny" (GS 25). *The Guardians* suggests the mutual service of guardianship as a compelling ethical model of the responsibility to which the church – and indeed all people – are called in the face of human grief and anguish. The spiritual ideal of guardian angels is concretized in flesh-and-blood humans who bring their imperfect efforts to one another in a dynamic interaction of care.

To be clear: *The Guardians* is hardly a triumphalist novel, even in its representation of the people of God. Its ending is hardly a happy one. The novel ends in a brutal, nearly unspeakable scene of violence. It ends in a martyrdom that ought not to be celebrated, one that is not redemptive but is rather the outcome of the terrors of linked injustices. Readers looking for epiphany, or grand redemption, or some other uplifting climax will find, instead, a thoroughly modern – or postmodern – sense of brokenness and loss. Neither the political officials, nor the church officials, nor indeed the community of guardians has been able to ward off the devastations that follow from such radically evil systems. In a sense, the novel reads as an exposé on how little success the church and modern culture have had in addressing those "more urgent problems" named in part two of *Gaudium et Spes*, even after forty years: broken family and social structures, economic and cultural injustices, rampant violence.

In the aftermath of this violence, however, the novel leaves us with a tentative kind of hope, an almost direct incarnation of a certain encouragement from *Gaudium et Spes*. Consider these words from the document: "Today, there is an inescapable duty to make ourselves the neighbor of every individual, without exception, and to take positive steps to help a neighbor whom we encounter, whether that neighbor be an elderly person abandoned by everyone, a foreign worker who suffers the injustice of being despised, a refugee, an illegitimate child wrongly suffering for a sin of which the child is innocent, or a starving human being who awakens our conscience by calling to mind the words of Christ: 'As you did it to one of the least of these my brothers or sisters, you did it to me' (Matt. 25:40)" (GS 27). In a novel that has already emphatically explored the needs of the elderly, the foreign worker, and the refugee, the final pages turn quite unexpectedly to the needs of the illegitimate child suffering for sins of which she is innocent. Regina, imperfect and divided within herself between faith and doubt, chooses to take in the unwanted infant of the person who has caused her the most devastating pain of her life. "My decision is to care for the child," she states, plainly claiming her own agency and also downplaying the extraordinary act of charity (210). In fact, she even visits the imprisoned teenage mother, Tiny Tears. Regina's choice to love Tiny Tears and the baby – whom she names "Gabriela," extending the human-angel resonance and memorializing her nephew – manifests the challenging work of actively *becoming* a neighbour, of actively loving "the least of these."

The resonance between the novel's conclusion and the passage from *Gaudium et Spes* quoted above continues in that both reference the Gospel of Matthew. As *Gaudium et Spes* quotes Matthew 25, Regina quotes Matthew 6: "For if ye forgive men their trespasses, your heavenly Father will also forgive you" (210). In both cases, the passages quote Jesus' teaching on the spiritual efficacy of earthly actions: in one case mercy (including visiting prisoners), in the other, forgiveness. Regina exemplifies both.

Still, Regina's actions are, again, hardly those of a pinnacle of piety. She does have Gabriella baptized at Father Juan Bosco's suggestion, but justifies her decision not with the vocabulary of the devout but with the claim, "I figured it couldn't hurt la baby to throw some holy water on her" (210). She reads the book of Matthew, not under the priest's instruction (though Father Bosco has his own doubts about the historicity of the Gospel) but for the very personal reason that it was Gabo's "favorite book of all" and that she feels her nephew speaking to her through it (210). She quotes Jesus' teaching on forgiveness but follows it up with the assertion, "Easier said than done" (210).

Regina exists in the paradoxical space between hope and anxiety, joy and grief, that *Gaudium et Spes* names as the modern condition. The novel's final pages stylistically parallel this paradoxical space by zigzagging back and forth between representing the beauty of Regina's forgiveness and active love and the literally fragmented story of what happens to Gabriel in the novel's terrible climax. There is no comfortable conclusion, no easy space to rest: only a heart-wrenching, disconcerting mix of grief and love.

"YOU CAN'T DO THAT IN REAL LIFE"

Regina's final words, the last paragraph and sentence of the novel – "You can't do that in real life" (211) – express her recognition that her experience is different from a documentary of it, which she would be able to rewind to before the terrible part and "press stop." This last musing, and its ultimate conclusion, emphasize the distinction between real-life agony and artistic representations. Artistic representations allow viewers (or readers) to go back, to dwell on an earlier scene; they *are not* real-life experience, which barrels onward, unfolding at its own rapid pace. Yet Regina herself, we must remember, is a fictional character: her own "real-life" experience is the imaginative creation of Ana Castillo. As readers, we both do and do not gain access to real-life suffering when we read of Regina's experience.

How ought we ultimately to understand the presence and function of *The Guardians* – and by extension, literature in general – in the modern world? I have suggested that *The Guardians* turns us to the world as a network of global inter-implications, first, through its representations of suffering and struggle at the borderlands, opening readers' eyes to the struggles of some global neighbours who might otherwise go unrecognized. Second, *The Guardians* turns us to the world by engaging us in a practice of more careful, self-suspending attention through its stylistic challenges and insistence on the mysterious existence of a spiritual dimension beyond the material, even as it explores the tensions of accepting such a spiritual realm in the skeptical modern world. Finally, *The Guardians* turns us to the world by exemplifying the risky, difficult work of mutual guardianship, forgiveness, and love in a modern world characterized by "situation[s] that challeng[e] and even oblig[e] people to respond" (GS 4).

Literature is not a documentary. Nor is it, as poet and essayist Adrienne Rich reminds us, a "blueprint." But in its imaginative representations, its engagement of the emotions, even its difficulty, literature can extend an invitation. It can begin a dialogue, that other key word of *Gaudium et Spes*: a dialogue between text and flesh, between contemplation and action. Literature offers us a space to reflect that is not often available in real life: it allows us to slow down, to rewind and consider, to mull over the provocation. At its best, then, literature eventually turns us away from itself.

The Guardians confronts us with grief and anguish; it consoles us with a vision of mutual aid and human dignity; it compels us both to admit our doubts and to look for a more-than-rational force at work in this world. And it disproves, definitively, any claim that contemporary literature offers only an anemic vision of belief, or that Catholic literature has declined and fallen in the years after the council. Instead, it painfully yet beautifully enacts the council's claim that "the future of humanity rests with people who are capable of providing the generations to come with reasons for living and for hope" (GS 31). "You can't do that in real life," Regina claims, but *The Guardians* turns our eyes and our hearts to the world with the passionate question that implicitly follows as we close its final pages: "What *can* you do in real life?"

NOTES

1 Invoking the label "Catholic literature" opens a debate beyond the scope of this chapter, especially because Ana Castillo has repeatedly claimed in interviews and essays that she is *not* a practising Catholic. In order to focus on the argument at hand, in these pages I follow Mary Reichardt in defining Catholic literature as "that which employs the history, traditions, culture, theology, and/or spirituality of Catholicism in a substantial and informed manner. Whether it involves Catholic subject matter or not, and whether its author is a Catholic or not, such literature is substantially grounded in a deep and realistic understanding of at least some aspects of the Catholic faith, Catholic life, or the Catholic tradition." Reichardt, *Between Human and Divine*, 3.

2 Sutton, *Catholic Modernists*, 157.

3 Ibid., 167; Griffiths, *Pen and the Cross*, 176.

4 Bergonzi, "Conspicuous Absentee"; Read, "Decline and Fall of the Catholic Novel."

5 Reichardt, *Between Human and Divine*, 1.

6 Elie, "Has Fiction Lost Its Faith?"

7 Wolfe, "Whispers of Faith."

8 Reichardt, *Between Human and Divine*, 3–4.

9 Young, "Hidden in Plain Sight," 29.

10 Those interested in broadening their familiarity with contemporary Catholic fiction might begin with Adichie's *Purple Hibiscus*, Erdrich's *The Last Report on the Miracles at Little No Horse*, Moraga's *Heroes and Saints*, or Castillo's *So Far from God*. Gordon's *Pearl* and Christopher Beha's *What Happened to Sophie Wilder* are also fascinating Anglo-American Catholic novels.

11 I develop an ethics of textual representation in *Of Women Borne*.
12 Hutcheon, *Poetics of Postmodernism*.
13 Reichardt, *Between Human and Divine*, 1.
14 In an interview with Katharina Kracht discussing her earlier novel *So Far from God*, Castillo claims, "What contemporary society wants to call magical or supernatural is really a question of faith. Do we believe that Christ, a man, died on a cross and was resurrected three days later on earth – is that magical realism or is that faith?" Kracht, "Question of Faith," 630–1.

8

An Integral Vision of Peace?
Assessing Catholic Social Teaching's
Contribution to Contemporary Green Cultures
of Peace from Vatican II to Benedict XVI

Christopher Hrynkow

This chapter maps specific examples of Catholic social teaching principles that can be helpful for understanding and imagining substantive peace. Such principles include social justice, participation, and nonviolence. *Pacem in Terris*, along with *Gaudium et Spes* and other documents of the Second Vatican Council, served to amplify, nuance, and open additional spaces where these principles can be taught and practiced. These spaces have been carried forward and recontextualized in the post-conciliar period. This process, in accord with Pope John XXIII's phrasing, helps to ensure that peace is not an empty word (PT 167).

After delineating this conciliar legacy, the present chapter will take a green, ecoethical approach to assess how this potential for peace has been brought forward in the exercise of the papal magisterial (teaching) office since the close of the Second Vatican Council. This approach is premised on the principles of green politics: ecological wisdom, social justice, participatory democracy, nonviolence, sustainability, and respect for diversity. It seeks to move beyond narrowly defined environmentalism and a concept of negative peace (the mere absence of war) toward a holistic conception of cultures of peace. The approach is also ethical and theological, in that it is grounded in a Christian ethic of peace. Specifically, in dialogue with Catholic social teaching from the conciliar period, this chapter assesses the contribution of Benedict XVI's World Day of Peace Messages to contemporary green cultures of peace.

CATHOLIC SOCIAL TEACHING ON PEACE DURING THE VATICAN II PERIOD

Catholic social teaching is generally defined as the exercise of the magisterial office of Catholic bishops, inclusive of the bishops teaching together (as in the case of the Second Vatican Council) or the Bishop of Rome exercising this imperative alone.[1] Despite being undertaken by some of its most prominent figures, Catholic social teaching is sometimes called the Catholic Church's "best kept secret."[2] Although Pope Francis is transforming that dynamic,[3] this characterization may be worth keeping in mind as this chapter works through the material from prior to his papacy.

Contemporary Catholic social teaching is generally traced to 1891, marking the promulgation of Pope Leo XIII's encyclical *Rerum Novarum*, which is significant for the way it addresses how workers and the poor ought to live in relationship to social, political, and religious institutions. Growing from *Rerum Novarum*, with a good deal of help from Vatican II, themes that have been prominent in Catholic social teaching include social justice, the common good, the preferential option for the poor, interdependence, solidarity, and – though relatively underdeveloped by anglophone scholars of Catholicism – peace.

As we mark a half-century since the conciliar period, it is important to unfold something of the context of the Second Vatican Council. Called by a man who may have been elected to be a "caretaker pope," Vatican II allowed Catholic social teaching to embrace a methodology of *aggiornamento* (bringing up to date, letting in fresh air) and *ressourcement* (rereading of the sources),[4] which served to shift the Roman Catholic Church out of a universalist, Tridentine expression into a more intimate relationship with both local and global concerns. In reflecting upon his motivations for calling a council, John XXIII recalled, "The idea of the Council did not ripen in me as the fruit of long meditation but came forth like the flower of an unexpected spring."[5] This ecological image invokes a freshness of approach – the Catholic Church interacting with and caring about the world in all its social, cultural, intellectual, and (lately, with more focus) biological diversity.[6] It is this "spring fresh" approach that I, as a result of my Jesuit education, have come to associate with that sometimes amorphous label, "the spirit of Vatican II."

According to Stephen Bevans's analysis, a significant consequence of the Second Vatican Council was a widening of the Catholic *locus theologicus* to include not only scripture and tradition but also context. Thus, data from disciplines like history, sociology, economics, and anthropology became valid sources for theological inquiry and Catholic social teaching.[7] It follows from such analysis that contextual issues such as war and peace would come into focus with a new intensity in Catholic social thought. Peace activist and writer John Dear argues that the Vatican II documents support new scholarly approaches to biblical interpretation that can serve to downplay the natural law and "just" war traditions, moving toward an active (re)embracing of the "Gospel of Peace," namely, Jesus' nonviolent peace witness.[8]

Another place to turn for the contemporary roots of an ethic for Catholic peace witness is *Pacem in Terris*, which is sometimes called John XXIII's "last will and testament."[9] This encyclical was promulgated after Vatican II's first session in 1963. It is noteworthy as the first papal encyclical addressed not just to bishops or Catholics but to everyone of good will.[10] In this same spirit of widening the remit of Catholic social teaching, *Pacem in Terris* outlines the rights and duties of persons in a world community in which people of different religions and political persuasions could (and ought to) live in harmony, justice, security, and freedom (see, in particular, PT section IV). It further predicts the imminent end of colonialism (PT 23) and, as a reading of the "sign of the times"[11] (just after the Cuban Missile Crisis), defines war, especially nuclear war and the stockpiling of nuclear weapons, as untenable (PT 109–19). Referencing the possibility of a nuclear holocaust, which was palpable at the time of its issue, *Pacem in Terris* states,

> There is a common belief that under modern conditions peace cannot be assured except on the basis of an equal balance of armaments ... And if one country is equipped with atomic weapons, others consider themselves justified in producing such weapons themselves, equal in destructive force ... Consequently people are living in the grip of constant fear ... While it is difficult to believe that anyone would dare to assume responsibility for initiating the appalling slaughter and destruction that war would bring in its wake, there is no denying that the conflagration could be started by some chance and unforeseen circumstance. (PT 110–11)

John XXIII continues this line of teaching on substantive peace with reference to concern not only for human dignity but also for all living things, ending with a definitive statement on the matter of nuclear arms: "Moreover, even though the monstrous power of modern weapons does indeed act as a deterrent, there is reason to fear that the very testing of nuclear devices for war purposes can, if continued, lead to serious danger for various forms of life on earth ... Hence justice, right reason, and the recognition of man's dignity cry out insistently for a cessation to the arms race. The stockpiles of armaments that have been built up in various countries must be reduced all round and simultaneously by the parties concerned. Nuclear weapons must be banned" (PT 112).

As these passages demonstrate, *Pacem in Terris* is representative of what theorists would call positive peace (i.e., a situation of peace that is inclusive of, but not just constituted by, the absence of war). We often assume that violence is located beyond our sphere of influence or takes place in far-off places, at the very least, "somewhere else." Yet a green, ecoethical perspective encourages us to discern our own levels of participation in overt and covert violence. With such a theoretical lens, we also become conscious of "structural violence" in the form of repressive social organizations. Johan Galtung, in his landmark article on peace research published in 1969, writes, "An extended concept of violence leads to an extended concept of peace. Just as a coin has two sides ... peace also has two sides: absence of personal violence, and absence of structural violence. We ... refer to them as negative peace and positive peace respectively."[12] Remarkably, *Pacem in Terris* predates Galtung's article, which is generally seen as the foundation for peace studies, by five years.

After John's death, a key papal moment dealing with peace occurred when Paul VI journeyed to New York to address the United Nations General Assembly. Paul chose to speak on 4 October 1965, the feast of St Francis, in part because Francis of Assisi is associated with peace-building among all members of the created world.[13] As an added advantage, the council was also in session. In the speech, he famously declared, "Never again war, never again war!"[14] As council father Remi De Roo notes, the speech had an impact in Rome; subsequently Paul was welcomed back from New York by those bishops gathered in St Peter's with vigorous applause.[15]

An important result of the momentum[16] signified by such applause was *Gaudium et Spes* (*Pastoral Constitution on the Church in the*

Modern World). Note that the church fathers did not reflect "on" the world; rather, they situated the church "in" the world. *Gaudium et Spes* affirms the task of the church to "preach the gospel to all nations" by promoting justice, peace, and cultural development. Promulgated as part of the council's last batch of documents on 7 December 1965, it is considered by many scholars of Vatican II to be the most intellectually developed document of the council. For example, Gregory Baum notes that the broader ethical horizon of *Gaudium et Spes*, in which the Catholic Church embraces its role in fostering freedom, equality, and participation within a framework of universal solidarity, marks an important new point in the life of the church.[17] In accord with this analysis, De Roo views his experience and that of the other council fathers at Vatican II as an educative process. The earlier documents of the council should therefore be read in light of the later ones, and in this regard De Roo sees *Gaudium et Spes* as generally the most authoritative.[18] It is particularly significant that *Gaudium et Spes* affirms that world issues matter to followers of Jesus: "The joys and hopes, the grief and anguish of the people of our time, especially of those who are poor or afflicted, are the joys and hopes, the grief and anguish of the followers of Christ as well" (GS 1). Further, as part of a renewed pastoral approach to "error," Vatican II issued few condemnations.

However, *Gaudium et Spes* explicitly condemns nuclear war (GS 80) and genocide (GS 79), and promotes substantive peace, especially in chapter IV, "Fostering of Peace and Establishment of a Community of Nations." As part of their "completely fresh appraisal of war" (GS 80) and teachings on peace, the council fathers

1   emphasize that war threatens the entire human family (GS 77);
2   declare that "advocates of peace" are blessed with reference to Matthew 5:9 (GS 77);
3   comment on the need to set up instruments of peace based on justice and love (GS 77), with love mediating the demands of justice;
4   endorse a concept of positive peace by writing, "Peace is more than the absence of war: it cannot be reduced to the maintenance of a balance of power between opposing forces nor does it arise out of despotic dominion, but it is appropriately called 'the effect of righteousness' (Is. 32:17)" (GS 78);

5   give qualified support to conscientious objection (based on alternative service) (GS 79);

6   provide a tempered embrace of principled nonviolence (GS 78);[19]

7   disallow the often-invoked principle that "all is fair between the warring parties" in a conflict (GS 79);

8   issue a general condemnation of total war due to its indiscriminate nature (GS 79–80);

9   affirm that arms racing is a trap that does not ensure a steady peace;

10   write about war as "age-old bondage" (GS 81);

11   speak of a "clear duty to spare no effort to achieve the complete outlawing of war by international agreement" (GS 82);[20]

12   endorse the need for an effective international authority to keep the peace among nation-states (GS 81) and allow for positive cooperation to "promote peace" (GS 83);

13   encourage leaders and educators to imagine alternatives to an unjust status quo and exercise their moral imaginations in the service of the "most important task to instill peaceful sentiments in people's minds" (GS 82);

14   speak of the need to free people from both want (GS 84) and economically oppressive structures (GS 85);[21]

15   further recognize several conflict stressors and, in this regard, encourage "Catholic experts" to study issues like demographic shifts (GS 87);

16   specifically recommend the establishment of Catholic aid organizations like Development and Peace[22] to address "hardships ... in areas which are in want" and stimulate the Catholic community to promote "social justice between nations" (GS 90); and

17   extol the need for dialogue and cooperation between Catholics and all those who "long for true peace" (GS 90), remarkably arguing that Catholics should work even with "those who oppose the church and persecute it in various ways ... together without violence and without deceit to build up the world in a spirit of genuine peace" (GS 92).

In this manner, taking up the salutary example of *Pacem in Terris*, the council fathers choose to address both the faithful and the whole of humanity, supporting the diversity necessary for a contagion of substantive peace. Although not without flaws, these teachings are impressive from a peace studies perspective. Seeing the principles the bishops advocate incarnated would certainly go a long way toward making cultures of peace alive in multiple contexts. My use of the plural "cultures of peace" is significant.[23] This chapter defines cultures of peace in nonimperialist terms, in the sense that they are transcultural, do not erase but transform individual cultures (e.g., Canadian culture, youth culture), and can be incarnated differently in different contexts while supporting substantive peace.

WHAT'S IN A WORD? SETTING A GREEN STANDARD

The word *green* and what it is meant to denote and connote when employed in this chapter is of more than passing significance. Herein, I am specifically seeking to distinguish green politics from environmental politics. Whereas environmental politics can be constructed in a manner that serves segmented interests, green politics is meant to be more holistic. It holds competing interests in creative tension and encompasses the interrelated themes of ecological health, cultural and biological diversity, participatory democracy, nonviolence, and gender equity.[24]

It is possible to have a sustainable but unjust society. In this scenario, governments would take a strictly managerial approach to "environment" and people that decouples ecological health from substantive peace and social justice. Indeed, such ecoelitism or ecofascism would have the "advantage" of holding the power to research and enact binding environmental legislation to preserve a segmented, livable environment for the dominant group. The natural world and those humans who are not part of the dominant group are viewed as objects to be disposed of as a means of managing and reducing ecological stresses. It is also possible to conceive of a global government holding such power for millennia. In fact, such an outcome may be representative of our current sociopolitical trajectory unless we bring more concerted attention to the implications of inequity and the increasingly present realities of unsustainability.[25]

By contrast, a green approach keeps social justice and ecological health closely coupled. From an ecojustice perspective, it is impossible to aim for a sustainable society that is not also a just society. This insight is affirmed by Pope Francis in his landmark encyclical *Laudato Si'*: "Today ... we have to realize that a true ecological approach *always* becomes a social approach; it must integrate questions of justice in debates on the environment, so as to hear *both the cry of the earth and the cry of the poor*" (LS 49). Ecologically minded Christians tend to advocate for such coupling to uphold human dignity. This approach is supported, for example, by a green reading of *imago Dei* – the idea that the image of God is especially present in each person, who is, in turn, understood to be intractably involved in human-earth-divine relationships.[26] Indeed, from an analytical viewpoint inspired by the work of the Passionist priest, monk, and self-described "geologian" Thomas Berry (1914–2009), it is crucial, in order to avoid untenable decoupling (for example, thinking of human rights in isolation), to recognize human dignity as existing within a web of relationships, so that moral worth is attributed to all people and, further, gives adequate spaces for the flourishing of other members of the earth community. Although Berry argues that human rights are relative,[27] he also helps us see that they are relational, existing in intertwined social and ecological webs (cf. LS 92).

Building on this articulation of relationality, the Canadian Berryite and ecofeminist theologian Heather Eaton reflects on the brokenness of our most nourishing relationships within a framework of "socio-ecological crisis."[28] This notion of interrelated crises, demanding a response that couples social justice and a concern for ecological health, is understood in light of the integrity of creation. Many Christian initiatives to address human-induced ecological degradation already frame their work as "responding to the ecological crisis."[29] By expanding the scope of crisis-response framing, we also expand the scope of Christian aspirations for faithful living on our planet "in light of making justice, of [nurturing] right relationships with women, men, and all living beings."[30]

The planet's more than two billion Christians[31] can help to build such holistic, nourishing relationships when they approach the task of faithful living with an understanding that the dignity of the human person and the integrity of the natural world are inextricably linked (cf. LS 49). This perspective has a long ecumenical pedigree, forged in dialogue between Christian traditions. For instance, the World Council of Churches and several Roman Catholic religious orders seek to have "Justice, Peace, and the Integrity of Creation" as a mutual set of commitments or a covenant underlying all their programming.[32] These groups often use the acronym JPIC,[33] which has the advantage of invoking these three concepts in such a way as to symbolize their rough parallel with the doctrine of the Trinity.

For people with privilege, applying JPIC principles means that we must humbly take up our duty to accept socioecological limits. A prime path of action here is embracing simple living. This need not be an overly austere asceticism, but there remains an imperative to limit consumption. Simple living, moreover, frequently activates the potential for joy among "deep greens" of both the secular and the religious variety.[34] Such intentional asceticism ultimately represents a more emancipatory dream for all members of the earth community than does the current American Dream (inaccessible for far too many) expressed through a big detached house, multiple carbon-burning vehicles, or processed food at every meal as part of a ubiquitous "addiction to commercial-industrial progress."[35] As Pope Francis notes, under present conditions people can be pulled in multiple directions away from simple living and their most essential relationships: "People get caught up in an abstract, globalized universe, falling into step behind everyone else, admiring the glitter of other people's world, gaping and applauding at all the right times. At the other extreme, they turn into a museum of local folklore, a world apart, doomed to doing the same things over and over, and incapable of being challenged by novelty or appreciating the beauty which God bestows beyond their borders."[36] Hence, a paradoxical mantra for our millennium may be "chosen limitations for ecological, social, and self-growth." That is, we learn to live simply so that others can simply live and, ultimately, have a chance to flourish.[37] Here, simplicity is recognized for its transformative potential to restore equality within an interconnected world and to heal gaps in personal relationships, our relationship with ourselves, and our orientation toward God.

This is not an abstract vision. It is brought home through the real joy of embracing humanity's status as relational beings. Yet, in the face of a saccharine waste world it requires a moral shift to be realized both in whole and in part.[38] Hope is active here, hope for a vital, more equal world.[39] Ecoliberation theologian Leonardo Boff grounds this hope in "alternality" – in imagining alternatives to the unjust status quo.[40] In other words, to drive transformative action we need a vision of something better than what the advertising industry promises.[41] Boff offers an ethical map to move a greater mass of humanity toward integral peace by placing the virtues of hospitality, co-living, respect, tolerance, and communality simultaneously at the centre and on the horizon of our moral imaginations. For Boff, these alternatives are at the heart of hope for a possible and necessary world.[42] This grounded hope is, further, intimately connected to the health benefits and joy that come from simple living.

In concert with green principles, Pope Francis situates proper Christian spirituality in a lived ethic of substantive peace and joy: "Christian spirituality proposes a growth marked by moderation and the capacity to be happy with little. It is a return to that simplicity which allows us to stop and appreciate the small things, to be grateful for the opportunities which life affords us, to be spiritually detached from what we possess, and not to succumb to sadness for what we lack. This implies avoiding the dynamic of dominion and the mere accumulation of pleasures" (LS 222). Francis's treatment of green joy in *Laudato Si'* situates peace, and the entirety of JPIC, in chosen simple living, which necessarily eschews domination and a consumerist orientation.[43] He invites us to appreciate "each person and each thing, learning familiarity with the simplest things and how to enjoy them. So [we] are able to shed unsatisfied needs, reducing [our] obsessiveness and weariness" (LS 223). Here, Francis offers an effective antidote to a "prosperity gospel" that equates God's favour with the "spiritual, physical and financial mastery that dominates not only much of the American religion scene but also some of the largest churches around the globe."[44] He urges us to understand growth in terms of positive relationships, as distinct from the violence of poverty.[45]

In describing green ascetic practices, Jeffrey Jacob notes that practitioners of voluntary simplicity often seek to connect what may at first seem paradoxical states: the inner peace flowing from simple living and world peace.[46] Pope Francis embraces this proposition with his concept of JPIC being firmly and integrally linked to inner peace within a spiritual worldview, which can cultivate wonder at the magnificence of creation: "An adequate understanding of spirituality consists in filling out what we mean by peace, which is much more than the absence of war. Inner peace is closely related to care for ecology and for the common good because, lived out authentically, it is reflected in a balanced lifestyle together with a capacity for wonder which takes us to a deeper understanding of life" (LS 225). Herein, voluntary simple living emerges as both a joyful and an accessible path to JPIC, a peace with the self that, in turn, contributes to world peace in line with the Gandhian insight that simple living supports wider spaces for the realization of socioecological flourishing. It follows that the Christian duty and virtue of growing positive, mutually enhancing relationships with all members of the socioecological world through simple living also becomes an act of peace-building. Hence, it is with an important measure of prophetic wisdom that the Canadian bishops name a chosen asceticism, that is, voluntary simple living, as essential to the Christian ecological imperative.[47]

Social teaching through the exercise of the magisterium, however, is not the last word on that imperative from within Catholic traditions. For example, several Catholic grassroots organizations and ecumenical coalitions involving Catholics are fostering and incarnating green cultures of peace. We might count here the presence of the Green Sisters whose stories are brought to the fore by Sarah McFarland Taylor's research.[48] These religious sisters live and work in places like the Genesis Farm and the Green Mountain Monastery to provide ecological literacy training and to model communities where sustainable living is possible, even amidst a high-consumption culture like the one that currently dominates North America.[49] Another tangible example is the Jesuit Ecology Project in Guelph, Ontario, which includes a peace pole next to twenty-five stations of the cosmos inspired by Thomas Berry, stations of the cross constructed in light of John Paul II's 1991 description of a scriptural way of the cross, and stations of the world religions.[50] The peace pole and these three sets of meditative aids, together with the natural surroundings, form a geography of peace. This green, spiritual response to the ecological crisis respects religious diversity and physically links traditional Catholic piety to both peace and ecology in one place.[51]

This brief mapping of an ethic of chosen green asceticism provides an interpretive framework to assess how Catholic social teaching serves rhetorically to support or detract from the promotion of green cultures of peace. Uhser, Bryant, and Johnston note that it is "precisely through the interplay between one's interpretative framework ... and that which one seeks to understand that knowledge is developed."[52] It is with such an epistemological dynamic in mind that this chapter employs a green, theological, ecoethical interpretive lens to assess the contribution of Benedict XVI to cultures of peace. The lens's nomenclature points to its four constitutive parts – its green, theological, ecological, and ethical dimensions. The lens employs the green principles – ecological wisdom, social justice, participatory democracy, nonviolence, sustainability, and respect for diversity – discerned through a cross-cultural process and affirmed at the Global Greens' conferences in Canberra (2001) and Dakar (2012).[53] The lens is *theological* since Christian ethical traditions serve to ground these green principles. The lens is *ecoethical* in that it is informed by contributions from ecological ethicists working not only within Christianity but also within other religious, spiritual, and secular traditions. These ethicists hold worldviews that locate humans in essential relationships with each other and the natural world. Each of these constitutive parts contributes contextual cogency to the analytical lens. When combined, the four dimensions take us beyond the analytical to the synthetic and the possible. Further, this lens provides for a methodology that is at once critical and normative, holding that a necessary response during a time of earth crisis is to turn the human project toward the interrelated goals of fostering substantive peace and incarnating visions of socioecological flourishing.

BENEDICT XVI'S TEACHING OFFICE AND CULTURES OF PEACE

Given the urgent teachings on peace and nuclear disarmament articulated by the council fathers, it becomes a cogent question a half-century on to consider what the popes have done with that momentum. To assess the papal contribution, I look to the World Day of Peace Messages, the first of which was promulgated in 1967, just after the conciliar period, at Paul VI's initiative. Notable in terms of Paul VI's contribution is his message in 1972, "if you want peace, work for justice,"[54] which has become a mantra often quoted in peace and justice circles. However, this chapter concentrates on Benedict XVI's contribution to this expression of the papal magisterial office (2005–12), which at the time of writing represents the last complete corpus of World Day of Peace Messages. This selection should not be taken as indicative of a progressive view of the history of Catholic social teaching. Nonetheless, the selection seems fitting given that Benedict notes in his inaugural World Day of Peace Message that he chose his papal name to invoke both the patron saint of Europe who helped bring peace to the continent, and Pope Benedict XV for his peacemaking efforts during World War I.[55]

More specifically, in light of some of the moral positions identified in *Gaudium et Spes*, my goal is to assess whether Benedict XVI continued the momentum of the council fathers in a manner that was substantively peaceful. Do his messages rhetorically foster (or detract from) social and ecological relationships that are mutually enhancing and supportive of the cosmic common good?[56] Because ecological worldviews are lightly represented in the conciliar documents, this section focuses on Benedict's treatment of three of the green principles as examples: social justice, participatory democracy, and nonviolence. I also compare the teachings of *Gaudium et Spes* with those of Benedict in his World Day of Peace Messages, bringing the council fathers into the conversation and building on the analysis above. This comparison is facilitated by the similar word counts: Benedict's messages are just under 30,000 words, about 5,000 less than *Gaudium et Spes*. A working premise here, as Bishop De Roo suggests, is that while the laity may not need episcopal or papal direction in the same manner that they did previously,[57] there may still be value in critically assessing the content of that direction when it is offered. The analysis offered here may be illustrative of what the laity ought to be doing with Catholic social teaching: wrestling with it on the level of their moral imaginations.[58]

Social Justice in Benedict XVI's World Day of Peace Messages

Gaudium et Spes notes the advantages of economic and cultural development being shared by everyone (cf. GS 87). Benedict adds much to this reflection. His position can be summed up in his last World Day of Peace Message that "integral, sustainable development in solidarity and the common good require a correct scale of goods and values which can be structured with God as the ultimate point of reference."[59] He also frequently invokes Paul VI's notion of integral human development involving whole persons in all their dimensions.[60] In his message for 2010, Benedict states that economic development must keep in mind the natural environment and future generations.[61] A green, theo-ethical perspective on cultures of peace would also put forward a view of integral development; it would, however, insist on checking this vision for development more firmly against ecological limits than does Benedict's rendering. Moreover, it would question the value of dominant framings of progress and success, and seek to more persistently place integral human development within complex webs of social and ecological relationships.

Turning to another area of social justice, Benedict employs inclusive language in the English version of his World Day of Peace Messages (though not always in French translations). As part of a series of lectures on the history of the papacy, the University of Notre Dame religious historian Thomas F.X. Noble called John Paul II's and Benedict's thought on women "feminism of the highest order."[62] Benedict decries many unjust realities related to gender, noting, for instance, that human rights are not enjoyed by men and women equally around the world and that women are subjugated to arbitrary decision-making by men.[63] Yet, the Pope Emeritus also reproduces limiting, stereotypical gender roles around, for example, marriage and child rearing.[64] A green, ecoethical perspective on cultures of peace would generally agree with Benedict's view that gender equality is related to peace. However, again because of the green preference for praxis, gender equality could never be a secondary issue. Specific issues, such as the pressures placed on some women by patriarchy-related "requirements" to "produce" large numbers of children, would have to be considered from within particular sociocultural contexts.[65] Moreover, the institutional features of the Catholic Church that exclude people based partly on biological essentialism, though not addressed in these messages, could not be far from consideration from a green, ecoethical perspective. Most especially, regarding gender, moral consistency as received within particular sociopolitical contexts seems necessary for moral legitimacy.

Participation in Benedict XVI's World Day of Peace Messages

The thrust of the Second Vatican Council was clearly connected to more (if, admittedly, not complete) participatory structures in the Catholic Church. Remi De Roo writes,

> One of the key teachings of *Lumen Gentium* is the image of the People of God, chosen by divine initiative, not just as separate individuals but as a community, with Christ as its Head, already here on earth offering a seed of unity, hope and salvation for all humankind and the entire cosmos. We reminded ourselves that servant-leadership needs to replace domination

or power. The vertical and hierarchical development that, through the centuries, had shaped the governing Church institutions into a pyramid of power was cautiously redirected towards the more primitive and traditional image of the circle. For the first time ever, an Ecumenical Council recognized the rights of all the baptized. The laity have the right and sometimes the duty to express their opinions on matters pertaining to the common good, and pastors should leave them the freedom and scope for activity.[66]

The council thus marked a reaffirmation of subsidiarity.[67] Benedict XVI explicitly mentions participation only twice in his World Day of Peace Messages, both times in relation to fighting poverty. However, his second reference is definitive, extolling the value of an "*ethical approach to participation* capable of harnessing the contributions of civil society at local and international levels."[68] For its part, a green, ecoethical perspective on cultures of peace places a high moral value on participatory governance at all levels. Such a perspective would support Benedict's call for an ethical approach to participation, but would also emphasize that this moral position must be consistently applied. Given the green preference for praxis, this perspective may start by questioning why participatory decision-making is not more adequately modelled in the institutional life of the Catholic Church (especially beyond the episcopal level). It should be remembered that the freshness of the council was limited in that only the bishops really experienced participatory governance, with the likes of Dorothy Day – despite her impactful spiritual writings and contributions to the Catholic Worker Movement – not even being able to address the council because of her gender.[69]

Nonviolence in Benedict's World Day of Peace Messages

A key constitutive dimension of a green, theo-ethical lens, understood as intertwined with nonviolence, is respect for diversity. This respect is based on foundations of tolerance, empathy, and solidarity acting in concert. For example, green solidarity extends in multiple directions in terms of both people (e.g., social justice) and the larger life community (e.g., ecological wisdom). This is a deep solidarity based on a full conception of subsidiarity that refrains from advocating for the necessity of intervention by a higher power (and seeks to limit the quantity of power held vertically) due to a strong normative prefer-ence for participatory decision-making on issues located both within and across cultural contexts. As such, a cogent goal would be to find ways to form identity in such a manner that it is never crafted in po-tentially violent, exclusivist, or exclusionary categories.[70]

As demonstrated above, both Paul VI and *Gaudium et Spes* pro-vided a remarkable macro-level peace witness that decries arms rac-ing and modern warfare as untenable, practically and morally. It follows that they, in no uncertain terms, oppose the premise that international peace and security requires military power backed by high-technology armaments. Benedict continued this teaching tra-jectory in his exercise of the papal magisterial office in the World Day of Peace Messages. In his 2009 message, Benedict emphasized that military expenditures are, in fact, a source of poverty, diverting money that ought to be spent on aid to the world's neediest citizens. He added that such misplaced expenditures risk accelerating the arms race.[71] In 2008, Benedict noted that even developing nations too often allot a disproportional amount of their spending to arms, and urged all nations to agree on dismantling nuclear weapons: "It is truly necessary for all persons of good will to come together to reach concrete agreements aimed at *an effective demilitarization,* especially in the area of nuclear arms. At a time when the process of nuclear non-proliferation is at a stand-still, I feel bound to entreat those in authority to resume with greater determination negotia-tions for a *progressive and mutually agreed dismantling of existing nuclear weapons.* In renewing this appeal, I know that I am echoing the desire of all those concerned for the future of humanity."[72] This statement builds on his earlier assertion, made during his first World Day of Peace Message, that the "truth of peace" requires disarma-ment and that indifference to this truth in global and juridical pro-cesses needs to be overcome by the international community for the sake of humanity.[73]

The popes have recently been very clear that modern armaments and arms racing detract from prospects for peace. Through *Gaudium et Spes,* the council concurred in no uncertain terms. This feature of contemporary Catholic social teaching deserves praise from a green, ecoethical perspective. Arms reduction builds on the green political commitment to nonviolence in practical terms, and as such may be the most promising area of cooperation between green politics and the Holy See as it is informed by Benedict XVI's legacy. One could envision theo-ecoethically informed green politics gaining legitimacy through coalitions of action on this matter, as the Holy See and non-violent green activists work in harmony to foster cultures of peace. Indeed, mutual collaboration on climate justice is increasingly evident under Pope Francis.[74]

CONCLUSION

Thomas Berry argues that there is no way the human project can succeed if the earth project fails.[75] Building on this insight, a green, ecoethical perspective on cultures of peace adds that the content of human success is important, especially as it relates to social justice and the cosmic common good. The question for us all as we head toward 8 billion people[76] sharing "spaceship Earth"[77] is how to ensure that we can flourish as a planetary community under these demographic conditions. This chapter posits that both peace ecology generally and a green, ecoethical perspective on cultures of peace can help by reducing the impact of conflict stressors and offering a path to fair living.

It would follow that the presence of greener elements in the World Day of Peace Messages and the personal lifestyle example of the person who holds the chair of St Peter become matters of importance. So far, Pope Francis has seemed promising in this regard on a number of levels including his choice of name, simple living, invocation of an ethic of creation care, and solidarity with the poor, along with hints at moving toward an ecclesiastical governance framework that more fully embraces pontifical humility and subsidiarity.[78] However, it is also important to acknowledge that transformation has already occurred in terms of papal contributions to fostering cultures of peace. As late as 1956, Pius XII employed his Christmas Message to teach that conscientious objection against war was incompatible with Catholic morality.[79] Yet, a generation later, John Paul II was essentially a pacifist pope.[80] Continuing the work in process since the conciliar period of filling in the content of substantive peace in a green way can help ensure that the exercise of the papal teaching office, perhaps undertaken in a more publicly transparent and consultative manner,[81] will serve to foster cultures of peace in diverse contexts around the world. Something of that potential is evident in the impact of Pope Francis's aforementioned first social encyclical *Laudato Si'* (*On Care for Our*

Common Home). In all the excitement around the document, it is sometimes forgotten that Francis drew upon and adapted the messages of Benedict XVI (e.g., LS 206) in framing care for our common home as a green, theo-ecoethical imperative.[82]

Given the mixed legacy of the Pope Emeritus in regard to an integral vision of peace, Pope Francis's selective harvest of his predecessor's insights concerning the ethical tasks of building peace and caring for creation is particularly prescient for the relevance of Catholic social teaching today. Indeed, in light of an imperative to foster socioecological flourishing combined with that sometimes amorphous spirit of Vatican II, such careful, critical selection emerges as essential from a green, theo-ecoethical perspective carried forward through methodologies of *ressourcement, aggiornamento*, and reading the signs of the times. In this manner, as it continues to integrate a deeper green vision and practice of peace, Catholic social teaching and its promulgators can more fully participate in a turning to the world that helps sustain our planet as home to a diverse and flourishing community of life.

NOTES

1 The use of "Catholic" here denotes a narrow and hierarchical ecclesiology. An ecclesiology that supports a narrow and hierarchical definition of Catholic social teaching can be challenged from a green, ecoethical perspective, which favours participatory and discursive structures. However, for example, the consulting drafting process of the US bishops' *The Challenge of Peace* may point to other possibilities for Catholic social teaching. See National Conference of Catholic Bishops, *Challenge of Peace.*

2 See, for example, DeBerri and Hug, *Catholic Social Teaching.*

3 See Hrynkow, "A True Ecological Approach."

4 See De Roo, *Chronicles of a Vatican II Bishop*, 51–6, and De Roo's prologue in the present volume.

5 Qtd in Costello, *Our Sunday Visitor's Treasury*, 75.

6 For a watershed document marking the embrace of ecology as a theme in Catholic social teaching, see John Paul II, "Message of His Holiness."

7 Bevans, *Models of Contextual Theology*, 4.

8 See Dear, *God of Peace*, 115–25. John Dear argues that Vatican's II orientation toward *ressourcement* and scripture allows for an important recovery of the Gospel of Peace.

9 For example, a notice for a 2013 conference at Georgetown University's
   Berkley Center for Religion, Peace and World Affairs, marking the fiftieth
   anniversary of *Pacem in Terris*'s promulgation, defined the encyclical as
   "the *decisive* last will and testament of Pope John and the charter Vatican
   II needed to embrace an agenda for peace, human dignity and human
   rights" (emphasis added). Berkley Center for Religion, Peace and World
   Affairs, "Human Dignity."
10 The address of the letter is quite remarkable in itself. Although the encyclical uses gender-exclusive language as translated into English on the Vatican
   website, it does make a concerted effort to be inclusive in terms of the audience addressed: "To Our Venerable Brethren the Patriarchs, Primates,
   Archbishops, Bishops, and all other Local Ordinaries who are at Peace and
   in Communion with the Apostolic See, and to the Clergy and Faithful of the
   entire Catholic World, and to all Men of Good Will" (PT 1). Pope Francis
   reproduces this formula in his encyclical *Laudato Si'* on caring for our common home (LS 62) but also extends it to include "every person living on this
   planet" (LS 3).
11 This methodology of reading the "signs of the times" is not only associated with the Second Vatican Council but can be considered a biblical
   imperative: "The Pharisees and Sadducees came to Jesus and tested him by
   asking him to show them a sign from heaven. He replied, 'When evening
   comes, you say, "It will be fair weather, for the sky is red," and in the mor-
   ning, "Today it will be stormy, for the sky is red and overcast." You know
   how to interpret the appearance of the sky, but you cannot interpret the
   signs of the times'" (Matt. 16:1–3 [NIV]). *Sign of the Times* is also the title
   of Christian Peacemaker Teams' newsletter. For more on this group see
   Hrynkow, "Christian Peacemakers Teams."
12 Galtung, "Violence, Peace, and Peace Research," 183; see Müller,
   "Violence Typology by Johan Galtung."
13 See, for example, Boff, *Francis of Assisi.*
14 Paul VI, "Address to the United Nations Organization."
15 De Roo, "New Pentecost."
16 Part of this momentum was also provided by the famous Catholic peace
   activists Dorothy Day and Dom Hélder Câmara, campaigning in Rome
   during the conciliar sessions to urge that the bishops "did not forget the
   poor" in their statements. See Kaiser, "Stories of Vatican II."
17 Baum, *Amazing Church*, 44.
18 De Roo, "New Pentecost."
19 Peace studies scholars and conflict transformation practitioners have
   made a distinction between principled and pragmatic nonviolence.

Principled nonviolence suggests a relational rather than a utilitarian approach to peace-building. As a result, the distinction implies a preference for moving beyond the tactical use of nonviolence. Accordingly, a definitive feature of principled nonviolence is that it seeks consistency between means and ends in projects actively fostering positive social change. There is also a realm of confluence here between principled nonviolence's relational underpinnings and the insights of Pope John XXIII and the council fathers in this section. Together they help discern a substantive vision of peace, which, in turn, generates an imperative for nonviolent transformative change. On the distinction between principled and pragmatic nonviolence from a Gandhian perspective, see Bharadwaj, "Principled Versus Pragmatic Nonviolence"; cf., Sharpe, *Waging Nonviolent Struggle*.

20 Remi De Roo, who attended Vatican II while serving as bishop of Victoria, reported in a lecture in November 2012 that it was the intention of several of the council fathers that *Gaudium et Spes* outlaw war altogether. He asserted that the document would have contained such a condemnation were it not for the fear of "communist threat" at that time. De Roo, "New Pentecost."

21 Earlier in the document, they also noted the misappropriation of resources that accompanies military buildup: "The arms race is one of the greatest curses on the human race and the harm it inflicts on the poor is more than can be endured" (GS 81).

22 Interestingly, the Canadian Catholic Organization for Development and Peace cites its Catholic social teaching origins not in *Gaudium et Spes* but in Paul VI's 1967 encyclical *Populorum Progressio*, which makes explicit the connection between the terms development and peace: *Development is the new word for Peace*. Peace cannot be seen simply as the absence of war. It must be built daily, and it must strive towards a more perfect justice among human beings" (PP 76)." Note the emphasis on a positive conception of peace. See Development and Peace, "History."

23 See Gregory Baum's discussion of "the culture of peace" in his monograph *Amazing Church*, 83–100, and my previous reflections on *cultures* of peace in "Ecotheology and Inculturation."

24 See Global Greens, "Global Greens Congress 2001." Particularly helpful for sourcing the above was the *Spinifex* newsletters compiled at this link (though these now have to be searched independently due to a website update). A literature search reveals citations of the *Global Greens Charter* in diverse academic fields from the study of politics to health research. For example, Bentley, "An Ecological Public Health Approach."

25 This connection between ecologically unsustainable outcomes and social oppression is brought to the fore by Leonardo Boff in a number of his books. See, for example, Boff, *Cry of the Earth*.

26 Cf. Hrynkow, *"Laudato Si'."*

27 Berry, "Ethics and Ecology." He writes, "Relatively trivial human rights prevail over the urgent rights of the natural world simply for survival."

28 Eaton, "Forces of Nature," 109.

29 For example, Bartlett, *Living by Surprise*.

30 Gebara, "Ecofeminism," 103.

31 The Pew Center calculates that there were 2.18 billion Christians in the world in 2010. See "Global Christianity."

32 World Council of Churches, "Justice, Peace, Creation."

33 Cf. Rajotte, "Integrity of Creation"; Robra, "Theology of Life."

34 Cf. Taylor, "Earth and Nature-Based."

35 Swimme and Berry, *The Universe Story*, 254.

36 Francis, *Evangelii Gaudium*.

37 In the first part of this formulation, I am borrowing from a phrase that is often credited to Gandhi but certainly has resonance for those concerned with issues of peace, justice, and the integrity of creation.

38 Cf. Berry, *Evening Thoughts*, 28.

39 Cf. O'Sullivan, "Emancipatory Hope," 71.

40 Boff, *Virtues for Another Possible World*, 79.

41 See Hrynkow, "New Story."

42 Boff, *Virtues for Another Possible World*.

43 See Wink, *Powers That Be*, 184–5.

44 Bowler, *Blessed*, 3.

45 Câmara, *Spiral of Violence*.

46 Jacob, *New Pioneers*, 93.

47 Canadian Conference of Catholic Bishops, "You Love All That Exists," 15–17.

48 See Taylor, *Green Sisters*.

49 See Dominican Sisters of Blairstown, "Genesis Farm"; Green Mountain Monastery, "About Us."

50 See Ignatius Centre, "Project News"; Karsh, "Stations of the Cosmos." Of particular interest is not only the allocation of space but also the existence of events to pray for the earth at the Peace Pole (in a manner that connects earth and peace). In recent years, one such event directing people to meet at the peace pole was advertised on a local site in Guelph: "Gather to pray with and for Earth. Walk together on the land in its changing seasons.

Celebrate life and the gifts of Earth. Pray for the healing of our world"
(webpage no longer available).

51 The Ignatius Jesuit Centre presents itself as a place of peace, even in its
logo and web design. As the centre's mission and vision statement puts
it, "The Ignatius Jesuit Centre is a place of peace that welcomes a global
community of people who seek to integrate their inner and outer life
with God and with all Creation ... especially through spiritual development in the tradition of the Spiritual Exercises of St Ignatius of Loyola
and through deep engagement with this land." See "Mission and
Vision."

52 Uhser, Bryant, and Johnston, *Adult Education*, 184.

53 These principles are sourced from the Global Greens Charter, the central
document of the worldwide Green movement. Global Greens is an
umbrella organization founded to link the world's Green parties, and
social and political movements, in a goal-oriented partnership to enact the
Green principles. See the Global Greens webpages "About Us," "Global
Greens Charter," and "Global Greens Congress 2001."

54 Paul VI, "If You Want Peace, Work for Justice."

55 Benedict XVI, "In Truth, Peace."

56 Daniel Scheid speaks of the "cosmic common good" (existing beyond
intra-human moral bounds to embrace the entire created cosmos) when
fashioning his Thomistic ecotheological insights. See, Scheid, "Thomas
Aquinas, the Cosmic Common Good, and Climate Change," 125–44.

57 De Roo, "Living the Vision of Vatican II."

58 Mennonite conflict transformation practitioner, theorist, and Kroc
Institute for Peace faculty member at the University of Notre Dame, John
Paul Lederach characterizes an exercise of the moral imagination as "the
pursuit of moving relationships from fear, mutual recrimination and violence towards those characterized by love, mutual respect and proactive
engagement." Lederach, *Moral Imagination*, 42. See also GS 82.

59 Benedict XVI, "Blessed Are the Peacemakers," 5.

60 See, for example, Benedict XVI, "The Human Person," 9.

61 Benedict XVI, "Cultivate Peace, Protect Creation," 9.

62 Noble, *Popes and the Papacy*.

63 Benedict XVI, "The Human Person," 6–7.

64 See, for example, Benedict XVI, "Fighting Poverty to Build Peace," 5.

65 For an example of such a consideration see Masenya, "An Eco*bosadi*
Reading of Psalm 127.3–5."

66 De Roo, *Chronicles of a Vatican II Bishop*, 57.

67 The Catholic social teaching principle of subsidiarity states, "Just as it is
   gravely wrong to take from individuals what they can accomplish by their
   own initiative and industry and give it to the community, so also it is an
   injustice and at the same time a grave evil and disturbance of right order
   to assign to a greater and higher association what lesser and subordinate
   organizations can do. For every social activity ought of its very nature to
   furnish help to the members of the body social, and never destroy and
   absorb them" (QA 79).

68 Benedict XVI, "Fighting Poverty to Build Peace," 12.

69 Kaiser, "Stories of Vatican II." Blair Kaiser further argues that the laity in a
   diocese ought to democratically elect their bishops, which would not be
   participatory governance in a green, ecoethical sense but would at least
   move to a geographically based representative democratic feature within
   the Catholic hierarchy.

70 From a green, ecoethical perspective, Benedict has at times struggled in
   this area. Consider for example the ill-chosen unfolding of an argument
   connecting Islam and violence during his lecture at the University of
   Regensburg. See Benedict XVI, "Apostolic Journey."

71 Benedict XVI, "Fighting Poverty to Build Peace," 6.

72 Benedict XVI, "The Human Family," 14.

73 Benedict XVI, "In Truth, Peace," 13–14.

74 See Hrynkow, "The Pope, the Planet, and Politics."

75 Berry, "Christianity's Role," 127.

76 At the time of the last edits for this chapter, there are just under 7.5 billion
   people in the world. We are projected to reach a global population of 8
   billion people in 2025. See Worldometers, "Real Time World Statistics."

77 This concept was developed by the Quaker peace theorist Kenneth
   Boulding during the same period as the Second Vatican Council. See
   Boulding, "Earth as a Space Ship."

78 These themes were, for example, raised in Francis's first homily as Bishop
   of Rome. See Francis, "Protect Creation Says Pope"; Hrynkow, "No to
   War."

79 See Genilo, *John Cuthbert Ford, SJ*, 35–9.

80 It should be noted that John Paul II rejected the label of pacifist in 1991,
   stating that Catholics do not want peace at any price, and adding that
   peace without justice was untenable (two positions that a green, ecoethical
   perspective might argue are compatible with pacifism). Nonetheless, he
   became widely known for his opposition to war under current technological conditions. See John Paul II, "We Are Not Pacifists," 625; Allman,

Who Would Jesus Kill? 188–92; and Yoder on "the pacifism of the honest study of cases" in *Nevertheless*, 22–8; cf. Francis, "Nonviolence: A Style of Politics for Peace."

81 The drafting process of *Laudato Si'* offers a case in point here, but a stronger antecedent is the consultative methodology that the US bishops employed in crafting *The Challenge of Peace: God's Promise and Our Response*. See Hrynkow, "Challenge of Peace," 130–1.

82 Benedict XVI, "The Human Family." Benedict introduced the concept of "responsible cooperation" in caring for our "common home" in this World Day of Peace Message for 2008.

9

The Priority of Social Justice at the Second Vatican Council: Canadian Contributions

Catherine E. Clifford

Any reflection on the last half-century of Catholic social teaching and its reception must give careful consideration to the context of the Second Vatican Council itself and the extent to which the church's understanding and commitment to peace and social justice were central elements of the council's agenda. These priorities are most apparent in the orientations for the council laid out by Pope John XXIII and further developed by Pope Paul VI. The centrality of peace and social justice can also be seen in the evolution of the council itself, as the council fathers redirected the conciliar agenda so that it might express more clearly the church's "turning to the world." As I hope to show, the Canadian bishops played a significant role in the council's embrace of the world *ad extra* in an attitude of humble service and solidarity. As well, they were instrumental in promoting the reception of the council's teaching on peace and justice in the Canadian context in a manner that was exemplary for the wider church.

POPE JOHN XXIII AND THE AGENDA OF THE COUNCIL

The encyclical letters of John XXIII provide an important orientation for the teaching of the Second Vatican Council on justice and peace. In his 1961 letter *Mater et Magistra* (*On Christianity and Social Progress*), published while preparations for the council were under way, John XXIII began to model a new openness and a style of discourse that was much more engaged with the modern world, recognizing much that was positive in the developments of secular society and in the aspirations of contemporary men and women for justice and human rights. Building on the teaching of his predecessors, he recognized a number of important developments that called for new thinking and new forms of action. The world was fast changing due to scientific and technological progress, including the nuclear science that had been used for both peaceful and destructive ends, and advances in technology that were changing the means of production, mass communication, and transportation. He recognized positive signs of social progress in the growing presence of worker movements, the establishment of social security nets, increased access to education, and improved standards of living. In the political sphere, he observed the end of overt European colonialism in Asia and Africa and new movements that favoured increased citizen participation and growing democratization (MM 47–9).

Nonetheless, he noted that these positive signs of social, economic, and political progress were at times accompanied by a growing disparity between rich and poor, unequal access to basic public services, and the failure to respect the rights of all to the basic necessities of human life: food, shelter, health care, education, a decent job, and a just wage. New social institutions were required to ensure that these basic needs were met. John XXIII called Catholics to promote these basic human rights and to work for the creation of social institutions that respect the dignity of every person in social, economic, and political life. Building on the teachings of Popes Leo XIII and Pius XI, he also argued for the need to limit the uses and distribution of private property to the extent that it might be placed at the service of the common good.

John XXIII's teaching in *Mater et Magistra* places an important emphasis on the increasing network of social relationships that accompanied this new phase of human history. In light of this new sense of interconnectedness, the processes of socialization and education in the principles of justice and the common good were taking on a new significance. He understood that Catholics are not only called to contribute to the common good, they are also shaped by it. By "common good," I mean the social conditions that enable each person to attain his or her fulfillment as a human being. The promotion of the common good entails respect for the person, including the right of each to follow his or her conscience. It seeks to balance the aspirations of individuals with the well-being of the wider community. The common good transcends the good of the individual person, which cannot be considered in isolation from the whole community. John XXIII knew that the manner in which we live, act, and structure our social interactions will have a profound effect on the formation of successive generations of citizens.

In a number of speeches leading up to the opening of the Second Vatican Council, John laid the themes of peace and justice on the hearts of the bishops who would gather to reflect on the life and mission of the church in the contemporary world. In the text of his announcement of the ecumenical council, delivered on 25 January 1959, he noted the "misuse and deprivation of human freedom" in the world and expressed concern that, while great strides were being made in technological and material progress, the spiritual vocation of humanity was not always kept in view.[1] He spoke with considerable optimism regarding social progress in his apostolic letter *Humanae Salutis*, of 25 December 1961, which contained an official convocation of the council for the following year. Noting that the world was "witnessing a crisis" in a society marked at once by great material progress and waning "values of the spirit," he called Catholic leaders to discern in "the signs of the times" (cf. Mark 16:4) a promise of hope and the desire for genuine human flourishing. Experiences of global conflict, of failed ideologies, and of scientific progress have "obliged human beings to become more thoughtful, more conscious of their own limitations, desirous of peace, and attentive to the importance of spiritual values."[2] This new consciousness presented the church with an opportunity to speak to the deepest aspirations of the human community. "The forthcoming council," he wrote, "must offer a possibility for all men of good will to turn their thoughts and their intentions toward peace, a peace which can and must, above all come from spiritual and supernatural realities, from human intelligence and conscience, enlightened and guided by God the Creator and Redeemer of humanity."[3] The council would therefore aim to show its solidarity with the whole human community, and work to bring the light of Christ to bear on a more human social order, helping others "to discover in themselves their own nature, their own dignity, their own end."[4] The church was to champion the rights and responsibilities of all persons and communities.

Just one month before the official opening of the council, John gave an important radio address to the Catholic faithful of the world.[5] In it, he spoke of the call of the church to reflect the light of Christ in the world, noting that the council was to be concerned with the renewal of the church both in its "internal vitality" and in its "external vitality." The church was preparing to speak on many of the problems of the modern world, and sought to foster "the administration and the distribution of created goods ... in a way that is to the benefit of everyone." Meeting seventeen years after the end of the Second World War, the council would proclaim a word about peace: "not just in its negative form – detestation of armed conflict – but much more in terms of its positive demands which call for every man to be aware of his own duties and to live up to them constantly."[6] In the historic Opening Address given in the presence of the bishops gathered from throughout the world on 11 October 1962, John reaffirmed his confidence in the opportunities presented by modern social progress. While remaining faithful to the heritage of the gospel, he observed that the church must attend to the present, in particular "to the new conditions and new forms of life introduced into the modern world which have opened new avenues to the Catholic apostolate."[7] The council, therefore, was to discern new ways and means to advance the church's mission in the service of justice and peace.

MESSAGE OF THE COUNCIL TO THE WORLD

The council opened officially on 11 October 1962, at a moment of great tension in the drawn-out conflict of the Cold War between the Western Alliance and the Soviet Union. Indeed, the first two weeks of the council took place against the backdrop of the October Crisis (14–28 October) – a confrontation between the Soviet Union and Cuba on one side and the United States on the other – that brought the world to the verge of nuclear war. On 20 October 1962, the bishops issued their first message from the council to the world.[8] It is striking to note the vision of the church as the humble servant of humankind that characterizes this brief message. This text also contains an important expression of solidarity with the whole human community, a theme that would be developed more fully just three years later in *Gaudium et Spes* (*Pastoral Constitution on the Church in the Modern World*): "Faith, hope, and the love of Christ impel us to serve our brothers, thereby, patterning ourselves after the example of the Divine Teacher, who 'came not to be served but to serve' (Matt. 20:28). Hence, the Church too was not born to dominate but to serve. He laid down his life for us, and we too ought to lay down our lives for our brothers (1 John 3:16)."[9]

The bishops gathered in Rome from the four corners of the earth were a reflection of a truly global community. They bore in themselves the lived experience of the churches and the aspirations of men and women from a remarkable variety of cultures and contexts. They were moved to a sense of profound solidarity with all humanity, as we can hear in the words of their message: "Coming together in unity from every nation under the sun, we carry in our hearts the hardships, the bodily and mental distress, the sorrows, longings, and hopes of all the peoples entrusted to us. We urgently turn our thoughts to all the anxieties by which modern man is afflicted. Hence, let our concern swiftly focus first of all on those who are especially lowly, poor, and weak. Like Christ, we would have pity on the multitude weighed down with hunger, misery, and lack of knowledge. We want to fix a steady gaze on those who still lack the opportune help to achieve a way of life worthy of human beings."[10] Very quickly, the bishops of Vatican II became aware of the importance of their coming together as a symbol of the gathered church from throughout the world and a hopeful sign for the unity and peace of the whole human community: "This very conciliar congress of ours, so impressive in the diversity of races, nations, and languages it represents, does it not bear witness to a community of brotherly love, and shine as a visible sign of it? We are giving witness that all men are brothers, whatever their race or nation."[11] Making their own the teaching of *Mater et Magistra* and the convictions of John XXIII's prophetic radio message, the council fathers committed themselves to working together with all people of good will for peace among all peoples and for the establishment of "social justice" informed by the gospel, recognizing these as issues of "special urgency."

John XXIII expanded on some of these themes in his final encyclical, *Pacem in Terris*, published in April 1963, in the period between the first and second sessions of the council and just a few months before his death. Reflecting this new consciousness of the vocation of the church as the servant of humanity, he called the nations to put an end to the arms race and redouble their efforts to work for genuine peace among nations. *Pacem in Terris* dealt with a number of themes that would be at the centre of the council's reflections: the basic human rights proper to each person, the relationship between authority and the individual conscience, peace and disarmament, and the common good. Foreshadowing the engaging and dialogical tone of the council's *Pastoral Constitution on the Church in the Modern World*, *Pacem in Terris* marks the first time in history that a papal teaching was addressed not only to members of the church, but to all people of good will. It proposes a vision of peace that is closely related to justice. More than the absence of war, John XXIII urged all peoples to work for a peace that is built on the pillars of truth, justice, charity, and freedom. In his view, authentic peace is not possible without full respect for the rights of others and without each and every member of society carrying out their responsibilities as fellow citizens.

POPE PAUL VI

Very soon after his election, Paul VI committed himself to carrying out the program set out by John XXIII for the council. Indeed, he was anxious to put the council's commitment to peace and justice into action through a number of prophetic gestures and symbolic voyages. In November 1963, in an act of renunciation of temporal power and to show his solidarity with the poor, he set aside his papal tiara and discontinued many ceremonial elements that surrounded an imperial model of the papacy. Soon afterward, in December 1964, Paul VI travelled to India as a humble pilgrim to signify the solidarity of the church with the poor and the dispossessed. Meeting with Hindu and Muslim leaders, Paul VI echoed the council's desire to collaborate with all people in the creation of a more just world order, asking, "Are we not all one in this struggle for a better world, in this effort to make available to all people those goods which are needed to fulfill their human destiny and to live lives worthy of the children of God?"[12] While in India he addressed a prophetic message to the world, asking the nations to put an end to the arms race, "devote their resources and energies instead to the fraternal assistance of the developing countries," and contribute to an international fund that would provide the basic needs of food, shelter, and medical care to those who live in poverty.[13]

Before the opening of the third session of Vatican II, where the bishops would deliberate on the draft document that formed the basis of *Gaudium et Spes*, Paul published an encyclical letter, *Ecclesiam Suam*, in which he reflected on the ways the church was called to carry out its mission in contemporary society. In his effort to promote a sincere dialogue between the church and the modern world, Paul drew attention once again to the urgent matter of world peace. He committed himself and the whole Catholic community to doing all in its power to foster justice and peace:

> It is a problem which demands our continuous personal involve-
> ment and practical concern, exercised of course within the limits
> of our ministry and entirely divorced from any set political
> theory and from considerations of our own personal and purely
> temporal advantage. Our aim must be to educate mankind to
> sentiments and policies which are opposed to violent and deadly
> conflicts and foster just, rational, and peaceful relations between
> states. We will do our utmost to promote harmonious relations
> and a spirit of cooperation between nations, and we will do so
> by proclaiming principles which represent the highest achieve-
> ment of human thought, and such as are best calculated to
> allay selfishness and greed from which war takes its rise ... Our
> mission is to bring men together in mutual love through that
> kingdom of justice and peace which Christ inaugurated by his
> coming into the world.[14]

On 4 October 1965, as the council was meeting for its final session, Paul VI was invited to address a special assembly of the United
Nations in New York. In that speech he made an impassioned plea
for peace, founded on justice. He urged, "No more war, never again
war. Peace, it is peace that must guide the destinies of people and of
all mankind."[15] Paul VI welcomed the opportunity to encourage the
members of the United Nations in their efforts to resolve international conflict and the challenges posed by social inequities by means
of reasoned negotiation, the rule of law, and the principles of justice,
rather than by force and violent means.

GAUDIUM ET SPES: CANADIAN CONTRIBUTIONS AND RECEPTION

Gaudium et Spes, the council's *Pastoral Constitution on the Church in the Modern World,* symbolizes, perhaps more than any other conciliar text, the church's turn to the world and conveys the council's teaching on the common good. Canadian bishops played a significant role in the council's engagement with the modern world and in the debates relating to this document. In the remainder of this chapter, I explore the role of some of these Canadians in the promotion and reception of the council's teaching and commitment to peace and social justice.

Cardinal Paul Émile Léger of Montreal was an important presence on the Central Preparatory Commission, which worked from 1960 to 1962. Prior to the opening of the council in October 1962, he had addressed a letter of great significance to John XXIII. This letter, co-signed by six other cardinals who would play leading roles in determining the direction of the council (Suenens, Frings, Alfrink, Döpfner, Liénart, and König), conveyed his deep concern regarding the inadequacy of the draft documents that were being presented to the bishops. In his estimation, they were scolding in their tone, overly scholastic in style, and failed to engage constructively with the signs of the times, in accordance with the pope's guiding vision. He wrote, "Several schemas consider the church too much as an institution under siege which the council must defend and fail to see her as the shining custodian of a salvation to be shared with others. The church appears there as more of a juridical than a missionary institution. One dare not turn freely toward the contemporary world, toward its needs, towards its new and legitimate demands."[16]

For Léger and many other bishops, if the council failed to turn to the world in compassion and solidarity, it would prove to be a dismal failure, and the church would have missed an opportunity to carry out its mission in a profoundly changed global context. His letter received a sympathetic hearing from John XXIII, who welcomed the initiative of Cardinal Suenens on 4 December 1962, in the concluding days of the first session, to substantially revise the work of the council and to orient its reflection along the axes of the life of the church *ad intra* and *ad extra*.[17] Léger, Suenens, and others were concerned not only about the content of the council's teaching, but about its style. They called for a more pastoral style and for a less juridical and scholastic language. The language and style of many of the schemata proposed by the Preparatory Commissions reflected an attitude that had dominated in official Catholic discourse and theology since the traumatic chapter of the French Revolution, a wound reinforced by the shocks of the Italian *Risorgimento* and the German *Kulturkampf*. Disoriented by the systematic unseating of the church from European centres of power and the end of the long marriage between throne and altar represented by the separation of church and state and the increasing prevalence of religious pluralism, the Catholic Church had assumed a stance that was insular and defensive. Catholicism was for the most part anti-Modern, anti-Enlightenment, and anti-Protestant.[18] The church's "turn to the world" at Vatican II signified a decisive break with anti-Modern reactionism and a commitment to a constructive engagement in, with, and for the world. It was, as John O'Malley has observed, "the end of the long nineteenth century."[19]

The council fathers called on the conciliar commissions to adopt a language and style of teaching that would be more dialogical and more engaging, one that would inspire contemporary men and women. Pope Paul VI's extended reflections on dialogue as the principal mode by which the church is to carry out its mission were contained in his encyclical *Ecclesiam Suam*, published mid-way through the council in August 1964. It exemplifies the council fathers' vision of the church's turn to the world. The modern Catholic Church could no longer dictate a set of abstract principles for living in the world from "on high" as it were, but had to rethink its place "in the world" – as a partner – in the process of transforming the world and working in the service of humanity.

Gaudium et Spes embodies the "pastoral" style of the church's mission and engagement in the world, in humility and in solidarity with the "joys and hopes, the grief and anguish" of humanity (GS 1). While others in this volume discuss the council's teaching on social justice and the common good in greater detail, I would like to draw attention to two key texts that can help us appreciate more fully the church's "turning to the world" and commitment to social justice at Vatican II. Article 55 of *Gaudium et Spes* is worth citing at length:

> In each nation and social group there is a growing number of men and women who are conscious that they themselves are the architects and molders of their community's culture. All over the world the sense of autonomy and responsibility increases with effects of the greatest importance for the spiritual and moral maturity of humankind. This will become clearer to us if we advert to the unification of the world and the duty imposed on us to build up a better world in truth and justice. We are witnessing the birth of a new humanism, where people are defined before all else by their responsibility to their sisters and brothers and at the court of history.

The American ecclesiologist and scholar of Vatican II Joseph Komonchak points to the importance of this particular text in helping us understand the extent to which the changing context of world history influenced the changing consciousness of the church.[20] The council speaks of a new age in human history where the human community is coming to awareness, as never before, of its capacity to determine the course of history and to shape the kind of world or society we desire to live in. As a corollary of this new consciousness, or "new humanism," the church as well is newly conscious of its life and mission, of its freedom and responsibility *in* the world, to be – with the help of God's grace – an artisan with others of culture and of a just society. The church, therefore, commits itself to cooperate with all people of good will in the promotion of the common good.

To embody the Catholic commitment to carry out this task on the international stage, the council exhorts competent members of the church to collaborate in national and international associations and organizations and to cooperate with other Christians in working for peace and a more just social order. In order to coordinate these many activities on the international level, *Gaudium et Spes* called for the establishment of "some organization of the universal church whose task it would be to encourage the catholic community to promote the progress in areas which are in want and foster social justice between nations" (GS 90). This new organization, the Pontifical Commission (today Pontifical Council) *Justitia et Pax* (Justice and Peace), was established by Paul VI on 6 January 1967 with the mandate of putting the council's teaching into practice.[21] To lead the new Pontifical Commission, Paul VI appointed Cardinal Maurice Roy. Roy would serve as president of the new dicasteries for the laity and for justice until his resignation in 1976. He did so while continuing to serve as the archbishop of the Diocese of Quebec.

When we revisit the history of the conciliar debates, it is interesting to note that there were probably more interventions on the part of Canadian bishops during the discussion of *Gaudium et Spes* than of any other schema at the council.[22] Cardinals Paul-Émile Léger and Maurice Roy, both members of the doctrinal commission, were actively involved in subcommissions charged with the drafting of the schema. Indeed, Roy had served on subcommissions that gave shape to important aspects of both the *Pastoral Constitution on the Church in the Modern World* and the council's *Decree on the Apostolate of the Laity (Apostolicam Actuositatem)*. The fact that Paul VI closely associated the activities of these two commissions is an indication that he and the council saw the church's engagement in the world and work for justice and peace as integral to the life and witness of every baptized member of the church.

During the Second Vatican Council, the Canadian Conference of Catholic Bishops (CCCB) established an office for Social Action. The Jesuit economist William Ryan served as the first co-director of the new Social Action (later Social Affairs) office (1964–70). Reflecting on the years immediately following the council, Ryan writes, "I believe that the CCCB was the primary agent in interpreting, communicating, and fostering a new way of being the Canadian church in the world, both domestically and globally."[23] In the early 1960s the Canadian government was moving toward the adoption of a system of universal health care. The staff of the Social Action office were actively engaged in studying the report of the Hall Royal Commission on universal medicare. This exploration quickly broadened to include collaboration in a coalition that included representatives of the Canadian labour movement and other Christian churches. In 1965, staff members took part in an important conference in Ottawa on Canada's Health Charter organized by the Canadian Council of Churches. In the decade that followed the council, there was close collaboration between the Social Action office and the newly established Pontifical Commission *Justitia et Pax*.[24]

Another important development that contributed to the converging efforts of the Commission for Justice and Peace and the Canadian Church was the establishment, in 1968, of the Canadian Catholic Organization for Development and Peace by the Canadian bishops. They did so in response to Paul VI's encyclical letter *Populorum Progressio* (*On the Development of Peoples*) of March 1967.[25] Paul VI's vision of development entailed far more than purely economic development and the just distribution of material goods. It extended to the integral development and flourishing of the human person and of human communities in all their diversity. Integral human development implies more than economic development, but entails the satisfaction of needs for food, water, shelter, security, intellectual and spiritual growth – in short, a holistic approach to the development of the whole person within a complex network of social relationships. In a theme that echoes *Gaudium et Spes,* Paul VI presented every person and every human community as an authentic subject that must be empowered to become "artisans of their own destiny" (PP 65). He called Christians in every context to a critical application of the principles of the pre-conciliar Catholic Action movement – "see, judge, act" – that is, to carry out an objective analysis, in their particular context, of concrete social problems of life using the best resources from the sciences, and to propose responses for action by church and society in light of the gospel. Development and Peace was to be an instrument for this study, reflection, and action for the Canadian context. Cardinal Roy's influence weighed heavily in the Canadian bishops' unanimous decision to launch Development and Peace.[26]

One of the hallmarks of Catholic engagement in favour of justice and peace in Canada was the church's commitment to act ecumenically whenever possible. Ryan was invited through ecumenical networks to be a Catholic participant in the World Council of Churches' international conference on Church and Society in 1966 – one of the first Catholics authorized to take part in an official WCC meeting. The Canadian participants at that meeting returned home determined to organize a conference on world poverty. This meeting was held in Montreal in 1968 and gathered together leaders of the Canadian churches as well as forty representatives of nongovernmental organizations working on issues of social concern. In sponsoring this event, the Canadian bishops were inspired by the exploratory agency for Social Development and Peace (SODEPAX), a joint project of the Pontifical Commission for Justice and Peace and the World Council of Churches that operated from 1966 until 1981.

Following the Montreal gathering, an effort was made to organize a broad coalition of actors from the Canadian churches, labour movements, and NGOs. While it did not survive, this experiment prepared the way for a uniquely Canadian approach to engagement in social justice initiatives, namely, the ecumenical coalitions, which included Project Ploughshares, Gatt-Fly, Project North, the Taskforce on the Churches and Corporate Responsibility, the Canada-Asia Working Group, the Interchurch Committee on Human Rights in Latin America, the Interchurch Committee for Refugees, and the Interchurch Coalition on Africa. By the 1990s, there were eleven coalitions in all. In 2001, these initiatives were reorganized under the umbrella of KAIROS.[27] The development of the Canadian coalitions for social justice was a model of effective ecumenical witness for the churches worldwide.

Ryan has commented that the establishment of the coalitions was something of a frustration for Roy, who hoped that the Canadian bishops would develop a National Justice and Peace Commission to work in parallel with the Pontifical Commission in Rome, one that might be an example for other countries.[28] For various reasons, no such commission emerged within the structures of the CCCB. However, a Commission on Justice and Peace took shape and continues to function in the context of the Canadian Council of Churches with the full participation of the CCCB.[29]

Another important and sometimes forgotten symbol of Canada's role in the reception of Vatican II's commitment to social justice can be found in the letter of Paul VI, *Octogesima Adveniens* (*A Call to Action*), published in 1971 to celebrate the eightieth anniversary of *Rerum Novarum*, the first of the modern social encyclicals. Written on the eve of the Synod on Justice in the World, it was framed as a letter to Cardinal Maurice Roy, president of the Council of Laity and of the Pontifical Commission on Justice and Peace. Jacques Racine has commented on the unique epistolary form of this papal document:

> [Paul VI] wanted in this way not so much to call attention to the person of the Cardinal, but to his role in two institutions established by Vatican II in the same line with the Pastoral Constitution *Gaudium et spes*. It is these institutions that were called – by the very fact that they were carrying it forward – to promote this new relationship with the world and the involvement of Christian communities in the transformation of society. He called them as well to nourish papal reflection and discourse. He entrusted them with the task of "awakening in the people of God a full understanding of their role" and of "promoting the apostolate on the international level." Paul VI wanted to maintain relations between Catholicism and the political world not only through the agency of nunciatures, but through a committed laity and through the Justice and Peace Commissions of the bishops' conferences which were more able to discern the modes of intervention best suited to the church in each place.[30]

Paul VI's letter to Roy is remarkable for the confidence it conveys in the co-responsibility of all the baptized for the mission of the church in the world and for the recognition of the role of the local churches. His recognition of the necessity for the churches to read and interpret the signs of the times in each context reflects a striking application of the principle of subsidiarity. Paul VI's insistence on the need for dialogue as the means by which this ongoing discernment is to be carried out reveals a profound understanding of the synergy and creativity that is generated in the church when the diverse gifts of all the faithful are brought together in the service of its mission. His letter might be characterized as a call to "action in communion," or perhaps to "communion in action."

Further receiving the council's vision, the 1971 Synod on Justice in the World would teach that "action on behalf of justice and participation in the transformation of the world fully appear ... as a constitutive dimension of preaching the Gospel" (JM 6). Inspired by this vision, the CCCB and its commissions produced more than a hundred statements from the conciliar period up until 1990, which were later compiled in Edward Sheridan's two volumes, *Do Justice!* and *Love Kindness!* These statements reflect a concerted effort to receive and apply to the Canadian context the insights of *Gaudium et Spes, Populorum Progressio, Octagesima Adveniens,* and *Justitia in Mundo.*

CONCLUSION

The Second Vatican Council marked an historic effort on the part of the Catholic Church to turn to the world in solidarity and in service. Concern for social justice and peace runs like a common thread through the conciliar teaching. Significantly, the council sought not only to teach *about* justice, but recognized that serious engagement in action for transformation of society would require new structures for study, dialogue, and action. As well, it recognized that the Catholic community could not exercise this constitutive aspect of proclaiming the gospel in isolation from others who shared its faith in Christ, or who were committed to the values of human dignity and the common good. This cursory effort to revisit the context of Vatican II reveals that Canadians made significant contributions both to the council's "turn to the world" and to the reception of that commitment into the structure, life, and witness of the Catholic Church in Canada. We may rightly ask how that commitment to read the signs of the times can be carried forward in the context of the twenty-first century.

NOTES
1 John XXIII, "Announcement," 398–401.
2 John XXIII, *Humanae Salutis,* 704.
3 Ibid., 706.

4 Ibid., 707.

5 John XXIII, "*Ecclesia Christi*," 105a–c.

6 Ibid., 105c.

7 John XXIII, "Pope John's Opening Speech," 714.

8 The impetus for this text came from Marie-Dominique Chenu; see *Notes*, 60–3.

9 "Message to Humanity," in *Documents of Vatican II*, 4–5.

10 Ibid., 5.

11 Ibid., 6.

12 Paul VI, "New Era," 153.

13 Paul VI, "Special Message," 158–9.

14 Paul VI, *Ecclesiam Suam*, 16.

15 Paul VI, "Discours du Pape Paul VI à l'organisation des Nations Unies."

16 Léger, "Lettre inédite du Cardinal Paul-Émile Léger au Pape Jean XXIII en août 1962," 107–8 (my translation). For a fuller discussion, see Routhier, "Les réactions du Cardinal Leger a la préparation de Vatican II."

17 For a fuller account of Suenens's plan to restructure the work of the council, see "Aux origines du concile Vatican II"; an English translation is found in "A Plan for the Whole Council." See also Suenens, *Souvenirs et espérances*, 55–131; Lamberigts and Declerck, "Role of Cardinal Léon-Joseph Suenens." Lamberigts and Declerck see parallels between Suenens's plan and John XXIII's Radio Address on 11 September 1962 on the eve of the council (ibid., 74). For the text of his speech, see *Acta Apostolicae Sedis*.

18 See Komonchak, "Modernity."

19 O'Malley, *What Happened at Vatican II?*; see John XXIII, "Announcement."

20 I am indebted to Fr Komonchak's lecture, "Legacy of Vatican II."

21 Paul VI, *Catholicam Christi Ecclesiam* (6 January 1967). After a ten-year experimental period, Paul VI gave the commission its definitive status with the Motu Proprio *Justitiam et Pacem* (10 December 1976). When the apostolic constitution *Pastor Bonus* (28 June 1988) reorganized the Roman Curia, Pope John Paul II changed its name from Commission to Pontifical Council and reconfirmed the general lines of its work.

22 See the interventions in the *Acta Synodalia Sacrosancti Concilii Oecumenici Vaticani II* (vol. 3, part 5), by Hermaniuk, 296–8; Roy, 322–3; and De Roo, 529–31.

23 Ryan, "Legacy of Gaudium et Spes," 2.

24 Ibid., 5.

25 See Beaudin, "*Populorum Progressio*."

26 Ryan, "Influence of Paul VI and Cardinal Roy," 204.
27 KAIROS, "Who We Are."
28 Ryan, "Influence of Paul VI and Cardinal Roy," 205.
29 Canadian Council of Churches, "Commission on Justice and Peace."
30 Racine, "Lettre de Paul VII au cardinal Maurice Roy," 146 (my translation).

10

The Search for the Common Good in Canada

Mary Jo Leddy

I remember hearing about Vatican II in my last years of high school in Saskatoon. It sounded like something important and yet very distant, far away, over there across oceans of difference.

Nevertheless, as the years passed, Vatican II would affect my life profoundly: how I thought and acted, what I believed, where I lived and with whom. In a mysterious way, the event that happened far away in Europe would lead me back to here, back to Canada, rediscovering the context of my faith *here*.

Throughout the documents of Vatican II, there is constant reference to the context of faith. Faith was not something dropped from heaven, not something abstracted from cultures and societies. The council took the context of Europe seriously, the joys and sufferings of the modern world, a world wrecked by war and prejudice, a world of the middle class and its modern questions about the existence of God. The council also encouraged scholars to study the context in which scripture was written.

After Vatican II, the challenge of taking context seriously was taken up by the churches of Latin America. While appreciating the answers of theologies shaped by the experience of Europe, these theologians began asking a different set of questions. Their burning question was not so much about the existence of God as about the existence of poverty. How could the church speak about the love of God in the face of such poverty? The emergence of a contextual theology in Latin America was exciting and challenging for many in the church. Liberation theology was debated intensely. Catholics throughout the world listened to the preaching of the gospel through the church of the martyrs. It seemed obvious that the common good had to include responding to the needs of the poor.

I was galvanized by the life and theology of Latin America, excited by the profound link between faith and justice that was being established in the church. I was drawn into an effort to articulate this through an independent, national Catholic newspaper called *Catholic New Times*. It became a voice for church groups across the country that were acting and speaking in ways that sought to integrate their faith with justice.

In the editorial team, we identified our challenge as that of trying to articulate a liberation theology for Canada. However, I began to notice that our efforts were not working. Only the most committed, the usual suspects, were interested in the issues raised by liberation theology. Our readers would be moved, but only for a while, by the suffering and martyrdom of the churches in Latin America. For a while we tried writing more, writing better about Latin America. We laid on the guilt. It became obvious that our words were not leaving the page, not lifting people to action.

Then a messenger came. He was an elderly gentleman, a business-man who worked with a large Canadian mining company. He came in once every two weeks to help us lay out the paper (an arduous task in the days before computers). His daughter was the design artist for the paper, and it was a chance for them to be together. He would read the stories about Latin America in a dubious sort of way: "I read these stories about the mining companies but I think you had better check your sources. I work for a mining company, and I'm sure they would never treat their employees that way." I told him that our sources were often Canadian missionaries who had seen the violence against union members and against the priests who worked with them. We would agree to disagree.

Then one day this messenger came in and said, simply, "I think the stories are true." I asked him why he had changed his mind. "I was fired yesterday, after thirty years. And I thought if they can do this to me here, they can do anything there." In a flash of insight I realized that we would never build a bridge to understanding liberation the-ology in Latin America until we began to write from *here*. And then we might bridge the gap between here and there.

WHERE IS HERE?

I soon learned that writing from here, not just about Canada but from within Canada, was a far more daunting task. It was not just a matter of taking some facts about Canada and splicing them together with some quotes from scripture or Vatican II or liberation theology. It was a matter of articulating, naming a context that was almost invisible to us because it was so near and so dear. The cadence of one's own language is the hardest to hear because it does not sound different. It is background noise, the silence between the words, a rhythm as familiar as a heartbeat.

Fortunately, I realized that a whole generation of Canadian writers and artists were engaged in the task of trying to "name" this place that we call Canada. They are the handmaidens of theology, those who "name" a reality before we know it in more analytic or systematic ways.

Given the limits of this chapter, I will mention only a few of the insights that led me back to here, to my place in the world. I am particularly indebted to Northrop Frye and Margaret Atwood in this effort. Although later writers and my experience of living with people of different cultures have also helped me to name this particular place on earth, the insights of Frye and Atwood are still a good place to begin.[1]

Northrop Frye was an internationally recognized literary critic who spent a lifetime identifying more abstract literary forms, and yet he had a definite interest in Canadian culture. Culture, he wrote, is always located, it is never general and abstract: "There is something vegetable about the imagination."[2] It arises from a specific place and time. However, he emphasized that we in Canada have a hard time imagining our place because of our colonial position in the world. Canada has always been a colony of some imperial power – first of France, then of England, and now of America. Thus we grow up thinking of our lives in reference to some place elsewhere, by *there* rather than *here*. Our ways of thinking, of acting, of conducting our lives are more influenced by centres of power elsewhere rather than here. We think the real political and economic decisions that determine our lives are made in head offices elsewhere. People in a colony look elsewhere to study, elsewhere to define art and ideas, elsewhere to blame for what is wrong in the world. We define our identities according to how we think other people see us, as rather boring and somewhat irrelevant.

Frye suggested that the most important question a writer in Canada must begin with is "Where is here?" He is saying this because *here* is what disappears if you live your personal and social life dominated by the culture and economics shaped by elsewhere. In other more established cultures, such as those in Europe or even in the United States, thinkers can afford to begin by asking "Who am I?" because they have a long and deep sense of where here is. They are burdened with a sense of history, weighed down by it but also grounded by its reality. However, in Canada we must ask prior questions: Where is here? How can we know our place in the world if we do not know where we are?

This question was taken up and developed by Frye's student, Margaret Atwood. In her now classic book *Survival: A Thematic Guide to Canadian Literature*, she explores the way in which the geography shaped the first encounter of the Europeans with this land – an encounter that would shape foundational attitudes in Canadian culture. Atwood argues that cultures are shaped by some defining image. England's culture is shaped by the experience of being an island; the United States by the experience of the frontier. Their literatures are shaped by and reflect these foundational metaphors. Canadian culture, she contends, is shaped by the struggle to survive.

The first larger groups of Europeans who arrived in this place had a shocking encounter with "a land so wide and savage."[3] As they journeyed down the St Lawrence and through the waterways of this region, they felt overwhelmed by the immensity of space and the daunting challenge of the weather, the cold, and the blackflies. Unlike the Americans who were stretched by the vast frontier that unfolded before them, those who would eventually be known as Canadians felt diminished and threatened by the space that surrounded them. Unlike the Americans who began to see themselves as conquerors, the imperative for the first Europeans who travelled the St Lawrence was simply to survive. These Europeans saw nature itself, and the peoples who lived in this place, as a threat – except for the ones who helped them survive the perils of nature.

This imperative of survival moved the first Europeans to build little garrisons in which they could huddle together and be protected from the forces of nature and the wild people they called Indians. Within these garrisons of survival, according to Frye, they developed an ethos of cooperation that would later become established within the various institutions of the emerging nation-state. There was a respect for law, order, and good government, something essential for survival. The greatest threat to this order within the garrison was that of pulling away from the group. Frye's contention is that these early experiences were translated into the laws that defined Confederation and the institutions that would implement the values learned in the early garrisons.

Many of the values that we now think of as "Canadian" can be linked to this garrison culture. It probably laid the foundation for the social safety net that many today see as characterizing Canada. It has often been noted that the Canadian culture is more cooperative than that of the Americans, who value the individual walking tall and taking the law into his own hands on the frontier. The importance of caring for each other in good times and in bad times, of cooperating in order to survive, seems to be part of our Canadian identity. The garrison culture also laid the foundation of respect for law and order and the sense of loyalty to the monarch, respect for the courts, and for the Royal Canadian Mounted Police.

However, the garrison mentality also has its shadow side, a shadow that seems to lengthen even unto today. The garrison is a culture in which people pull together because there is a common threat. In other words, it is a culture defined more by what/who it is against rather than by what/who it is for. It is also a culture that is not at home in nature and that is seriously separated from the people who are the original inhabitants of this place. It is a culture formed by exclusion.

Obviously, we no longer build little garrisons in the snow. Through the inventions of technology we have learned how to survive well in the cold, how to spray away mosquitoes and how to fly over difficult terrain. Through hard work and technology we have tamed nature. And more, we have learned how to use it to our own benefit. We have treated nature as a useful source of what we call "natural resources" – fur, then fish, and trees and wheat and metals and oil. We have used and abused nature but we have also parcelled off pieces of geography as beautiful landscapes to look at, to vacation in. Nature, for many, is no longer a threat but a place of refuge and renewal. It is where we dream of what Frye calls "the peaceable kingdom," a place where nature and community are in harmony.

However, most of us are still tourists and traders in this land. We have yet to feel at home here, to know our true place. Nowhere is this more evident than in the North today. It is a place of great natural resources and also a vast and unknown space accessible only to the few travellers who can afford it and the people who live there and call it their homeland. One of the most serious consequences of our ambivalence toward nature has been our ambivalence toward the Indigenous peoples – whom we have treated as either useless or as romantic artifacts to be looked at and preserved as some exotic beings. To some extent, the First Nations are the "inconvenient Indians" described by Thomas King because we are uncomfortable with the natural world we live in.[4]

Although we no longer build garrisons in the snow, we continue to huddle together in the face of threat. The only difference is that the threats now are from the vast socioeconomic forces, unleashed by the process of globalization, that seem to overwhelm us. In the face of these threats, we gather together with those like us and build walls. The walls are now invisible but real, constructed through paper and policies and prejudice. We exclude in order to survive.

Justice Thomas Berger has documented the various forms of exclusion that have shadowed the history of this country. In relatively peaceful times, he writes, Canada does seem to be a decent and tolerant country. Indeed, this is the way most Canadians think of themselves. However, he documents how that tolerance and decency seem to evaporate in times of social and economic stress. The garrison mentality reappears in new forms. He cites the treatment of the Jehovah's Witnesses in Quebec, the internment of Japanese Canadians, the exclusion of Jewish refugees during World War II, the War Measures Act, and the ongoing exclusion of the Indigenous peoples. His book *Fragile Freedoms* is aptly titled.

As I see it today, a large wall has been set up to exclude refugees from this country. They have been vilified as freeloaders, cheats, criminals, and terrorists. In a time when all national borders are under immense stress created by the process of globalization, it is refugees who have become the scapegoats for the fear that our borders are unprotected.

We are defining our country by who/what we are against. We are defining our common good by what we share with those like us. We who are in the garrison now have assumed the right to exclude those who are knocking at the door. We own this place, we say, and we have a right to say who is allowed to live here. How uncomfortable when we are reminded that there were others here before us, others who were willing to share the land with us.

Our problem is that our common good has been so shaped by the imperatives of survival that it is defined more by who/what it excludes than by who/what it includes. In times of threat, our country becomes a garrison of garrisons, a collection of small and stunted competing visions of the good.

Yet we cling to our myth of innocence, that we are good people who are incapable of doing bad things. It is one of the temptations of a colonial people to think that bad things are done to them rather than by them. The power to do great good and evil lies elsewhere, not here, not in a relatively powerless colony. We have developed what I would call a "branch plant morality" that puts the blame for wrongs at the head office, which is always elsewhere, anywhere but here. It is a dangerous innocence and blinds us to the very real good that we are capable of and the evil that we can manage on our own. For example, we protested mightily against the conduct of the American government during the Vietnam war but did not notice that Agent Orange was being produced in the lovely little town of Elmira, Ontario. Our myth of innocence not only blinds us to the evil we are capable of but to the very real goodness that exists within the heart of America.

Our colonial resentments against the head offices elsewhere fuel our tendencies to define ourselves in terms of who and what we are against. Being Canadian means being anti-American. Being Canadian means being against Toronto. I think these considerations situate the long and seemingly fruitless conversation about Canadian identity, a conversation that is really about whether we hold anything in common as a country. Is our national purpose simply to survive? If that is our only purpose, we will inevitably become a nation of garrisons held together by a series of real or invented threats.

WHY ARE WE HERE?

The story is told of the encounter between a Tsimshian chief who met the first European he had seen on the West Coast of what is now British Columbia. "Why are you here?" asked the Tsimshian chief. We do not know what the European answered. Why indeed? It is a question that is with us still: To trade? To make money? To civilize a barbarian people? To preach the gospel?

It is one of the most ancient questions and one that is deeply related to the Canadian question: Where is here? It is the question where identity and purpose meet and define each other.

There are those who will say that it is not the function of governments to answer the question of the meaning and purpose of a nation. The function of liberal governments, it is said, is to mediate various competing interests within a society so that the greatest good results. This is the role of governments in the market economy and in politics – the mediation and management of diverse interests. It is assumed that something good will come out of this process.

However, the more government defines its primary purpose as the generation of wealth, the more the common good recedes from our collective awareness. As governments abdicate responsibility for the common good, economic interests begin to define the good solely in materialistic terms: making money, making a living. In the process people are defined more as taxpayers and consumers than as citizens. Sometimes it seems as if the national purpose of Canada is just making money.

Some will celebrate this lack of a common vision or a common history, preferring instead a more postmodern sense of nationalism – in which a country is a collection of stories not bound by some large overarching metanarrative of nationalism. We may be left with a garrison country that is a collection of garrisons.

This barren situation invites people of faith to engage anew in a discussion of the common good in the Canadian context. We do so humbly aware of the many times that the church presumed to dictate the common good for others who did not share its faith, and with what disastrous consequences. Vatican II was rightly wary of blind nationalisms that had unleashed such suffering in the twentieth century.

Our participation in the search for the common good of Canada will be modest but meaningful. We ask not whether we can be a great nation but whether we can be a good country.

Interestingly enough, we will find little reference to the common good in the documents of Vatican II. As a concept, it is mentioned only once and then in the briefest of ways. However, as an image that inspires, it shapes all of the reflections of a church passionately committed to the good of all humanity.

So what might this great and common good look like in modest Canadian terms? Let me begin by describing rather than defining the common good in Canada. I want to do so through two stories drawn from my experience of living with refugees at Romero House in Toronto over the last twenty-five years.

The first story begins with my experience of radical exclusion when I first moved into a house with refugees in a small middle-class neighbourhood in the west end of Toronto. We were so preoccupied with getting the house in shape that we never noticed the neighbours on the very small street where we lived. But they noticed us! They noticed that the people in the house looked different, dressed differently, and talked differently. Their suspicions came to a head when we applied for a permit to renovate the two-storey garage at the back of the house. Our intention was to create a craft space but the neighbours saw only expansionary designs. When our application came before the city committee in charge of such things, many people in the neighbourhood went to City Hall and voiced their concerns that we would build a ten-storey addition, that there would be prostitution and drugs and peeping toms. The garrison walls were up!

The reaction of the neighbours was so intense that we abandoned all hope of renovating the garage and withdrew behind our own little protective garrison. Over the next five years things slowly changed, not through any great program but through daily efforts and kindnesses. Eventually we became a street and a neighbourhood that welcomed newcomers. Now all of us on that little street host one of the finest annual street parties in the whole city.

There were many times that I wondered what could hold us together as neighbours. We did not share a common history, a common language, common religion, culture, or class. Then one day I had this simple realization: what we held in common was the street.[5] This was the space that no one person or group owned but we all shared and were responsible for. Our small experience confirmed one of the key insights of the great urban thinker Jane Jacobs. She described the significance of the street and sidewalks in a neighbourhood as the space where people met as neighbours. While each person or group lived in a private place they called home, there was also a shared space that belonged to no one but was shared by all.

My second story takes place about five hours north of the city on Manitoulin Island. It is there that we take about fifty refugees every summer – men, women, and children from a variety of cultures. These are people who have been profoundly dislocated from their place in the world. Within minutes of our arrival at the camp, I begin to see people relax and seemingly become so at home in a place they had never seen or imagined before.

One day the children hiked to a large rock overlooking a deep and lovely lake. They jumped off and spun around as they fell into the water, saluting to some unseen flag. There they all felt Canadian. There, we all felt that Canada was our home and promised land.

I have often pondered why – why this experience of the Canadian Shield made them feel more at home than all the classes in Canadian history that they had taken as part of their introduction to the country. I have come to this understanding: anthropologists tell us that identity is formed along two key vectors: time and space, history and geography. When a culture has a weak sense of history (as it seems we do as Canadians), then I think our geography and sense of space become more important in terms of our identity. The refugee kids felt Canadian through their experience of the space, the landscape of the country. This did not mean that they stayed in the north. They did return to the city, but they had caught a glimpse of a space they could share – a space that no one owned but all were responsible for. They had a sense of their place in the world. They knew it was good to be *here*. They felt a sense of gratitude and a sense of responsibility for this good place.

Through the eyes of my neighbours and through the eyes of the refugee kids I have seen that we do have a common good in Canada, a good that is both obvious and elusive. We hold this place in common. I think it is this simple understanding that has shaped much of our theological thinking about the common good. In many small villages in Europe, there was a space called "the commons" that no one owned but all were free to use for grazing, for social events, for festivals and other social celebrations.[6] The common good was as real as a place and a state of mind.

Our turn to the world, which was voiced anew at Vatican II, must now become our turn to the earth and to this particular place on earth called Canada.

THIS PLACE AS OUR COMMON GOOD

Needless to say, the environment and climate change were not mentioned at Vatican II. Although the council expressed a strong awareness that the survival of each is tied to the survival of all because of the threat of nuclear war, it did not articulate this in terms of our interconnectedness given the reality of climate change.

We are now much more aware of our interconnectedness, for better or worse. We are aware of how we affect each other through global capitalism, global technology and communications, and the global reach of care and concern. Some are more focused on local efforts to connect with this and others by more global involvement.

There are dangers in either direction – becoming too local can disconnect us from wider realities but becoming globally aware can mean dissolving into abstractions, vague plans, and even vaguer spiritualities. These tendencies raise anew the importance of various intermediate political and social structures, such as the nation-state. As the exercise of political power becomes more local and more global, the nation-state has been increasingly threatened. Some will celebrate this fact, but this may also be a time to rethink and reimagine the significance of the nation-state in terms of the common good of the earth that we share.

Our national boundaries, the borders of Canada for example, are indeed artificial constructs. There is nothing sacred about these borders, which were constructed through wars, contracts, and the necessity of geography. These national borders have always been described as the area over which its citizens have rights. This kind of nationalism has always been somewhat dangerous. How many wars have been fought as nations sought to expand their national borders?

However, it is possible to imagine national borders not as defining the territory over which we have rights but as the place for which we are responsible. We cannot care for the whole earth. We may hope for the good of the earth, pray for it and contemplate it with care, but we cannot be practically responsible for the whole earth. We can, however, care for this particular place on earth called Canada. This is not the whole earth but neither is it the small space of a town or city. It is the space over which we as citizens have political, cultural, environmental, and economic responsibility. This is the space that we *inhabit*.

This particular space – from the West Coast to the northern Arctic along the 49th parallel through the Great Lakes and out to the Maritimes – this is the good that we hold in common. This is the good that we share with Quebec and with the First Nations of this place. Although there are particular places that are owned by individuals and groups and institutions, there remains a space held in common that none of us own but all of us share and are responsible for: the water, the air, the climate. Given the realities of climate change and our particular geographical location as a northern nation that is in meltdown, our responsibility is great. We are also responsible for public spaces of culture: museums, public broadcasters, schools, and libraries hold the culture we all share and are responsible for but that none of us own.

What this means in terms of particular public policies is something that must be worked out in every area of citizenship. The Catholic Church and other churches must be part of this public discussion without claiming any particular privileged voice in that discussion.

So much depends on whether the church can take responsibility for the sins of its past in relationship to the Indigenous peoples and to this land. The Truth and Reconciliation Commission has summoned us to recognize the ways in which we treated the Aboriginal people and this land as objects to be used and abused. Our repentance in this regard must be long and humble and sustained. It must be a repentance grounded not only in the memory of our original sin but also in the memory of the original blessing of this place on earth.

What the church can bring to this important public discussion is a new attitude toward the earth and this particular place on earth. What we Catholics have to bring is an attitude of gratitude for this space on earth. In gratitude we do not claim this earth as a possession that we can use and abuse and dominate. As people shaped by the biblical story of creation, we know we cannot and should not try to be masters of this place. In gratitude, we can dwell on this space of earth without trying to possess it for ourselves. In gratitude, we can rejoice in the gift of this good place. In gratitude, we can share real responsibility for this place with the First Nations. In gratitude, we know what we have been given, who and what we are responsible for, and what we are *for*. In gratitude, we can live in a community rather than a garrison; we can become a good country through the process of inclusion rather than patterns of exclusion.

It is our faith in the Creator who made heaven and earth that provides us with the foundational attitude toward this earth – which is a gift to be shared rather than an object to be owned. This is a great vision of our place on earth, our purpose on earth. We do not live on this earth, we live within it. And if we live closely enough, we can hear its call to care and responsibility.

The inhabitants of this place called Canada are those who care for this good that we hold in common. First Nations and settlers – we can share responsibility for this place. If we live together in gratitude, it will be easier to welcome those newcomers who are ready and willing to share the responsibility for this place.

NOTES

1 The key insights into the Canadian context are to be found in the now
classic *Survival* by Margaret Atwood and *Divisions on a Ground* by
Northrop Frye. Although other writers have refined and criticized some of
the interpretations of Frye and Atwood, their insights seem ever more rel-
evant when the sense of threat comes not so much from the natural world
as from vast socio-economic forces. See Linda Hutcheon's *The Canadian
Postmodern*.

2 O'Grady and Staines, *Northrop Frye on Canada*, 412.

3 The phrase "a land so wide and savage" is taken from Stan Rogers's 1981
song "Northwest Passage."

4 For a good reading of "Canadian" history from an Indigenous perspective,
see King, *Inconvenient Indian*.

5 Jane Jacobs's description of "the street" in urban life is found in her now
classic *The Death and Life of Great American Cities*.

6 The current interest in "the commons" was initially provoked by Garrett
Hardin in his essay "The Tragedy of the Commons." Initially an essay on
sustainability, it has generated a new interest in this concept/image.

Epilogue

Donald Bolen

When St Thomas More College in Saskatoon held its Turning to the World conference on Catholic social teaching and the Second Vatican Council, none of us knew what was just around the corner. The conference, which inspired the current volume, was held on 8–9 March 2013, and four days after it was over, Cardinal Jorge Bergoglio of Buenos Aires was elected pope. Exactly one week after the conference concluded, the new Bishop of Rome told journalists about his choice of the name Francis. He relayed how his friend Cardinal Claudio Hummes embraced him in the Sistine Chapel and told him, "Don't forget the poor!," how he thought immediately about St Francis, "the man of peace ... the poor man"; and then he exclaimed, in words which have become as good a description as any of his pontificate: "How I would like a Church which is poor and for the poor!"[1]

At the conference, at least from some participants such as Gregory Baum, there was a plea for greater commitment to justice issues from the church, and a sense that the turn to the world that marked the Second Vatican Council had not yet been fully received or implemented in the life of the church. People often say that change in the Catholic Church comes exceedingly slowly, and in many ways that is so. Yet by virtue of the authority vested in the Petrine Ministry, change can also come about quickly and unexpectedly. When John XXIII was elected pope, no one expected he would call an ecumenical council inviting *aggiornamento* and identifying the restoration of unity among Christians as one of the principal aims for calling the council. Prior to the election of John Paul II, who would have anticipated a pope who played a major role in the collapse of communism in Poland? Likewise, in the brief three years since the election of Pope Francis, we have witnessed and experienced an unexpected and significant transition, not in church doctrine but (among other things) in ecclesial culture, in consultation within the church and dialogue with the world, and in the manner that the Petrine Ministry engages in Catholic social teaching.

Since Francis's pontificate began, I have been serving on the Justice and Peace Commission of the Canadian Conference of Catholic Bishops (CCCB). It became clear very quickly that the pursuit of justice and the needs of prisoners and refugees, the unemployed and the homeless, the economically disadvantaged and many others on the peripheries of society were to be a central part of Francis's pontificate. This was so from the outset, not in major new documents on Catholic social teaching, but in daily speeches and encounters where those in need and the call to respond to them were near the heart of what he was saying. As a commission we decided to begin working on a document that would eventually be published under the title "A Church Seeking Justice: The Challenge of Pope Francis to the Church in Canada." I made it my responsibility to check the texts coming out of the papal office every day for elements of social teaching and references to those on the peripheries. What at first was exciting and energizing soon became exhausting; it was hard to keep up with him, and still is.

Francis's teaching on justice issues has certainly gained heightened attention because of lifestyle decisions he has made that give an added credibility to his message. As archbishop of Buenos Aires, Cardinal Bergoglio lived in a simple apartment, used public transportation, and often visited the slums. There he cultivated a pastoral approach to people that was characterized by listening and presence, sharing in their grief and joy, and preaching in a style that was down to earth and centred on the depths of God's mercy. As bishop of Rome, Francis has made similar decisions, communicating in word and action that his role does not exempt him from the daily challenges and difficult lifestyle decisions that are part of living the gospel. His decision not to live in the papal apartments but to reside in the Santa Marta residence with other Vatican officials, the invitation to homeless people to join him for breakfast on his birthday, and the establishment of a homeless shelter very near to St Peter's, are among the many actions that have communicated his own commitment to solidarity not only as a teaching but as a guide for his own daily lifestyle decisions.

Grounded in a profound understanding that Christ encounters us in those around us in need, and that Catholic social teaching rises directly from the heart of the gospel, Francis has also sought to put an end to any wedge driven between works of justice and acts of compassion. He sees responding to immediate needs and addressing structural injustices as two sides of the same coin. The church's response to material poverty is to be practical, concrete: "In imitation of our Master, we Christians are called to confront the poverty of our brothers and sisters, to touch it, to make it our own and to take practical steps to alleviate it."[2] Jesus himself calls us to simplicity of life, to practical and daily acts of service and renunciation, generosity and compassion. Yet our faith, Francis insists, also summons us to address the systemic issues of injustice and inequality. In the summary words of "A Church Seeking Justice," the Holy Father "challenges our practice of giving by saying that the world needs something more from us than a few sporadic acts of generosity. He calls us to promote the integral development of the poor, working for access to education, health care, employment with a just wage, and on another level, working to eliminate the structural causes of poverty, yet without overlooking the small daily acts of solidarity which meet the real needs of those we encounter."[3]

With a sense of urgency, and with passion, Francis has brought an immediacy and specificity to Catholic social teaching. He has drawn repeated attention to the dignity of the human person by speaking of areas where that dignity is not being respected. In his own neighbourhood around St Peter's, he asked how it was that a homeless person could die on the street and it was not news, while a small percentage drop in the stock market is considered a disaster. Travelling to the island of Lampedusa off the coast of Sicily where many North African asylum seekers have died at sea, he lamented the globalization of indifference that keeps us from truly empathizing with those who are suffering in our midst.

Reminiscent of the strong writing and preaching of Martin Luther King Jr, Francis has passionately addressed the terrors of war and the need for peace, pleading that "war begets war, violence begets violence,"[4] and calling for a daily commitment to peace, constructive negotiation, encounter, and dialogue. If we wish to build societies that are stable and a world that is sane, we need to directly address situations of poverty and systematic inequality, mindful that "inequality eventually engenders a violence which recourse to arms cannot and never will be able to resolve" (EG 60).

The pope has also spoken repeatedly about how our current economic system and relentless pursuit of economic growth excludes and marginalizes people and lacks "a truly human purpose" (EG 55; cf. 53–60). Challenging dominant economic assumptions has become a recurring theme in his ministry: "How long will we continue to defend systems of production and consumption which exclude most of the world's population even from the crumbs which fall from the tables of the rich?"[5] An economics of exclusion creates what he has termed a "throw-away culture" where the unborn, the poor and the marginalized, young people without work, families and the elderly are tossed aside because money, not the human person, is at the centre of the economic system.

With the publication of his monumental encyclical *Laudato Si': On Care for Our Common Home* in May 2015, Francis invited an even more profound engagement with the world. Intentionally published in time for the United Nations COP 21 Paris Conference on climate change, *Laudato Si'* offers a provocative reading of the signs of the times, drawing on a range of scientific and secular as well as ecclesial sources in a way that is new and presents a compelling call to action. Noting that our world is "falling into serious disrepair" (LS 61) and that in the past two centuries "we have hurt and mistreated our common home like never before" (LS 53), the encyclical details how our way of living is contaminating the earth's waters, its land and its air. Francis also draws attention to the human dimensions of the current crisis: billions of people in poverty, without access to safe drinking water, bearing the brunt of environmental degradation; the "structurally perverse" way in which the resources of developing nations enhance the quality of life in wealthy nations while the vital needs of their own citizens go unaddressed (LS 52; cf. 95); and how our technological and scientific discoveries have not been accompanied by a proportionate ethical maturity (LS 103–5). One of the strongest features of the text is the way in which it summons its readers to face reality. Francis laments and criticizes "obstructionist attitudes" (LS 14), the masking of problems and manipulation of information (LS 26, 54, 135), and the prioritizing of short-term gain and private or national interests above the global common good (LS 169, 184).

From the very start of his pontificate, Francis has been calling for and espousing a "culture of encounter," to the point where journalist

John Allen identified it as his "core signature phrase."[6] In *Laudato Si'*, and in his social teaching as a whole, Francis has stressed the need for dialogue and honest and open debate about the issues that matter most to us as a human family (e.g., LS 188). The encyclical is addressed to "every person living on this planet" and expresses the desire to "enter into dialogue with all people about our common home" (LS 3). In mapping a way forward, he outlines "the major paths of dialogue which can help us escape the spiral of self-destruction which currently engulfs us" (LS 163).

If it is right – and I believe it is – to say that the Second Vatican Council invited a turn toward the world, a new and profound engagement with "the joys and the hopes, the griefs and the anxieties" of the people of our day (GS 1), then I believe it is also true to say that this aspect of the council's teaching has blossomed in these early years of Francis's pontificate. In an address to political leaders in Brazil, he noted, "When leaders in various fields ask me for advice, my response is always the same: dialogue, dialogue, dialogue."[7] Through dialogue and practical deeds of compassion, through a deep listening to those in need and an intelligent commitment to justice and the common good, through a deep and abiding faith in the paschal mystery and the gospel's life-giving message, we are being summoned to be a church seeking justice, a church turned toward the world, a church that shows mercy. This is the witness the world needs from us today, and Francis is leading the way.

NOTES

1 Francis, "Address to Representatives of the Communications Media."
2 Francis, Lenten Message 2014.
3 Canadian Conference of Catholic Bishops, "A Church Seeking Justice," section 4.
4 Francis, "Angelus."
5 Francis, "Address on Ministry in Big Cities."
6 Allen, "Francis and the 'Culture of Encounter.'"
7 Francis, "Address to Brazil's Leaders of Society."

Bibliography

Abbott, Walter M., ed. *The Documents of Vatican II*. New York: Herder and Herder, 1966.

Achtemeier, Paul J., ed. *Society of Biblical Literature 1978 Seminar Papers*. 2 vols. Missoula, MT: Scholars Press, 1978.

Allen, John L., Jr. "Francis and the 'Culture of Encounter.'" *National Catholic Reporter*, 20 December 2013. https://www.ncronline.org/blogs/ncr-today/francis-and-culture-encounter.

Allman, Mark J. *Who Would Jesus Kill? War, Peace, and the Christian Tradition*. Winona, MN: Saint Mary's Press, 2008.

Allsopp, Michael E. "Subsidiarity, Principle of." In *The New Dictionary of Catholic Social Thought*, edited by Judith A. Dwyer, 927–9. Collegeville, MN: Liturgical Press, 1994.

Althusius, Johannes. *The Politics of Johannes Althusius*. Translated by Frederick S. Carney. London: Eyre & Spottiswoode, 1965.

Aquinas, Thomas. *Summa Theologiae*. 61 vols. Cambridge: Cambridge University Press, 2006.

Aroney, Nicholas. "Subsidiarity, Federalism and the Best Constitution: Thomas Aquinas on City, Province and Empire." *Law and Philosophy* 26, no. 2 (March 2007): 163.

Assemblée des évêques catholiques de Québec. "Catholiques dans un Québec pluraliste." Pastoral Message. November 2012. http://www.eveques.qc.ca/pluralisme/message.html.

Atwood, Margaret. *Survival: A Thematic Guide to Canadian Literature*. Toronto: Anansi Press, 1972.

Barry, Robert. "Thomas Aquinas, Contribution of." In *The New Dictionary of Catholic Social Thought*, edited by Judith A. Dwyer, 940–51. Collegeville, MN: Liturgical Press, 1994.

Bartlett, Woody. *Living by Surprise: A Christian Response to the Ecological Crisis*. New York: Paulist Press, 2003.

Baum, Gregory. *Amazing Church: A Catholic Theologian Remembers a Half-Century of Change*. Maryknoll, NY: Orbis, 2005.

– "Benedict XVI's First Encyclical." *The Ecumenist: A Journal of Theology, Culture, and Society* 43 (Spring 2006): 11–14.

– "The Forgotten Promises of Vatican II." *Historical Studies* 77 (2011): 7–22.

– *The Priority of Labour*. New York: Paulist Press, 1982.

Beaudin, Michel. "*Populorum Progressio:* Fécondité et actualité toujours prophétique d'une parole d'église risquée dans un tournant historique." In *Paul VI et Maurice Roy: un itinéraire pour la justice et la paix,* edited by Gilles Routhier, 73–94. Rome: Edizioni Studium; Brescia: Istituto Paulo VI, 2005.

Benedict XVI. *Caritas in Veritate* (*On Integral Development in Charity and Truth*). Encyclical. 29 June 2009. http://w2.vatican.va/content/vatican/it.html.

– *De Caritate Ministranda* (*On the Service of Charity*). Motu proprio. 11 November 2012. http://w2.vatican.va/content/benedict-xvi/en/motu_proprio/documents/hf_ben-xvi_motu-proprio_20121111_caritas.html.

– *Deus Caritas Est*. Encyclical. 25 December 2005. http://w2.vatican.va/content/benedict-xvi/en/encyclicals/documents/hf_ben-xvi_enc_20051225_deus-caritas-est.html.

– "Faith, Reason and the University: Memories and Reflections." Lecture of the Holy Father, Aula Magna of the University of Regensburg, 12 September 2006. https://w2.vatican.va/content/benedict-xvi/en/speeches/2006/september/documents/hf_ben-xvi_spe_20060912_university-regensburg.html.

– "Message of His Holiness Benedict XVI for the Celebration of the World Day of Peace 1 January 2006: In Truth, Peace." 8 December 2005. https://w2.vatican.va/content/benedict-xvi/en/messages/peace/documents/hf_ben-xvi_mes_20051213_xxxix-world-day-peace.html.

– "Message of His Holiness Benedict XVI for the Celebration of the World Day of Peace 1 January 2007: The Human Person, the Heart of Peace." 8 December 2006. http://w2.vatican.va/content/benedict-xvi/en/messages/peace/documents/hf_ben-xvi_mes_20061208_xl-world-day-peace.html

– "Message of His Holiness Pope Benedict XVI for the Celebration of the World Day of Peace 1 January 2008: The Human Family, a Community of Peace." 8 December 2007. http://w2.vatican.va/content/benedict-xvi/

en/messages/peace/documents/hf_ben-xvi_mes_20071208_xli-world-day-peace.html.

– "Message of His Holiness Benedict XVI for the Celebration of the World Day of Peace 1 January 2009: Fighting Poverty to Build Peace." 8 December 2008. https://w2.vatican.va/content/benedict-xvi/en/messages/peace/documents/hf_ben-xvi_mes_20081208_xlii-world-day-peace.html.

– "Message of His Holiness Pope Benedict XVI for the Celebration of the World Day of Peace 1 January 2010: If You Want to Cultivate Peace, Protect Creation." 8 December 2009. https://w2.vatican.va/content/benedict-xvi/en/messages/peace/documents/hf_ben-xvi_mes_20091208_xliii-world-day-peace.html.

– "Message of His Holiness Benedict XVI for the Celebration of the World Day of Peace 1 January 2013: Blessed are the Peacemakers." 8 December 2012. https://w2.vatican.va/content/benedict-xvi/en/messages/peace/documents/hf_ben-xvi_mes_20121208_xlvi-world-day-peace.html.

Bentley, Michael. "An Ecological Public Health Approach to Understanding the Relationships between Sustainable Urban Environments, Public Health and Social Equity." *Health Promotion International* 29, no. 3 (2014): 528–37.

Berger, Thomas R. *Fragile Freedoms: Human Rights and Dissent in Canada*. Toronto: Clarke, Irwin & Company, 1981.

Berkley Center for Religion, Peace and World Affairs. "Human Dignity in World Affairs: Celebrating *Pacem in Terris* and Its Legacy." https://berkleycenter.georgetown.edu/events/human-dignity-in-world-affairs-celebrating-i-pacem-in-terris-i-and-its-legacy.

Bernard Bergonzi. "A Conspicuous Absentee: The Decline and Fall of the Catholic Novel." *Encounter* 55, no. 2–3 (1980): 44–57.

Berry, Thomas. "Christianity's Role in the Earth Project." In *Christianity and Ecology*, edited by Dieter T. Hessel and Rosemary Radford Ruether, 127–34. Cambridge, MA: Harvard University Press, 2000.

– "Ethics and Ecology: A Paper Delivered to the Harvard Seminar on Environmental Values." 9 April 1996. https://intuerifarm.wordpress.com/philosophy/ethics-and-ecology-by-thomas-berry/.

– *Evening Thoughts: Reflecting on Earth as Sacred Community*. Edited by Mary Evelyn Tucker. San Francisco: Sierra Club Books, 2006.

Bevans, Stephen B. *Models of Contextual Theology*. Rev. ed. Maryknoll, NY: Orbis Books, 2002.

Bharadwaj, L.K. "Principled Versus Pragmatic Nonviolence." *Peace Review: A Journal of Social Justice* 10, no. 1 (1998): 79–81.

Blond, Phillip. "Introduction: Theology before Philosophy." In *Post-Secular Philosophy: Between Philosophy and Theology*, edited by Phillip Blond, 1–33. London: Routledge, 1998.

Boff, Leonardo. *Cry of the Earth, Cry of the Poor.* Translated by Philip Berryman. Maryknoll, NY: Orbis Books, 1997.

– *Francis of Assisi: A Model for Human Liberation.* Maryknoll, NY: Orbis, 2006.

– *Virtues for Another Possible World.* Eugene, OR: Cascade Books, 2011.

Boland, Vivian. "*Mater et Magistra.*" In *The New Dictionary of Catholic Social Thought*, edited by Judith A. Dwyer, 578–90. Collegeville, MN: Liturgical Press, 1994.

Booth, Ken. "Critical Explorations." In *Critical Security Studies and World Politics*, edited by Ken Booth, 1–20. London: Lynne Rienner Publishers, 2005.

Boulding, Kenneth E. "Earth as a Space Ship." 10 May 1965. http://www. colorado.edu/economics/morey/4999Ethics/Boulding-EARTH%20 AS%20A%20SPACE%20SHIP1965.pdf.

Bowler, Kate. *Blessed: A History of the American Prosperity Gospel.* New York, NY: Oxford University Press, 2013.

Boys, Mary C. "The *Nostra Aetate* Trajectory: Holding Our Theological Bow Differently." In *Never Revoked:* Nostra Aetate *as Ongoing Challenge for Jewish-Christian Dialogue*, edited by Marianne Moyaert and Didier Pollefeyt, 133–57. Leuven: Peeters, 2010.

Brown, Phillip J. "The 1983 Code and Vatican II Ecclesiology: The Principle of Subsidiarity in Book V." *The Jurist: Studies in Church Law and Ministry* 69, no. 2 (2009): 583–614.

Brueggemann, Walter. *The Prophetic Imagination.* 2nd ed. Minneapolis: Fortress Press, 2004.

– *Reality, Grief, Hope: Three Urgent Prophetic Tasks.* Grand Rapids, MI: Eerdmans, 2014.

Câmara, Hélder. *Spiral of Violence.* Translated by Della Couling. Denville, NJ: Dimension Books, 1971.

Canadian Conference of Catholic Bishops. "A Church Seeking Justice: The Challenge of Pope Francis to the Church in Canada." 2015. http://www. cccb.ca/site/images/stories/pdf/184-902.pdf.

– "Ethical Reflections on the Economic Crisis (1982)." In *Do Justice! The Social Teaching of the Canadian Bishops, 1945–1986*, edited by Edward F. Sheridan, 399–410. Montreal: Éditions Paulines, 1987.

– "Pastoral Letter on Freedom of Conscience and Religion." April 2012.
   http://www.cccb.ca/site/images/stories/pdf/Freedom_of_Conscience_
   and_Religion.pdf.

– "You Love All That Exists ... All Things Are Yours, God Lover of Life:
   A Pastoral Letter on the Christian Ecological Imperative." 4 October
   2003. http://www.cccb.ca/site/Files/pastoralenvironment.html.

Canadian Council of Churches. "The Commission on Justice and Peace."
   https://www.councilofchurches.ca/social-justice/.

Carroll, James. "Notre Dame's Stand against Catholic Fundamentalism."
   Salon, 17 May 2009. http://www.salon.com/2009/05/17/carroll_4.

Cassidy, Edward Idris. "Presentation of *We Remember: A Reflection on
   the Shoah*." http://www.vatican.va/roman_curia/pontifical_councils/
   chrstuni/documents/rc_pc_chrstuni_doc_16031998_shoah_en.html.

Castillo, Ana. *The Guardians*. New York: Random House, 2007.

Catechism of the Catholic Church. Vatican City: Libreria Editrice
   Vaticana, 1994.

Catholic Relief Services. "About Catholic Relief Services." http://www.crs.
   org/about.

Charles, Robert H., trans. *The Book of Enoch or 1 Enoch*. Oxford:
   Clarendon Press, 1912.

Charles, Rodger. "Christian Social Witness and Teaching: The Catholic
   Tradition from Genesis to 'Centesimus Annus.'" Vol. 2, *The Modern
   Social Teaching Context: Contexts, Summaries, Analysis*. Leominster:
   Gracewing, 1998.

Chenu, Marie-Dominique. *Notes quotidiennes au concile: journal de
   Vatican II: 1962–1963*. Edited by Alberto Melloni. Paris: Cerf, 1995.

Claffey, Patrick, and Joe Egan, eds. *Movement or Moment? Assessing
   Liberation Theology Forty Years after Medellín*. Bern: Peter Lang, 2009.

Cleary, Edward L. *How Latin America Saved the Soul of the Catholic
   Church*. New York: Pauline Press, 2009.

Collins, John J., ed. *Apocalypse: The Morphology of a Genre*. Semeia, 14.
   Chico, CA: Scholars Press, 1979.

– "Methodological Issues in the Study of I Enoch: Reflections on the
   Articles of P.D. Hanson and G.W. Nickelsburg." In *Society of Biblical
   Literature 1978 Seminar Papers*, vol. 1, edited by Paul J. Achtemeier,
   315–22. Missoula, MT: Scholars Press, 1978.

Commission of the Holy See for Religious Relations with the Jews. *The
   Gifts and the Calling of God Are Irrevocable (Rom 11:29): A Reflection
   on Theological Questions Pertaining to Catholic-Jewish Relations on
   the Occasion of the 50th Anniversary of 'Nostra Aetate' (No. 4)*. www.
   vatican.va.

- *Guidelines and Suggestions for Implementing the Conciliar Declaration "Nostra Aetate" (n. 4).* 1974. http://www.vatican.va/roman_curia/ pontifical_councils/chrstuni/relations-jews-docs/rc_pc_chrstuni_doc_ 19741201_nostra-aetate_en.html.
- *Notes on the Correct Way to Present the Jews and Judaism in Preaching and Catechesis in the Roman Catholic Church.* 1985. http://www.vatican.va/roman_curia/pontifical_councils/chrstuni/relations-jews-docs/ rc_pc_chrstuni_doc_19820306_jews-judaism_en.html.
- *Relations with the Jews.* http://www.vatican.va/roman_curia/pontifical_ councils/chrstuni/relations-jews-docs/rc_pc_chrstuni_doc_19750110_ setting-commission_en.html.
- *We Remember: A Reflection on the Shoah.* 1998. http://www.vatican. va/roman_curia/pontifical_councils/chrstuni/documents/ rc_pc_chrstuni_doc_16031998_shoah_en.html.
Committee on Doctrine and Committee on Ecumenical and Interreligious Affairs, US Conference of Catholic Bishops. "A Note on Ambiguities Contained in *Reflections on Covenant and Mission.*" Issued 18 June 2009, revised 13 October 2009. http://www.usccb.org/about/doctrine/ publications/upload/note-on-ambiguities-contained-in-reflections -on-covenant-and-mission.pdf.
Confalonieri, Luca Badini. *Democracy in the Christian Church: An Historical, Theological and Political Case.* London: Bloomsbury T & T Clark, 2012.
Conference of Latin American Bishops (CELAM). *I Conferencia General del CELAM: Documento Conclusivo.* 1955. http://www.iglesiacatolica. org.uy/departamento-de-catequesis/files/2012/08/rio.pdf.
- *II Conferencia General del CELAM: Documento Conclusivo.* 1968. http://www.celam.org /conferencia_Medellín.php.
- *III General Conference of Latin American Bishops: Evangelization at Present and in the Future of Latin America. Conclusions.* Official English ed. 1979. Washington: National Conference of Catholic Bishops, 1979.
- *IV Conferencia General del CELAM: Documento Conclusivo Santo Domingo.* Bogotá: CELAM, 1992. http://www.celam.org/conferencias/ Documento_Conclusivo_Santo_Domingo.pdf.
- *V Conferencia General del Episcopado Latinoamericano y del Caribe: Documento Conclusivo.* Bogotá: CELAM, 2007.
Congregation for the Doctrine of the Faith. "Instruction on Certain Aspects of the 'Theology of Liberation.'" 6 August 1984. http://www.

vatican.va/roman_curia/congregations/cfaith/documents/
rc_con_cfaith_doc_19840806_theology-liberation_en.html.

Consultation of the National Council of Synagogues and US Conference
of Catholic Bishops. *Reflections on Covenant and Mission*. 12 August
2002. http://www.usccb.org/beliefs-and-teachings/ecumenical-and
-interreligious/jewish/upload/Reflections-on-Covenant-and-Mission.pdf.

Coombs, Nathan. "The Political Theology of Red Toryism." *Journal of
Political Ideologies* 16, no. 1 (February 2011): 79–96.

Costello, Gerald M., ed. *Our Sunday Visitor's Treasury of Catholic Stories*.
Huntington, IN: Sunday Visitor Publishers, 1999.

Crockett, Clayton. *A Theology of the Sublime*. London: Routledge, 2001.

Curran, Charles E. *Catholic Social Teaching 1891–Present: A Historical,
Theological and Ethical Analysis*. Washington: Georgetown University
Press, 2002.

– *Directions in Catholic Social Ethics*. Notre Dame: University of Notre
Dame Press, 1985.

Davis, Creston, and Patrick Aaron Riches. "Metanoia: The Theological
Praxis of Revolution." In *Theology and the Political: The New Debate*,
edited by Creston Davis, John Milbank, and Slavoj Žižek, 22–51.
Durham, NC: Duke University Press, 2005.

Dawson, Maria Teresa. "The Concept of Popular Religion: A Literature
Review." *Journal of Iberian and Latin American Research* 7, no. 1
(2001): 105–32.

Dear, John. *The God of Peace: Toward a Theology of Nonviolence*.
Eugene, OR: Wipf and Stock, 2005.

DeBerri, Edward P., and James E. Hug. *Catholic Social Teaching: Our Best
Kept Secret*. With assistance from Peter J. Henriot and Micheal J.
Schultheris. Maryknoll, NY: Orbis, 2004.

De Lubac, Henri. *Le drame de l'humanisme athée*. Paris: Spes, 1945.

De Roo, Remi. *Chronicles of a Vatican II Bishop*. Toronto: Novalis, 2012.

– In *Acta Synodalia Sacrosancti Concilii Oecumenici Vaticani II*, 6 vols.
Vol. 3, part 5, 529–31. Vatican City: Typis polyglottis Vaticanis,
1970–2000.

– "Living the Vision of Vatican II." Lecture, Turning to the World: Social
Justice and the Common Good Since Vatican II conference, St Thomas
More College, University of Saskatchewan, Saskatoon, SK, 8 March 2013.

– "A New Pentecost: Vatican II Revisited." Lecture, Cathedral of the Holy
Family, Saskatoon, SK, 11 October 2012.

Deutsch, Celia, "Journey to Dialogue: Sisters of Our Lady of Sion and the
Writing of Nostra Aetate." *SCJR*, no. 1 (2016): 1–36.

Development and Peace. "Funding from CIDA Reduced: Development and
    Peace Members Mobilize in Large Numbers." News release, 29 March
    2012. http://www.devp.org/en/pressroom/2012/comm2012-03-29.
– "History." http://www.devp.org/en/aboutus/history.
Dimant, Devorah. "1 Enoch 6–11: A Methodological Perspective." In
    Society of Biblical Literature 1978 Seminar Papers, edited by Paul J.
    Achtemeier, 323–39. Missoula, MT: Scholars Press, 1978.
Dominican Sisters of Blairstown, New Jersey. "Genesis Farm: Since 1980."
    http://www.genesisfarm.org/.
Dorr, Donal. *Option for the Poor and for the Earth: Catholic Social
    Teaching*. Maryknoll, NY: Orbis, 2012.
Dulles, Avery. "Covenant and Mission." *America*, 21 October 2002. www.
    americamagazine.org.
Dupont, Jacques. "La Chiesa e la povertà." In *La Chiesa del Vaticano II*,
    edited by Guilherme Baraúna, 387–418. Florence: Vallecchi, 1965.
Dwyer, Judith A., ed. *The New Dictionary of Catholic Social Thought*.
    Collegeville, MN: Liturgical Press, 1994.
Eagelson, John, and Philip Sharper, eds. *Puebla and Beyond*. Maryknoll,
    NY: Orbis Books, 1979.
Eaton, Heather. "Forces of Nature: Aesthetics and Ethics." In *Aesth/Ethics
    in Environmental Change: Hiking through the Arts, Ecology, Religion
    and Ethics of the Environment*, edited by Sigurd Bergmann, Irmgard
    Blindow, and Konrad Ott, 109–26. Berlin: LIT Verlag, 2013.
Elie, Paul. "Has Fiction Lost Its Faith?" *New York Times*, 19 December
    2012.
Fe y Alegria. *Cuantos Somos*. 2013. http://www.feyalegria.org/es/
    cuantos-somos.
Filteau, Jerry. "Notre Dame Faculty Members Call on Bishop to Retract
    'Incendiary Statement' on Obama." *National Catholic Reporter*, 23
    April 2012. http://ncronline.org/news/politics/notre-dame-faculty
    -members-call-bishop-retract-incendiary-statement-obama.
Fisher, Eugene J. "The Evolution of a Tradition: From *Nostra Aetate* to the
    'Notes.'" *Christian Jewish Relations* 18, no. 4 (1985): 32.
Fitzmyer, Joseph A. *Romans: A New Translation with Introduction and
    Commentary*. Anchor Bible 33. New York: Doubleday, 1993.
Flannery, Austin, ed. *Vatican Council II: Constitutions, Decrees,
    Declarations: A Completely Revised Translation in Inclusive Language*.
    Collegeville, MN: Liturgical Press, 2014.

Francis. "Address to the Brazilian Bishops." 28 July 2013. http://w2.
vatican.va/content /francesco/en/speeches/2013/july/documents/
papa-francesco_20130727_gmg-episcopato-brasile.html.

– "Address to Brazil's Leaders of Society." 27 July 2013. http://w2.vatican.
va/content/francesco/en/speeches/2013/july/documents/papa-francesco
_20130727_gmg-classe-dirigente-rio.html.

– "Address to the Workers of Cagliari." 22 September 2013. https://
w2.vatican.va/content/francesco/en/speeches/2013/september/
documents/papa-francesco_20130922_lavoratori-cagliari.html.

– "Address on Ministry in Big Cities." Vatican City, 29 November 2014.

– "Address to the Ecclesial Movements." 18 May 2013. http://w2.vatican.
va/content/francesco/en/speeches/2013/may/documents/papa-francesco
_20130518_veglia-pentecoste.html.

– "Address to Representatives of the Communications Media." 16 March
2013. http://w2.vatican.va/content/francesco/en/speeches/2013/march/
documents/papa-francesco_20130316_rappresentanti-media.html.

– "Address to the Young People from Argentina." 25 July 2013. http://
w2.vatican.va/content/francesco/en/speeches/2013/july/documents/
papa-francesco_20130725_gmg-argentini-rio.html.

– "Angelus." 1 September 2013. https://w2.vatican.va/content/francesco/
en/angelus/2013/documents/papa-francesco_angelus_20130901.html.

– The Church of Mercy: A Vision for the Church. Chicago: Loyola Press,
2014.

– Evangelii Gaudium (The Joy of the Gospel). Apostolic Exhortation of
the Holy Father to the Bishops, Clergy, Consecrated Persons and the
Lay Faithfull on the Proclamation of the Gospel in Today's World. 24
November 2013. Vatican City: Libreria Editrice Vaticana. http://w2.
vatican.va/content/francesco/en/apost_exhortations/documents/
papa-francesco_esortazione-ap_20131124_evangelii-gaudium.html.

– Laudato Si' (On Care for Our Common Home). Encyclical. 24 May
2015. http://w2.vatican.va/content/francesco/en/encyclicals/documents/
papa-francesco_20150524_enciclica-laudato-si.html.

– Lenten Message 2014. https://w2.vatican.va/content/francesco/en/
messages/lent/documents/papa-francesco_20131226_messaggio
-quaresima2014.html.

– "Message of His Holiness Pope Francis for the Celebration of the Fiftieth
World Day of Peace 1 January 2017: Nonviolence: A Style of Politics for
Peace." Vatican City: Libreria Editrice Vaticana. https://w2.vatican.va/
content/francesco/en/messages/peace/documents/papa-francesco_
20161208_messaggio-l-giornata-mondiale-pace-2017.html.

– "Protect Creation Says Pope in First Address." Euronews, 19 March 2013. http://www.euronews.com/2013/03/19/ protect-creation-says-pope-francis-in-first-address/.

Freire, Paulo. *Pedagogy of the Oppressed*. Translated by Myra Bergman Ramos. New York: Continuum, 1970.

Frye, Northrop. *Divisions on a Ground: Essays in Canadian Culture*. Toronto: House of Anansi Press, 1989.

Galtung, Johan. "Violence, Peace, and Peace Research." *Journal of Peace Research* 6, no. 3 (1969): 167–91.

Gattegna, Renzo. "The Importance of Symbolic Gestures." January 2016. http://www.ccjr.us/dialogika-resources/documents-and-statements/ jewish/1372-jewish-2016jan17.

Gebara, Ivone. "Ecofeminism: A Latin American Perspective." *Cross Currents* 53, no. 1 (Spring 2003): 93–103.

Genilo, Eric Marcelo. *John Cuthbert Ford, sj: Moral Theologian at the End of the Manualist Era*. Washington: Georgetown University Press, 2007.

George, Cardinal Francis. "U.S. Bishops' Reply to Jewish Letter of Concern." 2 October 2009. http://www.ccjr.us/dialogika-resources/ documents-and-statements/roman-catholic/us-conference-of-catholic -bishops/585-usccb09oct2-1.

Giblin, Marie J. "*Quadragesimo Anno*." In *The New Dictionary of Catholic Social Thought*, edited by Judith A. Dwyer, 802–13. Collegeville, MN: Liturgical Press, 1994.

Global Greens. "About Us." 2013. http://www.globalgreens.org/about-us.

– "Global Greens Charter." 2001, 2012. http://www.globalgreens.org/ globalcharter-english.

– "Global Greens Congress 2001." Canberra, Australia, 14–16 April. https://www.globalgreens.org/canberra2001.

– "Global Greens Congress, Dakar 2012." 29 March–1 April. https:// www.globalgreens.org/dakar2012.

Goff, Matthew J. "Monstrous Appetites: Giants, Cannibalism and Insatiable Eating in Enochic Literature." *Journal of Ancient Judaism* 1 (2010): 19–42.

Goodstein, Laurie. "Pope Says Church Is 'Obsessed' with Gays, Abortion and Birth Control." *New York Times*, 19 September 2013.

Green Mountain Monastery. "About Us." 2016. http://www. greenmountainmonastery.org/about-us/.

Gregory XVI. *Mirari Vos (On Liberalism and Religious Indifferentism)*. Encyclical. 15 August 1832. http://www.papalencyclicals.net/Greg16/g16mirar.htm.

Gremillion, Joseph, ed. *The Gospel of Peace and Justice: Catholic Social Teaching since Pope John*. Maryknoll, NY: Orbis Books, 1975.

Griffiths, Richard. *The Pen and the Cross: Catholicism and English Literature 1850–2000*. London: Continuum, 2010.

Gruending, Dennis. "Development and Peace Kneecapped by Canadian Catholic Bishops Conference." *Pulpit and Politics* (blog). http://www.pulpitandpolitics.ca/2012/11/development-and-peace-knee-capped-by-catholic-bishops/.

Hagopian, Frances. *Religious Pluralism, Democracy and the Catholic Church in Latin America*. Notre Dame: University of Notre Dame Press, 2009.

Hanson, Paul D. *The Dawn of Apocalyptic*. Philadelphia: Fortress Press, 1975.

– "Rebellion in Heaven, Azazel, and Euhemeristic Heroes in 1 Enoch 6–11." *Journal of Biblical Literature* 96, no. 2 (1977): 195–233.

Hardin, Garrett. "The Tragedy of the Commons." *Science Magazine* 162, no. 3859 (13 December 1968): 1243–8.

Hastings, Adrian, ed. *Modern Catholicism: Vatican II and After*. New York: Oxford University Press, 1991.

Hauerwas, Stanley. *The Peaceable Kingdom: A Primer in Christian Ethics*. Notre Dame: University of Notre Dame Press, 1983.

Hebblethwaite, Peter. "John XXIII." In *Modern Catholicism: Vatican II and After*, edited by Adrian Hastings, 27–34. New York: Oxford University Press, 1991.

Hegel, Georg W.F. *Grundlinien der Philosophie des Rechts oder Naturrecht und Staatwissenschaft im Grundrisse*. Frankfurt: Suhrkamp Taschenbuch, 1973.

Hemming, Laurence Paul, ed. *Radical Orthodoxy? A Catholic Enquiry*. Burlington, VT: Ashgate, 2000.

Hengel, Martin. *Judaism and Hellenism: Studies in Their Encounter in Palestine during the Early Hellenistic Period*. 2 vols. London: SCM, 1974.

Hennelly, Alfred T. "*Populorum Progressio*." In *The New Dictionary of Catholic Social Thought*, edited by Judith A. Dwyer, 762–70. Collegeville, MN: Liturgical Press, 1994.

Henrix, Hans Hermann. "The Covenant Has Never Been Revoked: Basis of the Christian-Jewish Relationship." http://www.jcrelations.net/ The_covenant_has_never_been_revoked.2250.0.html.

Hermaniuk, Maxim. In *Acta Synodalia Sacrosancti Concilii Oecumenici Vaticani II*. 6 vols. Vol. 3, part 5, 296–8. Vatican City: Typis polyglottis Vaticanis, 1970–2000.

Herms, Ronald. *An Apocalypse for the Church and for the World: The Narrative Function of Universal Language in the Book of Revelation*. Berlin: Walter de Gruyter, 2006.

Himes, Kenneth R. "Commentary on *Justitia in Mundo* (*Justice in the World*)." In *Modern Catholic Social Teaching: Commentaries & Interpretations*, edited by Kenneth R. Himes, 333–62. Washington: Georgetown University Press, 2011.

Hobson, Theo. *Anarchy, Church and Utopia: Rowan Williams on Church*. London: Dartman, Longman and Todd, 2005.

Hrynkow, Christopher. "Challenge of Peace." In *Religion and Politics in America: An Encyclopedia of Church and State in American Life*, edited by Frank J. Smith, 130–1. Santa Barbara, CA: ABC-CLIO, 2016.

– "Christian Peacemakers Teams, Solidarist Nonviolent Activism and the Politics of Peace: Peace Witness That Challenges Militarism and Destructive Violence." *Peace Research: The Canadian Journal of Peace and Conflict Studies* 40, no. 1 (2009): 111–34.

– "*Laudato Si'*, Transformative Learning, and the Healing of Human-Earth-Divine Relationships." *The Ecumenist: A Journal of Theology, Culture, and Society* 53, no. 4 (Fall 2016): 10–15.

– "The New Story, Transformative Learning and Socio-Ecological Flourishing: Education at Crucial Juncture in Planetary History." In *Sustainable Well-Being: Concepts, Issues, and Educational Practices*, edited by Frank Deer, Thomas Falkenberg, Barbara McMillan, and Laura Sims, 105–20. Winnipeg, MB: Education for Sustainable Well-Being Press, 2014.

– "No to War and Yes to So Much More: Pope Francis, Principled Nonviolence, and Positive Peace." In *Advancing Nonviolence and Social Transformation: New Perspectives on Nonviolence Theories*, edited by Heather Eaton and Lauren Michelle Levesque, 135–52. Sheffield, UK: Equinox, 2016.

– "The Pope, the Planet, and Politics: A Mapping of How Francis Is Calling for More than the Paris Agreement." *Journal of Church and State* 59, no. 3 (2017): 377–408. doi:10.1093/jcs/csw030.

- "'A True Ecological Approach Always Becomes a Social Approach': A Green Theo-Ecoethical Lens, Pope Francis' Teaching, and Integral Social Justice." *Heythrop Journal* (August 2016). doi:10.1111/heyj.12350.

Hrynkow, Christopher, Sean Byrne, and Matthew Hendzel. "Ecotheology and Inculturation: Implications for Theory and Practice in Peace and Conflict Studies." *Peace and Change: A Journal of Peace Research* 35, no. 2 (April 2010): 295–327.

Hurtado, Alberto. *Moral Social – Acción Social: Obra Póstuma in Obras Completas de San Alberto Hurtado.* CD-ROM. Santiago de Chile: Universidad Católica de Chile, 1952.

Hutcheon, Linda. *The Canadian Postmodern: A Study of Contemporary Canadian Fiction.* Don Mills, ON: Oxford University Press, 2012.

- *A Poetics of Postmodernism: History, Theory, Fiction.* New York: Routledge, 1988.

Hyman, Gavin. *The Predicament of Postmodern Theology: Radical Orthodoxy or Nihilist Textualism?* Louisville: Westminster John Knox, 2001.

Ignatius Jesuit Centre. "Mission and Vision." https://ignatiusguelph.ca/about/mission-vision/.

- "Project News: The Peace Pole Project." http://www.ignatiusguelph.ca/about/mission.html.

Insole, Christopher J. "Against Radical Orthodoxy: The Dangers of Overcoming Political Liberalism." *Modern Theology* 20, no. 2 (2004): 214–41.

Inter-American Human Rights Court. *Sentencia del Caso Myrna Mack Chang vs. Guatemala.* 25 November 2003. http://www.corteidh.or.cr/docs/casos/articulos/seriec_101_esp.pdf.

International Catholic-Jewish Liaison Committee. "Joint Statement of the 22nd International Catholic-Jewish Liaison Committee Meeting, Madrid (October 13–16, 2013)." Holy See Press Office, 18 October 2013. http://press.vatican.va/content/salastampa/en/bollettino/pubblico/2013/10/18/0674/01515.html.

International Group of Orthodox Rabbis. *To Do the Will of Our Father in Heaven: Toward a Partnership between Jews and Christians.* 2015. http://ccjr.us/dialogika-resources/documents-and-statements/jewish/1359-orthodox-2015dec4.

International Jewish Committee on Interreligious Consultations. "Response to Vatican Document 'We Remember: A Reflection on the Shoah.'" 1998. https://www.bc.edu/content/dam/files/research_sites/cjl/texts/cjrelations/resources/documents/jewish/response_We_Remember.html.

Isaac, Jules. "Notes about a Crucial Meeting with John XXIII." Council of
Centers on Jewish-Christian Relations, 13 June 1960. http://www.ccjr.
us/dialogika-resources/documents-and-statements/jewish/
1123-isaac1960.

Jacob, Jeffrey. *New Pioneers: The Back-to-the-Land Movement and the
Search for a Sustainable Future*. University Park: Pennsylvania State
University Press, 1997.

Jacobs, Jane. *The Death and Life of Great American Cities*. Toronto:
Random House of Canada, 1968.

John XXIII. "Announcement of Ecumenical Council and Roman Synod
(January 25, 1959)." *The Pope Speaks* 5, no. 4 (1959): 398–401.

– *"Ecclesia Christi, Lumen Gentium."* *The Pope Speaks* 8, no. 1 (1962):
105.

– *Humanae Salutis*. Apostolic Constitution. In *The Documents of Vatican
II*, edited by Walter M. Abbott, 703–9. New York: Herder and Herder,
1966.

– *Mater et Magistra* (*On Christianity and Social Progress*). Encyclical. 15
May 1961. http://www.vatican.va/holy_father/john_xxiii/encyclicals/
documents/hf_j-xxiii_enc_15051961_mater_en.html.

– *Pacem in Terris* (*On Establishing Universal Peace in Truth, Justice,
Charity, and Liberty*). Encyclical. 11 April 1963. http://www.vatican.va/
holy_father/john_xxiii/encyclicals/documents/hf_j-xxiii_enc_11041963
_pacem_en.html.

– "Pope John's Opening Speech to the Council [*Gaudet Mater Ecclesia*]."
In *The Documents of Vatican II*, edited by Walter M. Abbott, 710–19.
New York: Herder and Herder, 1966.

– Radio Address on 11 September 1962. *Acta Apostolicae Sedis* 54
(1962): 678–85.

John Paul II. "Address of John Paul II to the Representatives of the
Christian Churches and Ecclesial Communities and of the World
Religions." 27 October 1986. http://www.vatican.va/holy_father/john_
paul_ii/speeches/1986/october/documents/hf_jp-ii_spe_19861027_
prayer-peace-assisi-final_en.html.

– "Address on the 50th Anniversary of the Warsaw Ghetto Uprising."
L'Osservatore Romano, 17 August 1993.

– *Centesimus Annus* (*On the Hundredth Anniversary of* Rerum
Novarum). Encyclical. 1 May 1991. http://www.vatican.va/holy_father/
john_paul_ii/encyclicals/documents/hf_jp-ii_enc_01051991_
centesimus-annus_en.html.

– *Ecclesia in America*. Apostolic exhortation. 22 January 1999. http://
w2.vatican.va/content /john-paul-ii/en/apost_exhortations/documents/
hf_jp-ii_exh_22011999_ecclesia-in-america.html.

– *Evangelium Vitae*. Encyclical. 25 March 1995. http://w2.vatican.va/
content/john-paul-ii/en/encyclicals/documents/hf_jp-ii_enc_25031995_
evangelium-vitae.html.

– *Laborem Exercens (On Human Work)*. Encyclical. 14 September 1981.
http://w2.vatican.va/content/john-paul-ii/en/encyclicals/documents/hf_
jp-ii_enc_14091981_laborem-exercens.html.

– "Letter to Cardinal Edward Idris Cassidy." In *We Remember: A
Reflection on the Shoah*. 1998. http://www.vatican.va/roman_curia/
pontifical_councils/chrstuni/documents/rc_pc_chrstuni_doc_16031998
_shoah_en.html.

– "Letter to the Latin-Rite Diocese of Jerusalem." In *We Remember: A
Reflection on the Shoah*. 1998. http://www.vatican.va/roman_curia/
pontifical_councils/chrstuni/documents/rc_pc_chrstuni_doc_16031998
_shoah_en.html.

– "Message of His Holiness Pope John Paul II for the Celebration of the
World Day of Peace 1 January 1990: Peace with God the Creator, Peace
with All of Creation." 8 December 1989. http://w2.vatican.va/content/
john-paul-ii/en/messages/peace/documents/hf_jp-ii_mes_19891208_
xxiii-world-day-for-peace.html.

– *Pastor Bonus*. Apostolic Constitution. 28 June 1988. http://w2.vatican.
va/content/john-paul-ii/en/apost_constitutions/documents/hf_jp-ii_
apc_19880628_pastor-bonus-appendix.html.

– *Sollicitudo Rei Socialis (On Social Concern)*. Encyclical. 30 December
1987. http://www.vatican.va/holy_father/john_paul_ii/encyclicals/
documents/hf_jp-ii_enc_30121987_sollicitudo-rei-socialis_en.html.

– "We Are Not Pacifists." *Origins* 20 (1991): 625.

KAIROS. "KAIROS and CIDA Funding." https://www.kairoscanada.
org/?s=kairos+and+cida+funding.

– "Who We Are." https://www.kairoscanada.org/who-we-are.

Kaiser, Robert Blair. "Stories of Vatican II: The Human Side of the
Council." Lecture, Heythrop College, London, 5 October 2012. http://
www.thetablet.co.uk/page/lectureTablet2012.

Kant, Immanuel. *Kritik der Urteilskraft*. Frankfurt: Suhrkamp
Taschenbuch, 1974.

Karsh, Marianne. "Stations of the Cosmos." *The Ignatius-Loyola News*
(2009). http://oen.ca/uploads/2009Newsletter.pdf.

Kaufmann, Franz-Xaver. "The Principle of Subsidiarity Viewed by the Sociology of Organizations." *The Jurist* 48 (1988): 275–91.

Kavunkal, Jacob, Errol D'Lima, and Evelyn Monteiro. *Vatican II: A Gift and a Task*. Mumbai: Bombay Saint Paul Society, 2006.

Kessler, Edward. *An Introduction to Jewish-Christian Relations*. Cambridge: Cambridge University Press, 2010.

Ketteler, Wilhelm Emmanuel. *The Social Teachings of Wilhelm Emmanuel von Ketteler*. Edited and translated by Rupert Ederer. Lanham, MD: University Press of America, 1981.

King, Martin Luther, Jr. "Letter from Birmingham Jail." 16 April 1963. http://mlk-kpp01.stanford.edu/index.php/encyclopedia/documentsentry/annotated_letter_from_birmingham.

King, Thomas. *The Inconvenient Indian*. Toronto: Anchor Canada, 2012.

Kohler, Thomas C. "In Praise of Little Platoons, *Quadragesimo Anno* (1931)." In *Building the Free Society: Democracy, Capitalism, and Catholic Social Teaching*, edited by George Weigel and Robert Royal, 31–50. Grand Rapids, MI: Eerdmans, 1993.

– "Lessons from the Social Charter: State, Corporation, and the Meaning of Subsidiarity." *University of Toronto Law Journal* 43, no. 3 (Summer 1993): 617–18.

Komonchak, Joseph A. "Legacy of Vatican II: Historical Context of the Council." Lecture, Creighton University, Omaha, NE, 12 November 2012. https://www.youtube.com/watch?v=XxtbpDBMe_0.

– "Modernity and the Construction of Roman Catholicism." *Cristianesimo nella storia* 18 (1997): 353–85.

– "Subsidiarity in the Church: The State of the Question." *The Jurist* 48 (1988): 298–349.

Kracht, Katharina. "'A Question of Faith': An Interview with Ana Castillo." In *Voces de América: Entrevias a Escritores Americanos*, edited by Laura P. Alonso Gallo, 623–38. Cádiz, Spain: Aduana Veija, 2004.

Lamberigts, Mathijs. "Vatican II on the Jews: A Historical Survey." In *Never Revoked: "Nostra Aetate" as Ongoing Challenge for Jewish-Christian Dialogue*, edited by Marianne Moyaert and Didier Pollefeyt, 13–56. Leuven: Peeters, 2010.

Lamberigts, Mathijs, and Leo Declerck. "The Role of Cardinal Léon-Joseph Suenens at Vatican II." In *The Belgian Contribution to the Second Vatican Council,* edited by D. Donnelly, J. Famarée, M. Lamberigts, and K. Schelkens, 61–217. Leuven: Peeters, 2008.

Leal, Claudia. "La Noción de Justicia Social en la *Gaudium et Spes*." *Teología y Vida* 54 (2013): 181–204.

Leclerc, Jean-Claude. "L'angoisse de l'organisme Développement et Paix." *Le Devoir*, 26 November 2012.

Leddy, Mary Jo. *The Other Face of God: When the Stranger Calls Us Home*. Maryknoll, NY: Orbis Books, 2011.

Lederach, John Paul. *The Moral Imagination: The Art and Soul of Building Peace*. New York: Oxford University Press, 2005.

Léger, Paul-Émile. "Lettre inédite du Cardinal Paul-Émile Léger au Pape Jean XXIII en août 1962." In *Mémoires de Vatican II*, edited by Brigitte Caulier and Gilles Routhier, 93–113. Saint-Laurent, QC: Fides, 1997.

Leo XIII. *Aeterni Patris: On the Restoration of Christian Philosophy*. Encyclical. 4 August 1879. http://www.vatican.va/holy_father/leo_xiii/encyclicals/documents/hf_l-xiii_enc_04081879_aeterni-patris_en.htm.

– *Rerum Novarum (On the Condition of Labour)*. Encyclical. 15 May 1891. http://w2.vatican.va/content/leo-xiii/en/encyclicals/documents/hf_l-xiii_enc_15051891_rerum-novarum.html.

Leys, Adrianus. *Ecclesiological Impacts of the Principle of Subsidiarity*. Kampen, Netherlands: Uitgeverij Kok-Kampen, 1995.

Longley, Clifford. "Structures of Sin and the Free Market: John Paul II on Capitalism." In *The New Politics: Catholic Social Teaching for the Twenty-First Century*, edited by Paul Vallely, 97–113. London: SCM Press, 1998.

López García, J. *Dos defensores de los esclavos negros en el siglo XVII: Francisco José de Jaca y Epifanio de Moirans*. Caracas: Universidad Católica Andrés Bello, 1981.

Lorentzen, Lois Ann. "*Gaudium et Spes.*" In *The New Dictionary of Catholic Social Thought*, edited by Judith A. Dwyer, 406–16. Collegeville, MN: Liturgical Press, 1994.

Losada, Angel. *Fray Bartolomé de Las Casas a luz de la moderna crítica histórica*. Madrid: Tecnos, 1970.

Losada, Joaquin. "Subsidiarity from an Ecclesiologist's Point of View." *The Jurist* 48 (1988): 350–4.

Lundbom, Jack R. *Jeremiah 21–36: A New Translation with Introduction and Commentary*. Anchor Bible 21B. New York: Doubleday, 2004.

Maritain, Jacques. *L'humanisme integral*. Paris: Aubier, 1936.

– *Man and the State*. Chicago: University of Chicago Press, 1956.

Masenya, Madipoane. "An Eco*bosadi* Reading of Psalm 127.3–5." In *The Earth Bible Series*, Vol, 4, *The Earth Story in Psalms and Prophets*, edited by Norman C. Habel, 109–22. Sheffield, UK: Sheffield Academic Press, 2001.

McBrien, Richard. *Catholicism*. San Francisco: HarperCollins, 1994.

McCormick, Patrick T. "*Centesimus Annus*." In *The New Dictionary of Catholic Social Thought*, edited by Judith A. Dwyer, 132–42. Collegeville, MN: Liturgical Press, 1994.

McNabb, Vincent, ed. *The Decrees of the Vatican Council*. London: Burns and Oates, 1907.

Mendez, Ramón Ignacio. *Reflexiones que el Arzobispo de Caracas y Venezuela, Dr. Ramón Ignacio Mendez, dirige a sus diocesanos sobre varios errores que se propagan en el Diócesis*. Caracas: Damiron y Dupuy, 1834.

"Message to Humanity." In *The Documents of Vatican II*, edited by Walter M. Abbott, 3–7. New York: Herder and Herder, 1966.

Meyer, David. "*Nostra Aetate*: Past, Present, Future: A Jewish Perspective." In *Never Revoked: Nostra Aetate as Ongoing Challenge for Jewish-Christian Dialogue*, edited by Marianne Moyaert and Didier Pollefeyt, 117–32. Leuven: Peeters, 2010.

Milbank, John. *Being Reconciled: Ontology and Pardon*. London: Routledge, 2003.

– *The Future of Love: Essays in Political Theology*. London: SCM Press, 2009.

– "A Real Third Way." In *The Crisis of Global Capitalism: Pope Benedict XVI's Social Encyclical and the Future of the Political Economy*, edited by Adrian Pabst, 27–70. Eugene, OR: Cascade Books, 2011. Kindle.

– *Theology and Social Theory: Beyond Secular Reason*. Oxford: Blackwell, 1990.

– *The Word Made Strange: Theology, Language, Culture*. Oxford: Blackwell, 1997.

Milbank, John, Graham Ward, and Catherine Pickstock. "Introduction: Suspending the Material: The Turn of Radical Orthodoxy." In *Radical Orthodoxy: A New Theology*, edited by John Milbank, Catherine Pickstock, and Graham Ward, 1–20. London: Routledge, 1999.

Millon-Delsol, Chantal. *L'État subsidiaire: ingérence et non-ingérence de l'État: le principe de subsidiarité aux fondements de l'histoire euro-péenne*. Paris: Presses universitaires de France, 1992.

Moyaert, Marianne, and Didier Pollefeyt, eds. *Never Revoked: Nostra Aetate as Ongoing Challenge for Jewish-Christian Dialogue*. Leuven: Peeters, 2010.

Mulcahy, Richard. *The Economics of Heinrich Pesch*. New York: Holt, 1952.

Müller, Ragnar. "Violence Typology by Johan Galtung (Direct, Structural and Cultural Violence)." http://www.friedenspaedagogik.de/content/pdf/2754.

National Conference of Catholic Bishops. *The Challenge of Peace: God's Call and Our Response.* 3 May 1983. http://www.usccb.org/upload/challenge-peace-gods-promise-our-response-1983.pdf.

Newsom, Carol A. "The Development of 1 Enoch 6–19: Cosmology and Judgment." *Catholic Biblical Quarterly* 42 (1980): 310–29.

Nickelsburg, George W.E. *1 Enoch 1: A Commentary on the Book of 1 Enoch Chapters 1–36; 81–108.* Edited by Klaus Baltzer. Hermeneia series. Minneapolis: Fortress Press, 2001.

– "Apocalyptic and Myth in 1 Enoch 6–11." *Journal of Biblical Literature* 96 (1977): 383–405.

– *Jewish Literature between the Bible and the Mishnah: A Historical and Literary Introduction.* 2nd ed. Philadelphia: Fortress Press, 2005.

Nickelsburg, George W.E., and James C. VanderKam. *Enoch 2: A Commentary on the Book of Enoch Chapters 37–82.* Edited by Klaus Baltzer. Hermeneia series. Minneapolis: Fortress Press, 2012.

Noble, Thomas F.X. *Popes and the Papacy: A History.* Great Courses DVD. Chantilly, VA: The Teaching Company, 2006.

Novak, Michael. *Catholic Social Thought and Liberal Institutions: Freedom with Justice.* 2nd ed. New Brunswick, NJ: Transaction Publishers, 1989.

– *The Spirit of Democratic Capitalism.* New York: Simon and Schuster, 1983.

O'Brien, David J., and Thomas A. Shannon, eds. *Catholic Social Thought: The Documentary Heritage.* Expanded ed. Maryknoll, NY: Orbis, 2010.

O'Donovan, Joan Lockwood. "Subsidiarity and Political Authority in Theological Perspective." In *Bonds of Imperfection: Christian Politics, Past and Present,* edited by Oliver O'Donovan and Joan Lockwood O'Donovan, 225–45. Grand Rapids, MI: Eerdmans, 2004.

Oesterreicher, John M. "Declaration on the Relationship of the Church to Non-Christian Religions." In *Commentary on the Documents of Vatican II: Volume III,* edited by Herbert Vorgrimler, 1–136. New York: Herder and Herder, 1969.

– "A New Beginning: Reflections on *Nostra Aetate* after 25 Years." *Ecumenical Trends* 20, no. 3 (1991): 44–46.

O'Grady, Jean, and David Staines, eds. *Northrop Frye on Canada.* Toronto: University of Toronto Press, 2003.

Oliver, Simon. "Introducing Radical Orthodoxy: From Participation to Late Modernity." In *The Radical Orthodoxy Reader*, edited by John Milbank and Simon Oliver, 1–27. London: Routledge, 2009.

O'Malley, John W. "*Ressourcement* and Reform at Vatican II." In *Vatican II*, edited by Silvia Scatena, Dennis Gira, Jon Sobrino, and Maria Clara Bingemer, 47–55. London: SCM Press, 2012.

— "Trent and Vatican II: Two Styles of Church." In *From Trent to Vatican II: Historical and Theological Investigations*, edited by Raymond F. Bulman and Frederick J. Parrella, 301–20. New York: Oxford University Press, 2006.

— *What Happened at Vatican II*. Cambridge, MA: Belknap of Harvard University, 2008.

O'Sullivan, Edmund. "Emancipatory Hope: Transformative Learning and the 'Strange Attractors.'" In *Holistic Learning and Spirituality in Education: Breaking New Ground*, edited by John P. Miller, Selia Karsten, Diana Denton, Deborah Orr, and Isabella Colalillo Kates, 69–78. Albany: University of New York Press, 2005.

Pabst, Adrian, ed. *The Crisis of Global Capitalism: Pope Benedict XVI's Social Encyclical and the Future of the Political Economy*. Eugene, OR: Cascade Books, 2011. Kindle.

Paul VI. "Address to the United Nations Organization." 4 October 1965. https://w2.vatican.va/content/paul-vi/en/speeches/1965/documents/hf_p-vi_spe_19651004_united-nations.html.

— *Catholicam Christi Ecclesiam*. Motu proprio. 6 January 1967. http://w2.vatican.va/content/paul-vi/la/motu_proprio/documents/hf_p-vi_motu-proprio_19670106_catholicam-christi-ecclesiam.html.

— *Christus Dominus* (*Decree concerning the Pastoral Office of Bishops in the Church*). 28 October 1965. http://www.vatican.va/archive/hist_councils/ii_vatican_council/documents/vat-ii_decree_19651028_christus-dominus_en.html.

— "Discours du Pape Paul VI à l'organisation des Nations Unies." 4 October 1965. http://w2.vatican.va/content/paul-vi/fr/speeches/1965/documents/hf_p-vi_spe_19651004_united-nations.html.

— *Ecclesiam Suam* (*On the Church*). Encyclical. 6 August 1964. http://www.vatican.va/holy_father/paul_vi/encyclicals/documents/hf_p-vi_enc_06081964_ecclesiam_en.html.

— *Evangelii Nuntiandi*. Apostolic exhortation. 8 December 1975. http://w2.vatican.va/content/paul-vi/en/apost_exhortations/documents/hf_p-vi_exh_19751208_evangelii-nuntiandi.html.

– *Justitiam et Pacem*. Motu proprio. 10 December 1976. http://w2. vatican.va/content/paul-vi/la/motu_proprio/documents/hf_p-vi _motu-proprio_19761210_iustitia-et-pacem.html.

– "Message of His Holiness Pope Paul VI for the Celebration of the World Day of Peace 1 January 1972: If You Want Peace, Work for Justice." 8 December 1971. http://www.vatican.va/holy_father/paul_vi/messages/ peace/documents/hf_p-vi_mes_19711208_v-world-day-for-peace_ en.html.

– "New Era for the Human Race." *The Pope Speaks* 10, no. 2 (1965): 152–4.

– *Octogesima Adveniens (A Call to Action)*. Apostolic Letter. 14 May 1971. http://www.vatican.va/holy_father/paul_vi/apost_letters/ documents/hf_p-vi_apl_19710514_octogesima-adveniens_en.html.

– *Populorum Progressio (On the Development of Peoples)*. Encyclical. 26 March 1967. http://www.vatican.va/holy_father/paul_vi/encyclicals/ documents/hf_p-vi_enc_26031967_populorum_en.html.

– "Special Message to the World." *The Pope Speaks* 10, no. 2 (1965): 158–9.

Pawlikowski, John T. "Reflections on Covenant and Mission: Forty Years after Nostra Aetate." In *Never Revoked: Nostra Aetate as Ongoing Challenge for Jewish-Christian Dialogue*, edited by Marianne Moyaert and Didier Pollefeyt, 57–91. Leuven: Peeters, 2010.

Pew Research Center. "Global Christianity: A Report on the Size and Distribution of the World's Christian Population." 19 December 2011. http://www.pewforum.org/2011/12/19/global-christianity-exec/.

Pius IX. *Quanta Cura (Condemning Current Errors)*. Encyclical. 8 December 1864. http://www.papalencyclicals.net/Pius09/p9quanta.htm.

– *Syllabus Errorum (Syllabus of Errors)*. Encyclical. 8 December 1864. http://www.papalencyclicals.net/Pius09/p9syll.htm.

Pius XI. *Quadragesimo Anno (On Reconstruction of the Social Order)*. Encyclical. 15 May 1931. http://w2.vatican.va/content/pius-xi/en/ encyclicals/documents/hf_p-xi_enc_19310515_quadragesimo-anno. html.

Pius XII. *Humani Generis*. Encyclical. 12 August 1950. http://w2.vatican. va/content/pius-xii/en/encyclicals/documents/hf_p-xii_enc_12081950_ humani-generis.html.

– *Radiomessaggio di sua santità Pio XII in occasione della "Giornata della Famiglia."* 23 March 1952. http://www.vatican.va/roman_curia/ congregations/cfaith/pcb_documents/rc_con_cfaith_doc_20020212_ popolo-ebraico_en.html.

Pontifical Biblical Commission. "The Jewish People and Their Sacred Scriptures in the Christian Bible." Vatican City: Libreria Editrice Vaticana, 2001. http://www.vatican.va/roman_curia/congregations/ cfaith/pcb_documents/rc_con_cfaith_doc_20020212_popolo-ebraico _en.html.

Pontifical Council for Justice and Peace. *Compendium of the Social Doctrine of the Church.* http://www.vatican.va/roman_curia/pontifical_ councils/justpeace/documents/rc_pc_justpeace_doc_20060526_ compendio-dott-soc_en.html.

Portier-Young, Anathea E. *Apocalypse against Empire: Theologies of Resistance in Early Judaism.* Grand Rapids, MI: Eerdmans, 2011.

Racine, Jacques. "Lettre de Paul VII au cardinal Maurice Roy à l'occasion du 80ᵉ anniversaire de *Rerum novarum.*" In *Paul VI et Maurice Roy: un itinéraire pour la justice et la paix,* edited by Gilles Routhier, 143–70. Rome: Edizioni Studium; Brescia: Istituto Paulo VI, 2005.

Rajotte, Freda. "Justice, Peace, and the Integrity of Creation." *Religious Education* 85, no. 1 (2006): 5–14.

Ratzinger, Joseph. "Cardinal Ratzinger's Memo on Communion Principles. *Denver Catholic Register,* 21 July 2004, 13.

– "The Dignity of the Human Person." In *Commentary on the Documents of Vatican II,* Vol. 5, *Pastoral Constitution on the Church in the Modern World,* translated by W.J. O'Hara. Freiburg: Herder; Montreal: Palm, 1969.

– Homily on 18 April 2005. http://www.vatican.va/gpII/documents/ homily-pro-eligendo-pontifice_20050418_en.html.

Read, Paul. "Decline and Fall of the Catholic Novel: Opinion." Business Insights, *Times* (London, England), 29 March 1997.

Reed, Annette Yoshiko. *Fallen Angels and the History of Judaism and Christianity: The Reception of Enochic Literature.* Cambridge: Cambridge University Press, 2005.

Reichardt, Mary R., ed. *Between Human and Divine: The Catholic Vision in Contemporary Literature.* Washington: Catholic University of America Press, 2010.

Robra, Martin. "Theology of Life – Justice, Peace, Creation: An Ecumenical Study." *Ecumenical Review* 48, no. 1 (1996): 28–37.

Rosen, David. "Fifty Years Since Nostra Aetate: A Historical Retrospective." www.rabbidavidrosen.net.

– "Jerusalem, from Pain to Peace." http://rabbidavidrosen.net/Articles/ Christian-Jewish%20Relations/Jerusalem_from_Pain_to_Peace_ English_Feb9_2012.pdf.

- "Jewish and Israeli Perspectives 40 Years after Vatican II." In *"Nostra Aetate"*: *Origins, Promulgation, Impact on Jewish-Christian Relations,* edited by Uri Bialer, Neville Lamdan, and Alberto Melloni, 176–89. Berlin: LIT Verlag, 2007.

- "'Nostra Aetate,' Forty Years after Vatican II: Present and Future Perspectives." http://www.vatican.va/roman_curia/pontifical_councils/ chrstuni/relations-jews-docs/rc_pc_chrstuni_doc_20051027_rabbi -rosen_en.html.

Routhier, Gilles. "Les réactions du Cardinal Leger à la préparation de Vatican II." *Revue de l'histoire de l'Eglise de France* 80 (1994): 281–302.

- ed. *Paul VI et Maurice Roy: un itinéraire pour la justice et la paix.* Rome: Edizioni Studium; Brescia: Istituto Paulo VI, 2005.

Roy, Maurice. In *Acta Synodalia Sacrosancti Concilii Oecumenici Vaticani II.* 6 vols. Vol. 3, part 5, 322–3. Vatican City: Typis polyglottis Vaticanis, 1970–2000.

Rubin, Sergio, and Francesca Ambrogetti. *Pope Francis: Conversations with Jorge Bergolio.* New York: Penguin Group, 2013.

Ryan, Thomas. "Catholic Fundamentalism." http://tomryancsp.org/ fundamentalism.htm.

Ryan, William. "The Influence of Paul VI and Cardinal Roy in the Mission for Justice and Peace in the North American Church." In *Paul VI et Maurice Roy: un itinéraire pour la justice et la paix,* edited by Gilles Routhier, 201–8. Rome: Edizioni Studium; Brescia: Istituto Paulo VI, 2005.

- "The Legacy of *Gaudium et Spes* in Canada (1965–1990)." https:// www.stthomas.edu/media/catholicstudies/center/ryan/conferences/ 2005-vatican/Ryan.pdf.

Sacks, Jonathan. *To Heal a Fractured World: The Ethics of Responsibility.* Montreal: McGill-Queen's University Press, 2005.

Scheid, Daniel P. "Thomas Aquinas, the Common Good, and Climate Change." In *Confronting the Climate Crisis: Catholic Theological Perspectives,* edited by James Schaefer, 125–44. Milwaukee; WI: Marquette University Press, 2011.

Schuck, Michael J. "Modern Catholic Social Thought." In *The New Dictionary of Catholic Social Thought,* edited by Judith A. Dwyer, 611–32. Collegeville, MN: Liturgical Press, 1994.

Schürer, Emil. *The History of the Jewish People in the Age of Jesus Christ.* 3 vols. Revised and edited by Geza Vermes, Fergus Millar, and Matthew Black. Edinburgh: T & T Clark, 1973–87.

Schwaller, J.F. *The History of the Catholic Church in Latin America*. New York: New York University Press, 2001.

Secretariat for Christian Unity. *Decretum de Iudaeis (Decree on the Jews)*. 1961. http://www.ccjr.us/dialogika-resources/documents-and -statements/roman-catholic/second-vatican-council/na-drafts/1024-1961.

Sharpe, Gene. *Waging Nonviolent Struggle: 20th Century Practice and 21st Century Potential*. Boston, MA: Porter Sergant Publishers, 1995.

Sheridan, Edward F. *Do Justice! The Social Teaching of the Canadian Catholic Bishops (1945–1986)*. Sherbrooke, QC: Éditions Paulines, 1987.

– *Love Kindness! The Social Teaching of the Canadian Catholic Bishops (1958–1989): A Second Collection*. Montreal: Éditions Paulines; Toronto: Jesuit Centre for Social Faith and Justice, 1991.

Smith, James K.A. *Introducing Radical Orthodoxy: Mapping a Post-Secular Theology*. Grand Rapids, MI: Baker Academic, 2004.

Sobrino, Jon. "The 'Church of the Poor' Did Not Prosper at Vatican II." In *Vatican II*, edited by Silvia Scatena, Dennis Gira, Jon Sobrino, and Maria Clara Bingemer, 75–84. London: SCM Press, 2012.

Spadaro, Anthonio. "A Big Heart Open to God: The Exclusive Interview with Pope Francis." *America*, 30 September 2013. http://america magazine.org/pope-interview.

Stuckenbruck, Loren T. *1 Enoch 91–108*. Commentaries on Early Jewish Literature. Berlin: Walter de Gruyter, 2007.

– "The Book of Enoch: Its Reception in Jewish and Christian Tradition." In *Early Christianity* 1 (2013): 8–40.

– *The Book of Giants from Qumran: Texts, Translation, and Commentary*. Texte und Studien zum antiken Judentum 63. Tübingen: Mohr Siebeck, 1997.

– "The Epistle of Enoch: Genre and Authorial Presentation." *Dead Sea Discoveries* 17 (2010): 387–417.

– "Giant Mythology and Demonology: From the Ancient Near East to the Dead Sea Scrolls." In *Die Dämonen*, edited by A. Lange, H. Lichtenberger, and K.T. Diethard Römheld, 318–38. Tübingen: Mohr Siebeck, 2003.

– *The Myth of the Rebellious Angels*. Grand Rapids: Eerdmans, 2017.

– "The Origins of Evil in Jewish Apocalyptic Tradition: The Interpretation of Genesis 6:1–4 in the Second and Third Centuries B.C.E." In *The Fall of the Angels*, edited by Christoph Auffarth and Loren T. Stuckenbruck, 87–118. Themes in Biblical Narrative 6. Leiden: Brill, 2004.

– "'Reading the Present' in the Animal Apocalypse (1 Enoch 85–90)." In *Reading the Present in the Qumran Library: The Perception of the Contemporary by Means of Scriptural Interpretations*, edited by Kristin De Troyer and Armin Lange, 91–102. Society of Biblical Literature Symposium Series 30. Atlanta: Society of Biblical Literature, 2005.

Suenens, Léon-Joseph. "Aux origines du concile Vatican II." *Nouvelle Revue Théologique* 107 (1985): 3–21.

– "A Plan for the Whole Council." In *Vatican II by Those Who Were There*, edited by A. Stacpoole, 88–105. London: G. Chapman, 1986.

– *Souvenirs et espérances*. Paris: Fayard, 1991.

Sutton, Timothy J. *Catholic Modernists, English Nationalists*. Newark: University of Delaware Press, 2010.

Swimme, Brian, and Thomas Berry. *The Universe Story*. New York: HarperCollins, 1992.

Synod of Bishops. *Justitia in Mundo (Justice in the World)*. Vatican City: Typis Polyglottis Vaticanis, 1971.

Taylor, Bron. "Earth and Nature-Based Spirituality (Part 1): From Deep Ecology to Radical Environmentalism." *Religion* 31, no. 2 (2001): 175–93.

Taylor, Sarah McFarland. *Green Sisters: A Spiritual Ecology*. Cambridge, MA: Harvard University Press, 2007.

32nd General Congregation of the Society of Jesus. "Our Mission Today: The Service of Faith and the Promotion of Justice." Decree 4, 2 December 1974–7 March 1975. http://onlineministries.creighton.edu/CollaborativeMinistry/our-mission-today.html.

Tiller, Patrick A. *A Commentary on the Animal Apocalypse of 1 Enoch*. Early Judaism and Its Literature 4. Atlanta: Scholars Press, 1993.

Uhser, Robin, Ian Bryant, and Rennie Johnston. *Adult Education and the Postmodern Challenge: Learning beyond the Limits*. New York: Routledge, 1997.

Valiente, O. Ernesto. "The Reception of Vatican II in Latin America." *Theological Studies* 13, no. 4 (December 2012): 795–824.

Vallely, Paul, ed. *The New Politics: Catholic Social Teaching for the Twenty-First Century*. London: SCM Press, 1998.

Vatican I. "Dogmatic Constitution on the Catholic Faith." In *The Decrees of the Vatican Council*, edited by Vincent McNabb, 19–21. London: Burns and Oates, 1907.

Wallace, Cynthia R. *Of Women Borne: A Literary Ethics of Suffering*. New York: Columbia University Press, 2016.

Walsh, Michael. "Laying the Foundations: From *Rerum Novarum* to the Second Vatican Council." In *The New Politics: Catholic Social Teaching for the Twenty-First Century*, edited by Paul Vallely, 28–41. London: SCM Press, 1998.

Weaver, Darlene Fozard. "Vatican II and Moral Theology." In *After Vatican II: Trajectories and Hermeneutics*, edited by James L. Heft with John O'Malley, 23–42. Grand Rapids, MI: Eerdmans, 2012.

Williams, Rowan. "Logic and Spirit in Hegel." In *Post-Secular Philosophy: Between Philosophy and Theology*, edited by Phillip Blond, 60–7. London: Routledge, 1998.

– *Lost Icons: Reflections on Cultural Bereavement*. Edinburgh: T & T Clark, 2006.

– "Mission and Christology." J.C. Jones Memorial Lecture. Church Missionary Society, 1994.

– *On Christian Theology*. Oxford: Blackwell, 1999.

– "Saving Time: Thoughts on Practice, Patience and Vision." *New Blackfriars* 73, no. 861 (June 1992): 319–26.

Wink, Walter. *The Powers That Be: A Theology for the New Millennium*. New York: Galilee Doubleday, 1999.

Wolfe, Gregory. "Whispers of Faith in a Postmodern World." *Wall Street Journal*, 10 January 2013. http://www.wsj.com/articles/SB10001424127 887324081704578231634123976600.

World Council of Churches. "Justice, Peace, Creation: History." http://www.wcc-coe.org/wcc/what/jpc/hist-e.html.

Worldometers. "Real Time World Statistics: Current World Population." http://www.worldometers.info/world-population.

Wyschogrod, Michael. *Abraham's Promise: Judaism and Jewish-Christian Relations*. Grand Rapids, MI: Eerdmans, 2004.

Yoder, John Howard. *Nevertheless: Varieties of Religious Pacifism*. Waterloo, ON: Abington Press, 1992.

Young, Julia G. "Hidden in Plain Sight." Review of *Latino Catholicism: Transformation in America's Largest Church*, by Timothy Matovina. *Commonweal* 140, no. 3 (8 February 2013): 28–9.

Contributors

GREGORY BAUM, OC, was professor emeritus in the Faculty of Religious Studies at McGill University in Montreal, Canada.

ANNA BLACKMAN is a doctoral student at the Centre for Catholic Studies at Durham University in Durham, UK.

DONALD BOLEN is the archbishop of the Roman Catholic Archdiocese of Regina, Canada, and was previously bishop of the Roman Catholic Diocese of Saskatoon, Canada.

CATHERINE E. CLIFFORD is a professor of systematic and historical theology at Saint-Paul University in Ottawa, Canada.

BISHOP REMI DE ROO is bishop emeritus of the Roman Catholic Diocese of Victoria, Canada.

MICHAEL W. DUGGAN is a professor of religious studies and theology and the CWL Chair for Catholic Studies at St Mary's University in Calgary, Canada.

CHRISTOPHER HRYNKOW is an associate professor specializing in eco-theology in the Department of Religion and Culture at St Thomas More College in Saskatoon, Canada.

MARY JO LEDDY, OC, is a lecturer in religion and society at Regis College at the University of Toronto, Canada, and co-founder of Romero House in Toronto.

ALISHA POMAZON is an assistant professor specializing in Judaic studies in the Department of Religion and Culture at St Thomas More College in Saskatoon, Canada.

EDUARDO SOTO PARRA, SJ, is a doctoral student at the Arthur V. Mauro Centre for Peace and Justice, St Paul's College, University of Manitoba in Winnipeg, Canada.

LOREN STUCKENBRUCK is a professor of New Testament studies at the Ludwig-Maximilans-Universität München in Munich, Germany.

CYNTHIA R. WALLACE is an assistant professor specializing in Catholic literature in the Department of English at St Thomas More College in Saskatoon, Canada.

Index